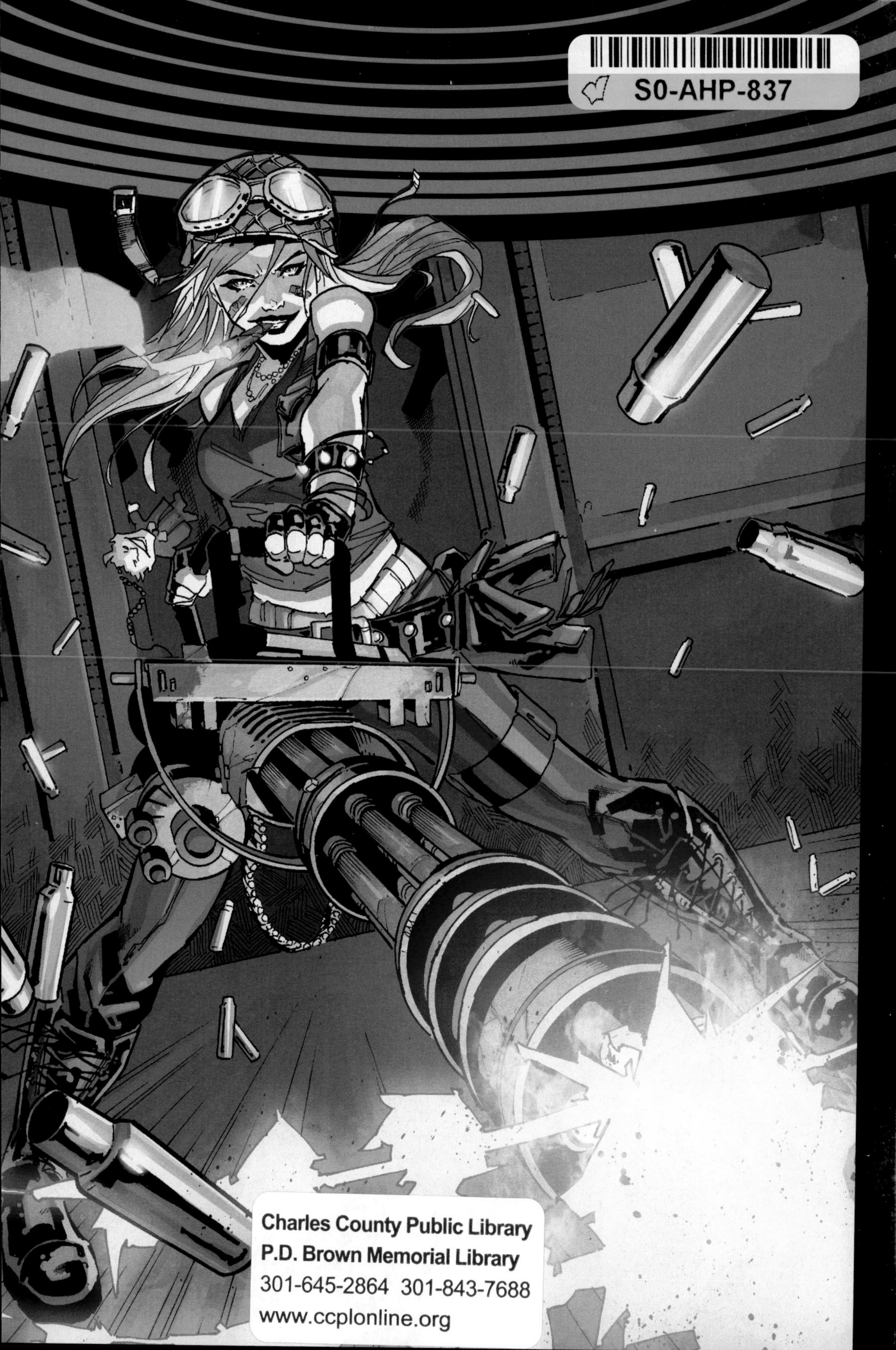

SUICIDE SQUAD

VOL.5 KILL YOUR DARLINGS

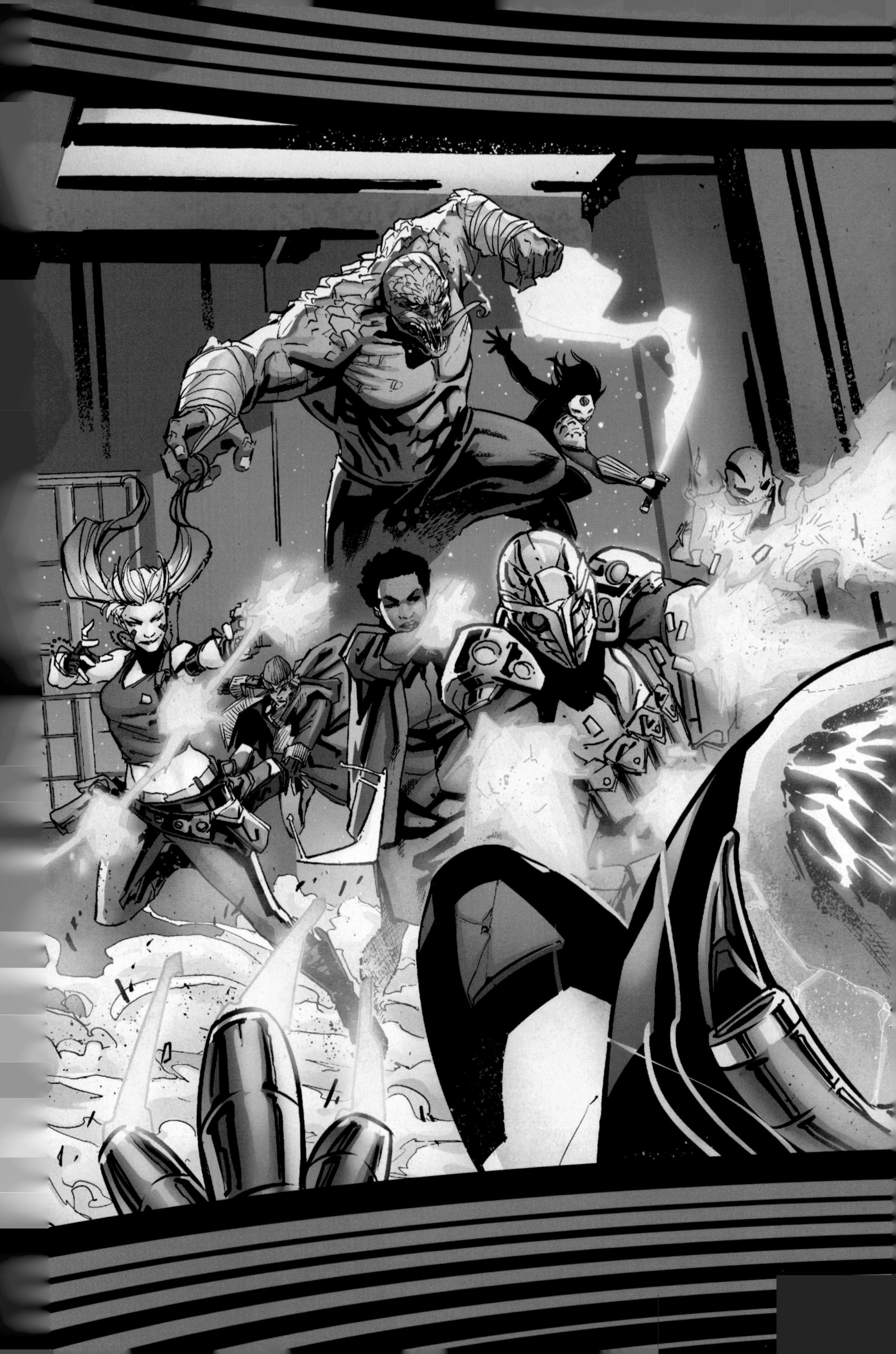

SUICIDE SQUAD
VOL.5 KILL YOUR DARLINGS

ROB WILLIAMS
writer

GUS VAZQUEZ * **AGUSTIN PADILLA**
JUAN FERREYRA * **GIUSEPPE CAFARO**
artists

ADRIANO LUCAS * **HI-FI**
colorists

PAT BROSSEAU
letterer

EDDY BARROWS, EBER FERREIRA and ADRIANO LUCAS
collection cover art

EDDY BARROWS, EBER FERREIRA and ADRIANO LUCAS
JUAN FERREYRA
original series covers

KILLER FROST created by **GERRY CONWAY** and **ALLEN MILGROM**
AMANDA WALLER created by **JOHN OSTRANDER** and **JOHN BYRNE**
TUNGUSKA created by **ROB WILLIAMS** and **JIM LEE**
SUPERMAN created by **JERRY SIEGEL** and **JOE SHUSTER**
By special arrangement with the Jerry Siegel family

ANDY KHOURI Editor - Original Series ✳ **HARVEY RICHARDS** Associate Editor - Original Series
JEB WOODARD Group Editor - Collected Editions ✳ **SCOTT NYBAKKEN** Editor - Collected Edition
STEVE COOK Design Director - Books ✳ **MEGEN BELLERSEN** Publication Design

BOB HARRAS Senior VP - Editor-in-Chief, DC Comics
PAT McCALLUM Executive Editor, DC Comics

DIANE NELSON President ✳ **DAN DiDIO** Publisher ✳ **JIM LEE** Publisher ✳ **GEOFF JOHNS** President & Chief Creative Officer
AMIT DESAI Executive VP - Business & Marketing Strategy, Direct to Consumer & Global Franchise Management
SAM ADES Senior VP & General Manager, Digital Services ✳ **BOBBIE CHASE** VP & Executive Editor, Young Reader & Talent Development
MARK CHIARELLO Senior VP - Art, Design & Collected Editions ✳ **JOHN CUNNINGHAM** Senior VP - Sales & Trade Marketing
ANNE DePIES Senior VP - Business Strategy, Finance & Administration ✳ **DON FALLETTI** VP - Manufacturing Operations
LAWRENCE GANEM VP - Editorial Administration & Talent Relations ✳ **ALISON GILL** Senior VP - Manufacturing & Operations
HANK KANALZ Senior VP - Editorial Strategy & Administration ✳ **JAY KOGAN** VP - Legal Affairs ✳ **JACK MAHAN** VP - Business Affairs
NICK J. NAPOLITANO VP - Manufacturing Administration ✳ **EDDIE SCANNELL** VP - Consumer Marketing
COURTNEY SIMMONS Senior VP - Publicity & Communications ✳ **JIM (SKI) SOKOLOWSKI** VP - Comic Book Specialty Sales & Trade Marketing
NANCY SPEARS VP - Mass, Book, Digital Sales & Trade Marketing ✳ **MICHELE R. WELLS** VP - Content Strategy

SUICIDE SQUAD VOL. 5: KILL YOUR DARLINGS

Published by DC Comics. Compilation and all new material Copyright © 2018 DC Comics. All Rights Reserved.
Originally published in single magazine form in SUICIDE SQUAD 21-25. Copyright © 2017 DC Comics. All Rights Reserved.
All characters, their distinctive likenesses and related elements featured in this publication are trademarks of DC Comics.
The stories, characters and incidents featured in this publication are entirely fictional.
DC Comics does not read or accept unsolicited ideas, stories or artwork.

DC Comics, 2900 West Alameda Ave., Burbank, CA 91505
Printed by LSC Communications, Kendallville, IN, USA. 3/9/18. First Printing.
ISBN: 978-1-4012-7880-9

Library of Congress Cataloging-in-Publication Data is available.

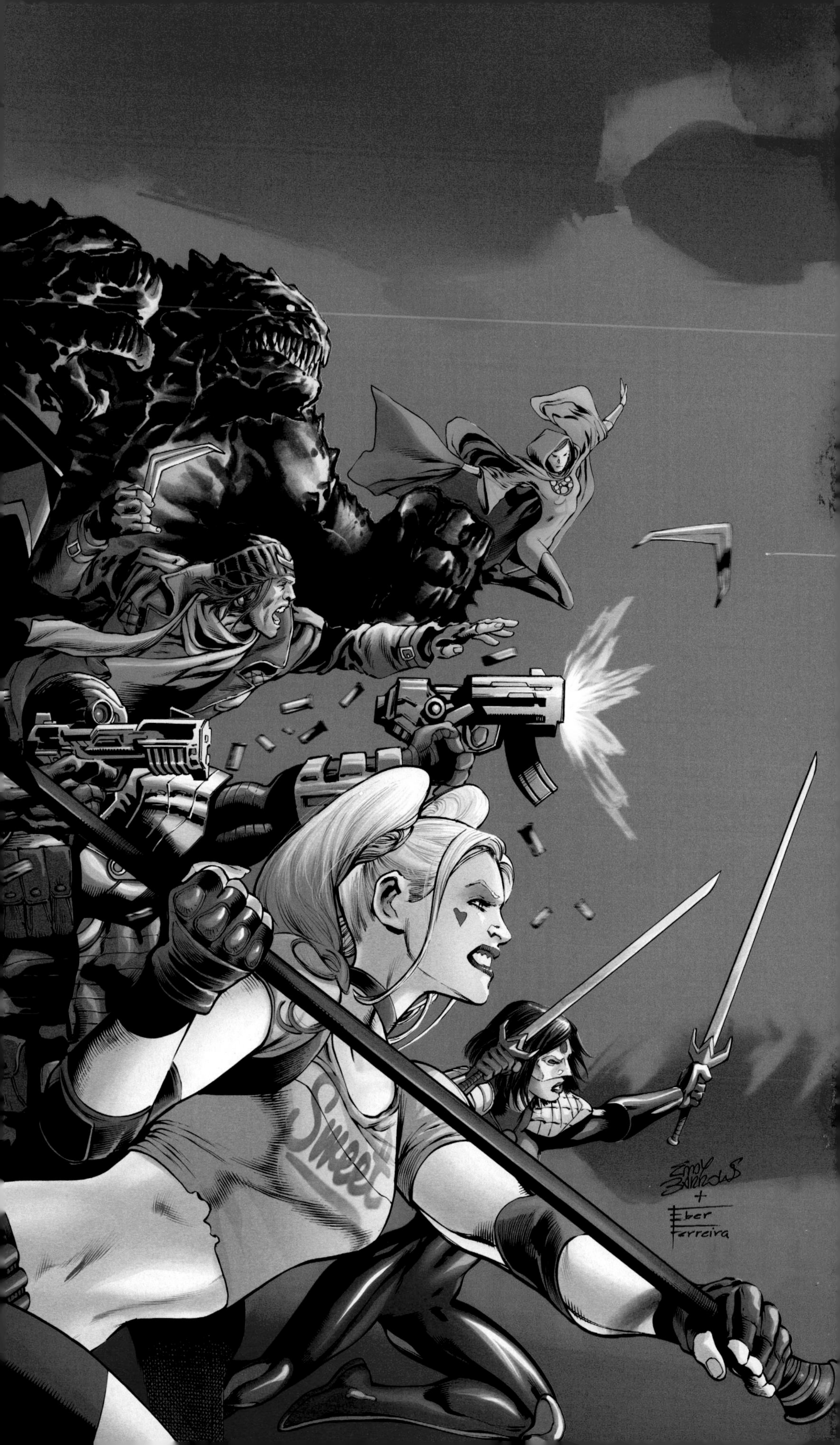
Sweet
Eber
Ferreira

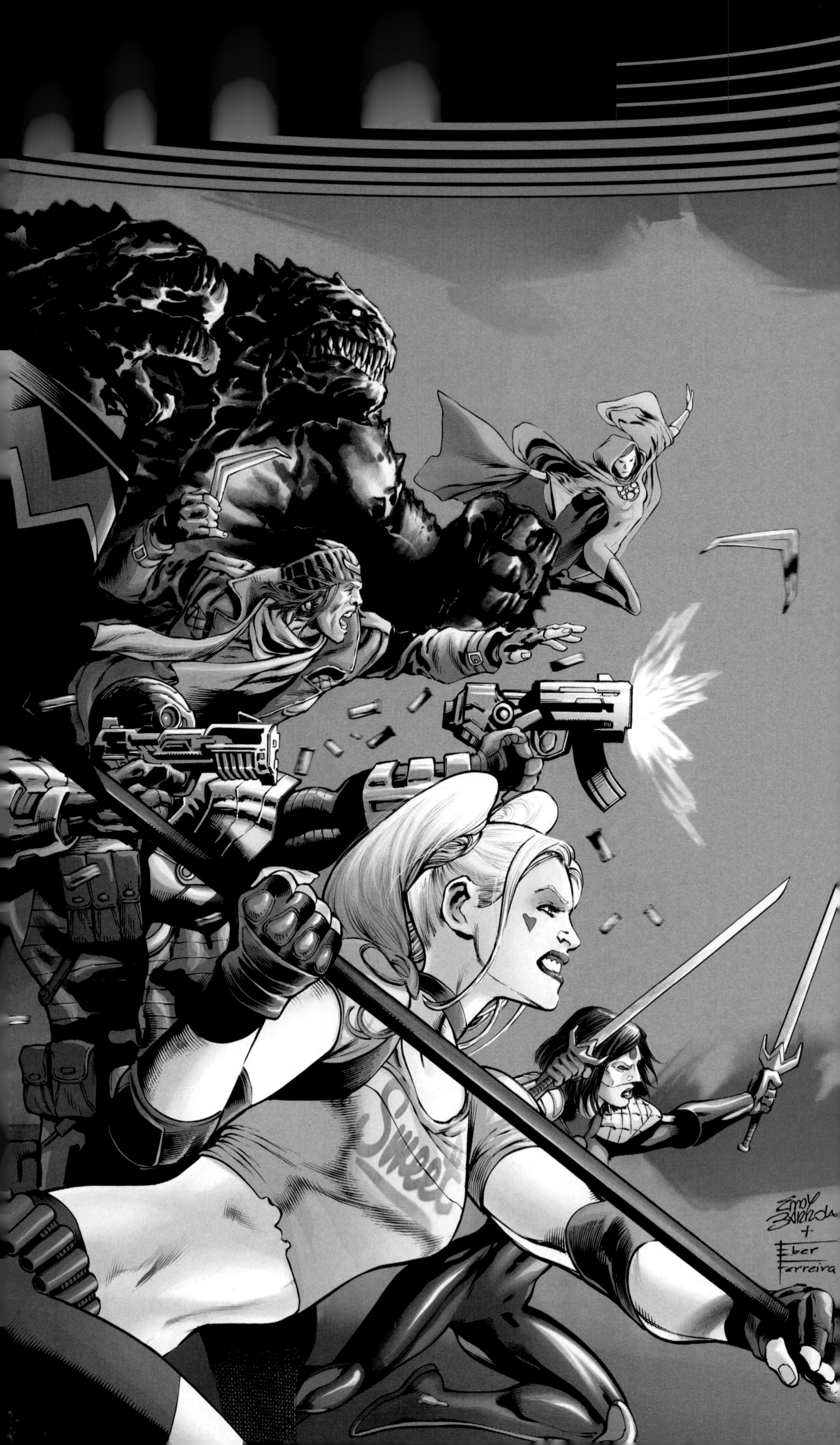
Sweet
Eber Ferreira

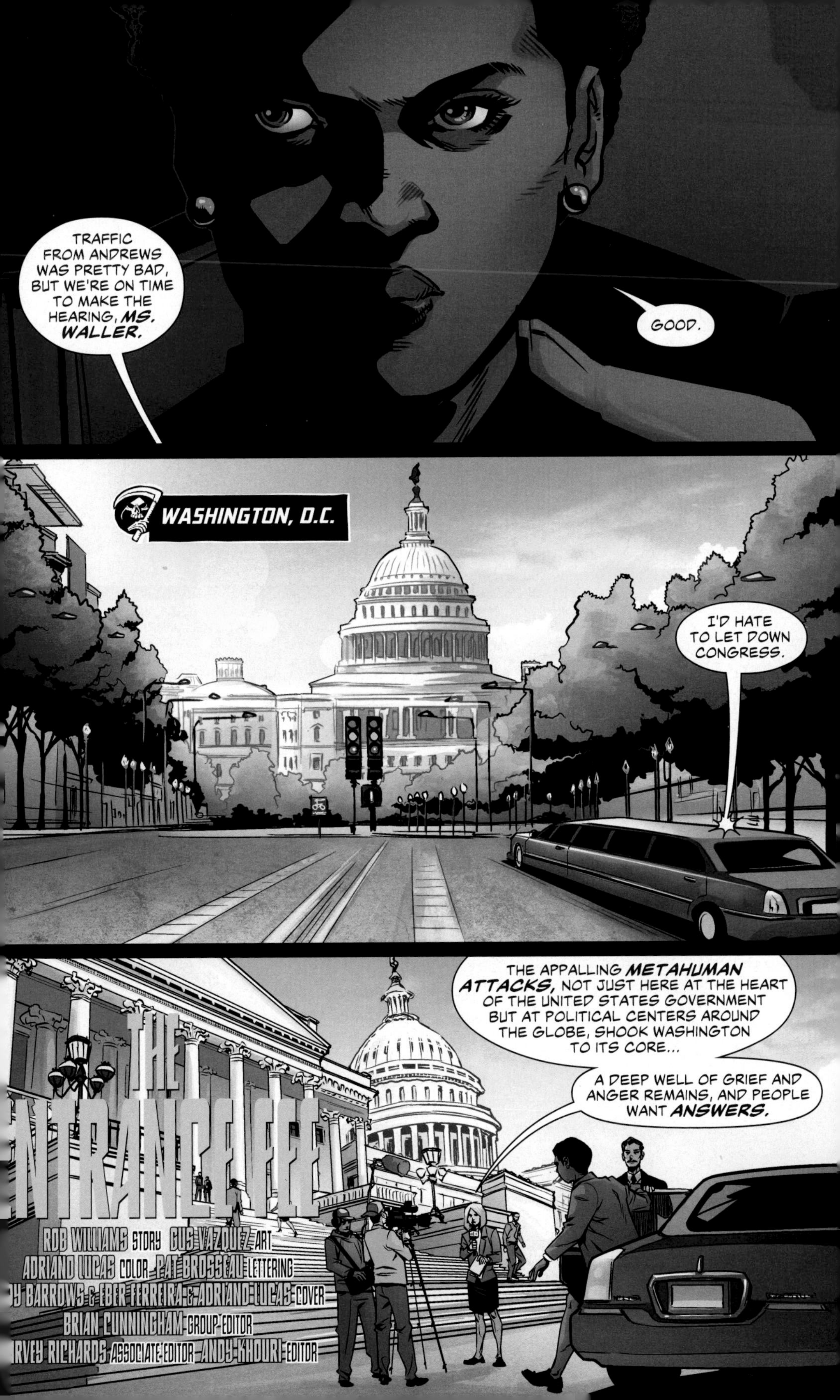
TRAFFIC FROM ANDREWS WAS PRETTY BAD, BUT WE'RE ON TIME TO MAKE THE HEARING, MS. WALLER.
GOOD.
WASHINGTON, D.C.
I'D HATE TO LET DOWN CONGRESS.
THE APPALLING METAHUMAN ATTACKS, NOT JUST HERE AT THE HEART OF THE UNITED STATES GOVERNMENT BUT AT POLITICAL CENTERS AROUND THE GLOBE, SHOOK WASHINGTON TO ITS CORE...
A DEEP WELL OF GRIEF AND ANGER REMAINS, AND PEOPLE WANT ANSWERS.
THE NTRANCE FEE
ROB WILLIAMS STORY GUS VAZQUEZ ART
ADRIANO LUCAS COLOR PAT BROSSEAU LETTERING
Y BARROWS & EBER FERREIRA & ADRIANO LUCAS COVER
BRIAN CUNNINGHAM GROUP EDITOR
RVEY RICHARDS ASSOCIATE EDITOR ANDY KHOURI EDITOR

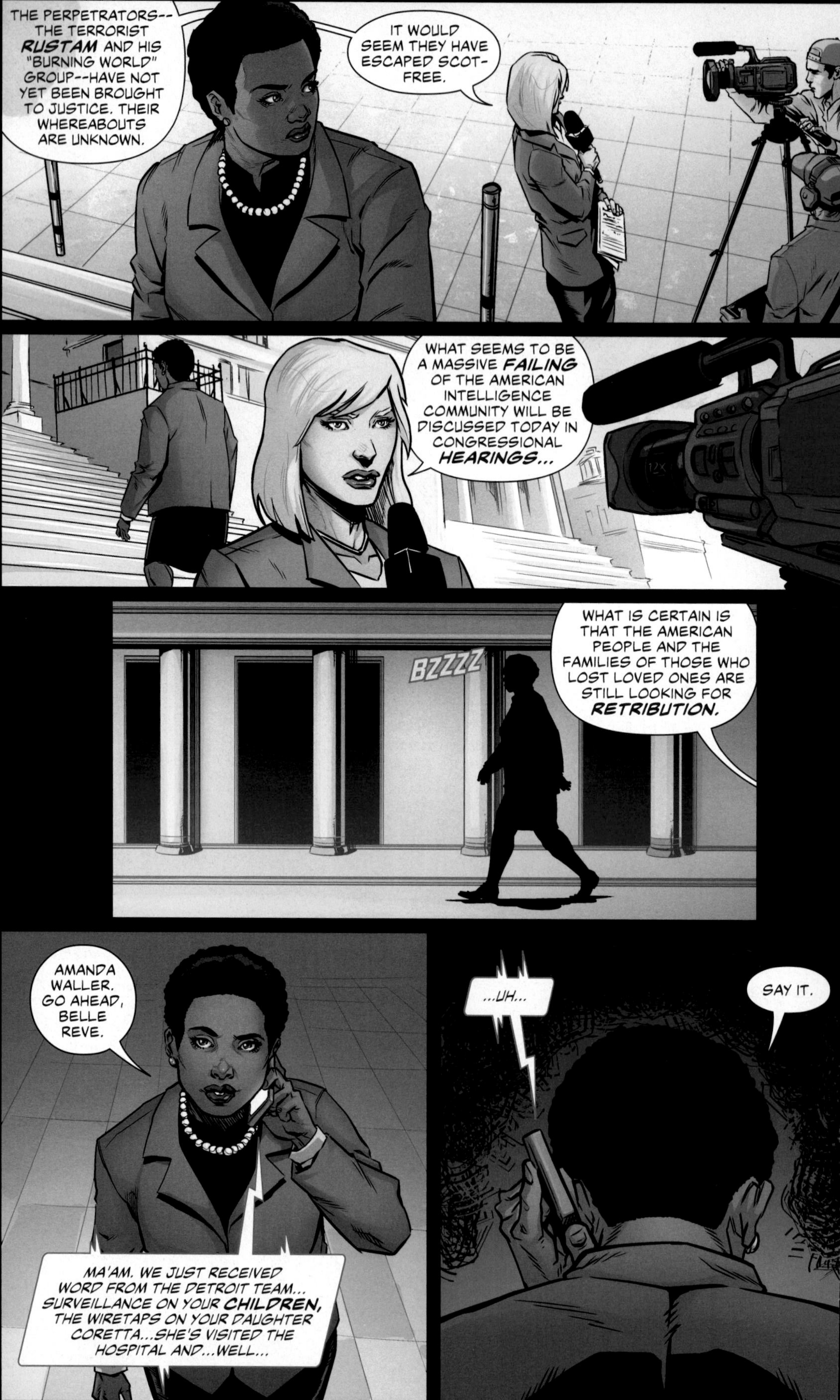
THE PERPETRATORS-- THE TERRORIST RUSTAM AND HIS "BURNING WORLD" GROUP--HAVE NOT YET BEEN BROUGHT TO JUSTICE. THEIR WHEREABOUTS ARE UNKNOWN.
IT WOULD SEEM THEY HAVE ESCAPED SCOT-FREE.
WHAT SEEMS TO BE A MASSIVE FAILING OF THE AMERICAN INTELLIGENCE COMMUNITY WILL BE DISCUSSED TODAY IN CONGRESSIONAL HEARINGS...
WHAT IS CERTAIN IS THAT THE AMERICAN PEOPLE AND THE FAMILIES OF THOSE WHO LOST LOVED ONES ARE STILL LOOKING FOR RETRIBUTION.
BZZZZ
AMANDA WALLER. GO AHEAD, BELLE REVE.
MA'AM. WE JUST RECEIVED WORD FROM THE DETROIT TEAM... SURVEILLANCE ON YOUR CHILDREN, THE WIRETAPS ON YOUR DAUGHTER CORETTA...SHE'S VISITED THE HOSPITAL AND...WELL...
...UH...
SAY IT.

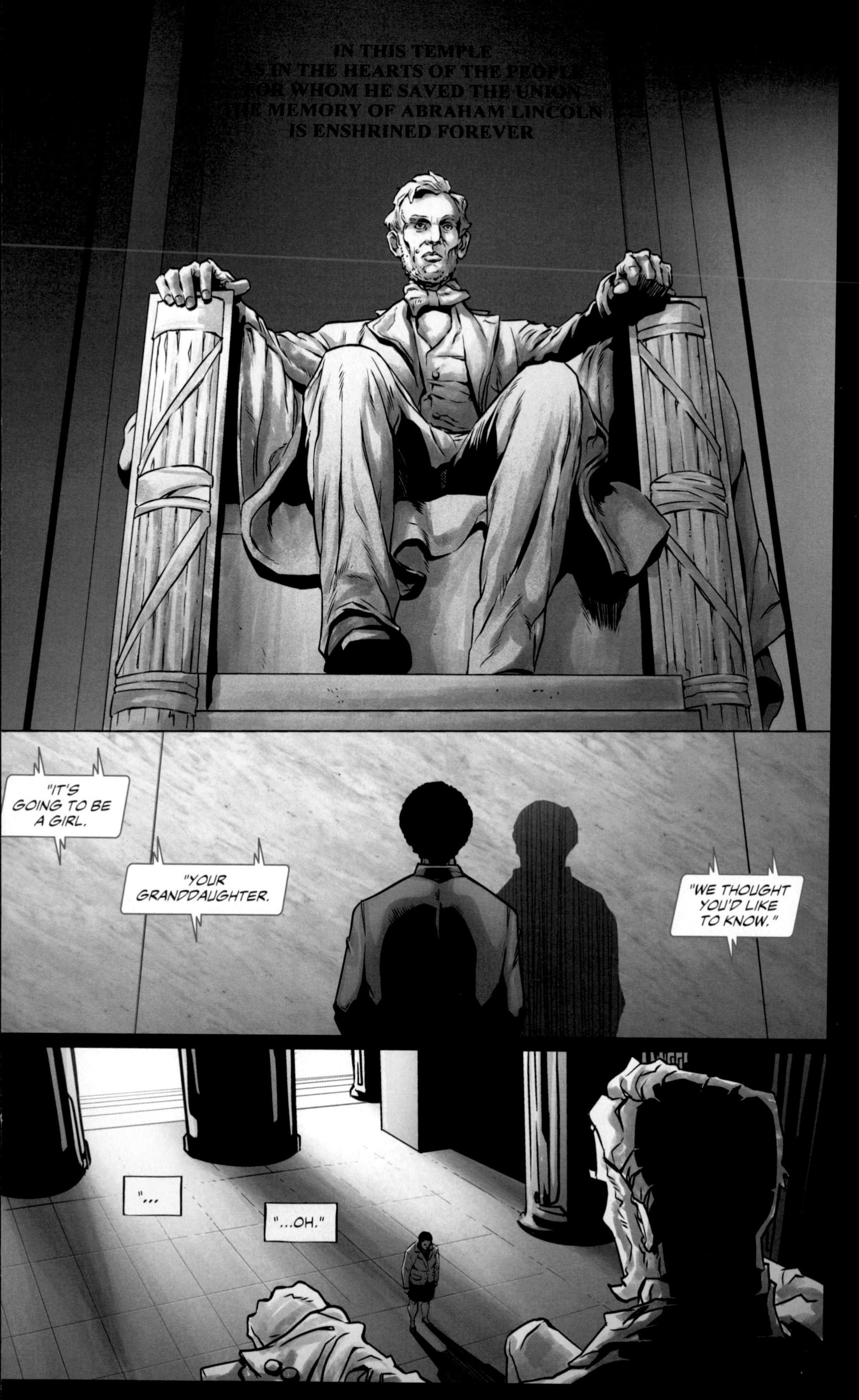
IN THIS TEMPLE
IN THE HEARTS OF THE PEOPLE
WHOM HE SAVED THE UNION
MEMORY OF ABRAHAM LINCOLN
IS ENSHRINED FOREVER
"IT'S GOING TO BE A GIRL.
"YOUR GRANDDAUGHTER.
"WE THOUGHT YOU'D LIKE TO KNOW."
"...
"...OH."

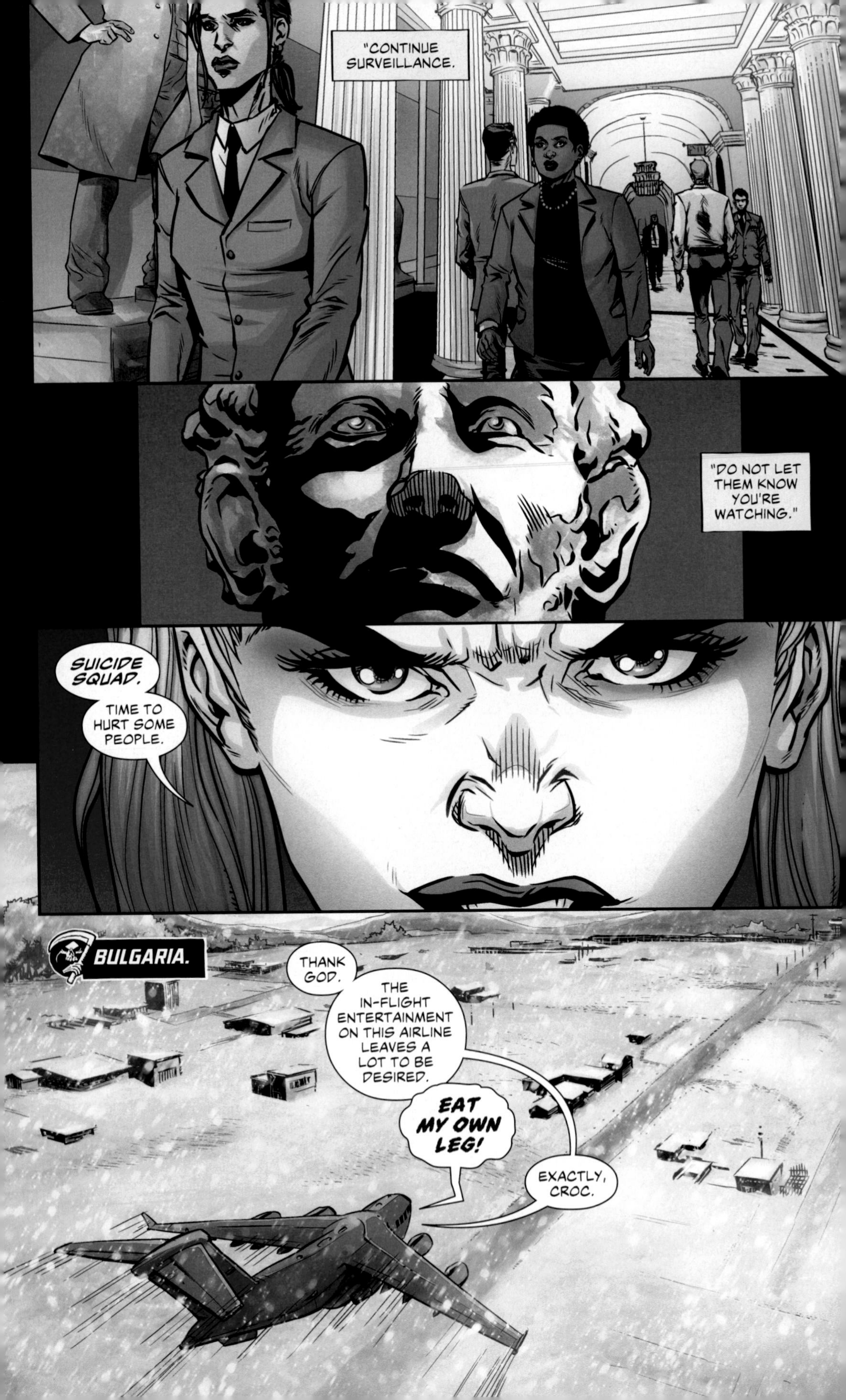
"CONTINUE SURVEILLANCE.
"DO NOT LET THEM KNOW YOU'RE WATCHING."
SUICIDE SQUAD.
TIME TO HURT SOME PEOPLE.
BULGARIA.
THANK GOD.
THE IN-FLIGHT ENTERTAINMENT ON THIS AIRLINE LEAVES A LOT TO BE DESIRED.
EAT MY OWN LEG!
EXACTLY, CROC.

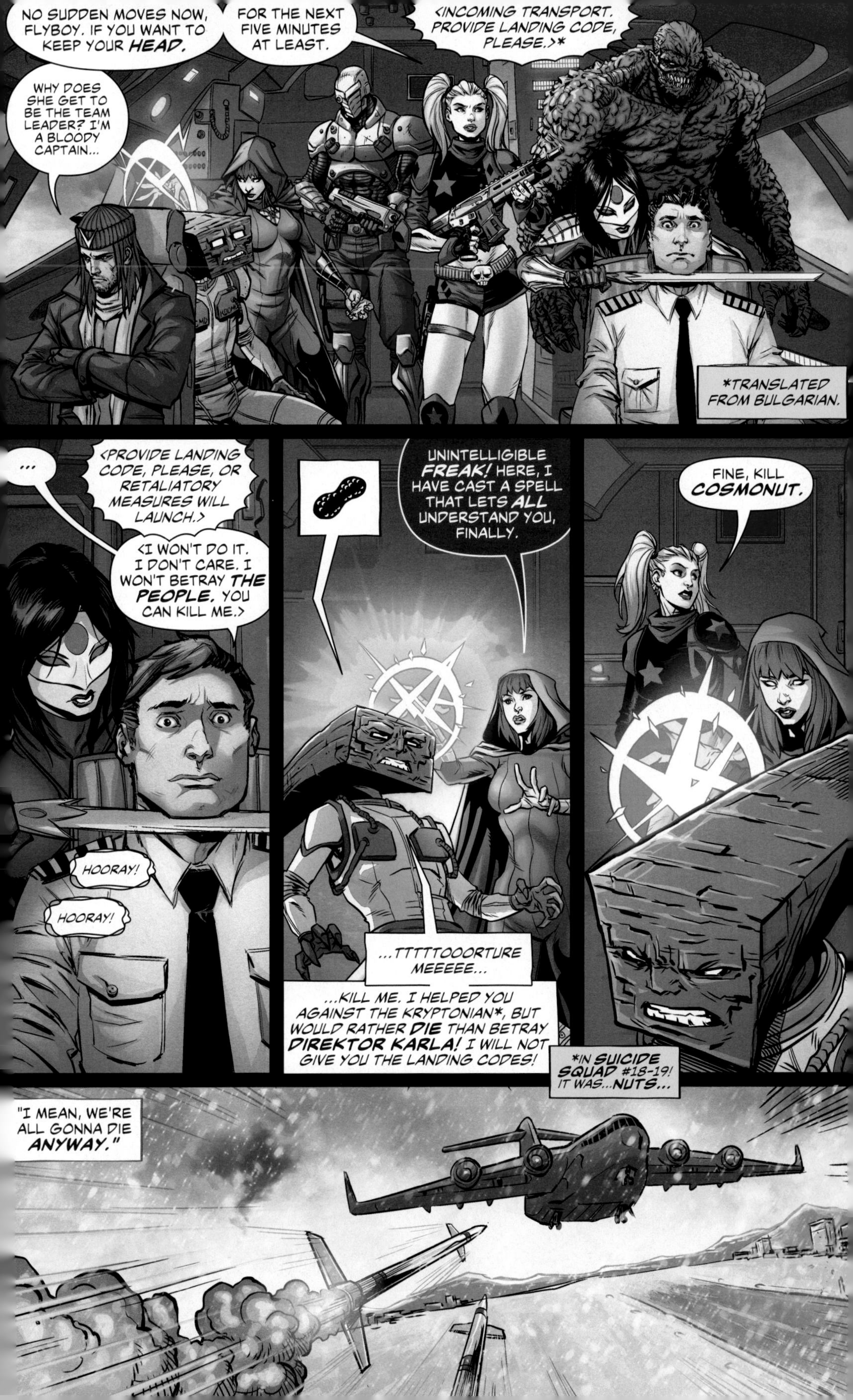
NO SUDDEN MOVES NOW, FLYBOY. IF YOU WANT TO KEEP YOUR HEAD.
FOR THE NEXT FIVE MINUTES AT LEAST.
<INCOMING TRANSPORT. PROVIDE LANDING CODE, PLEASE.>*
WHY DOES SHE GET TO BE THE TEAM LEADER? I'M A BLOODY CAPTAIN...
*TRANSLATED FROM BULGARIAN.
...
<PROVIDE LANDING CODE, PLEASE, OR RETALIATORY MEASURES WILL LAUNCH.>
<I WON'T DO IT. I DON'T CARE. I WON'T BETRAY THE PEOPLE. YOU CAN KILL ME.>
HOORAY!
HOORAY!
UNINTELLIGIBLE FREAK! HERE, I HAVE CAST A SPELL THAT LETS ALL UNDERSTAND YOU, FINALLY.
...TTTTTOOORTURE MEEEEE...
...KILL ME. I HELPED YOU AGAINST THE KRYPTONIAN*, BUT WOULD RATHER DIE THAN BETRAY DIREKTOR KARLA! I WILL NOT GIVE YOU THE LANDING CODES!
FINE, KILL COSMONUT.
*IN SUICIDE SQUAD #18-19! IT WAS...NUTS...
"I MEAN, WE'RE ALL GONNA DIE ANYWAY."

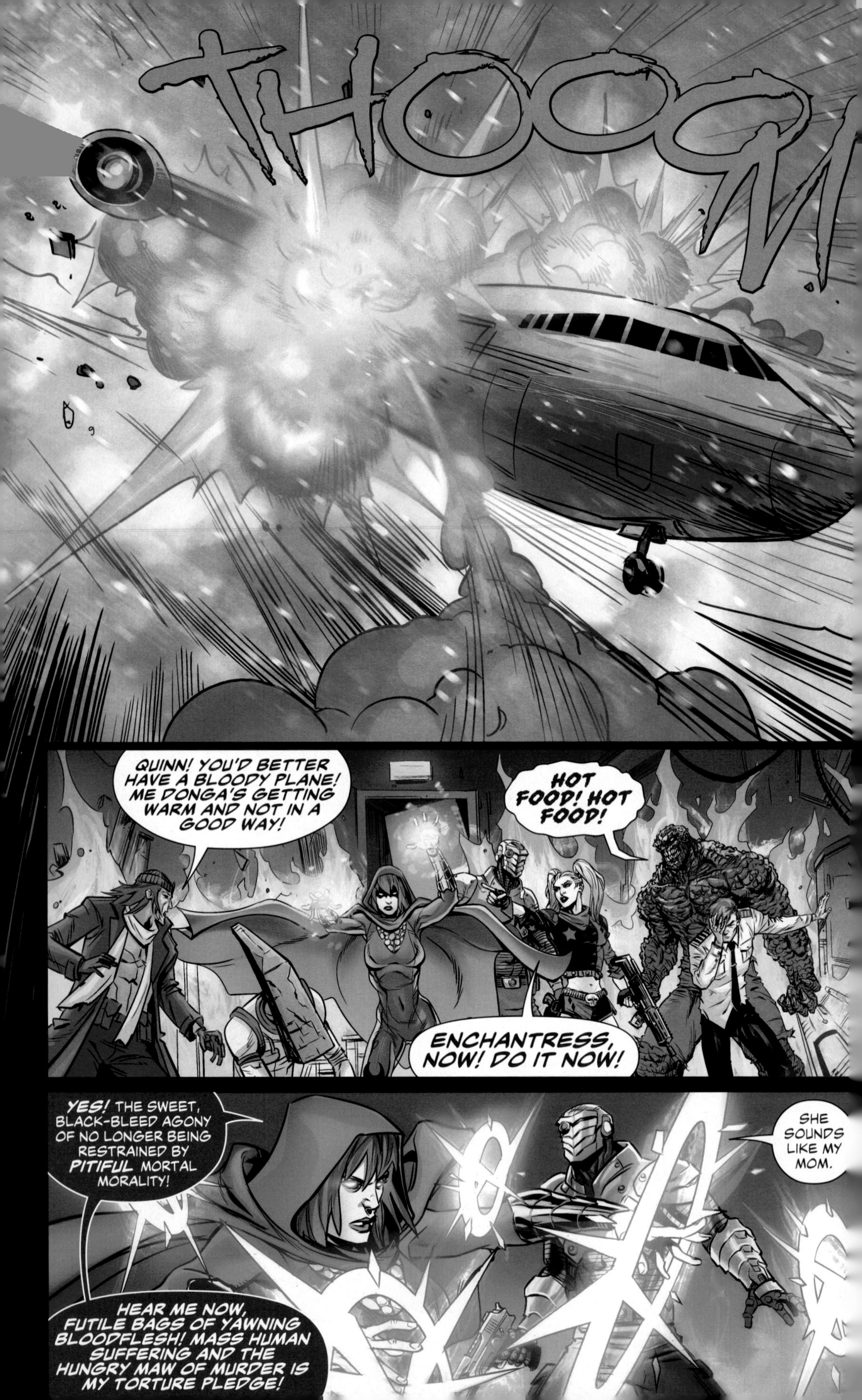
THOOOM
QUINN! YOU'D BETTER HAVE A BLOODY PLANE! ME DONGA'S GETTING WARM AND NOT IN A GOOD WAY!
HOT FOOD! HOT FOOD!
ENCHANTRESS, NOW! DO IT NOW!
YES! THE SWEET, BLACK-BLEED AGONY OF NO LONGER BEING RESTRAINED BY PITIFUL MORTAL MORALITY!
SHE SOUNDS LIKE MY MOM.
HEAR ME NOW, FUTILE BAGS OF YAWNING BLOODFLESH! MASS HUMAN SUFFERING AND THE HUNGRY MAW OF MURDER IS MY TORTURE PLEDGE!

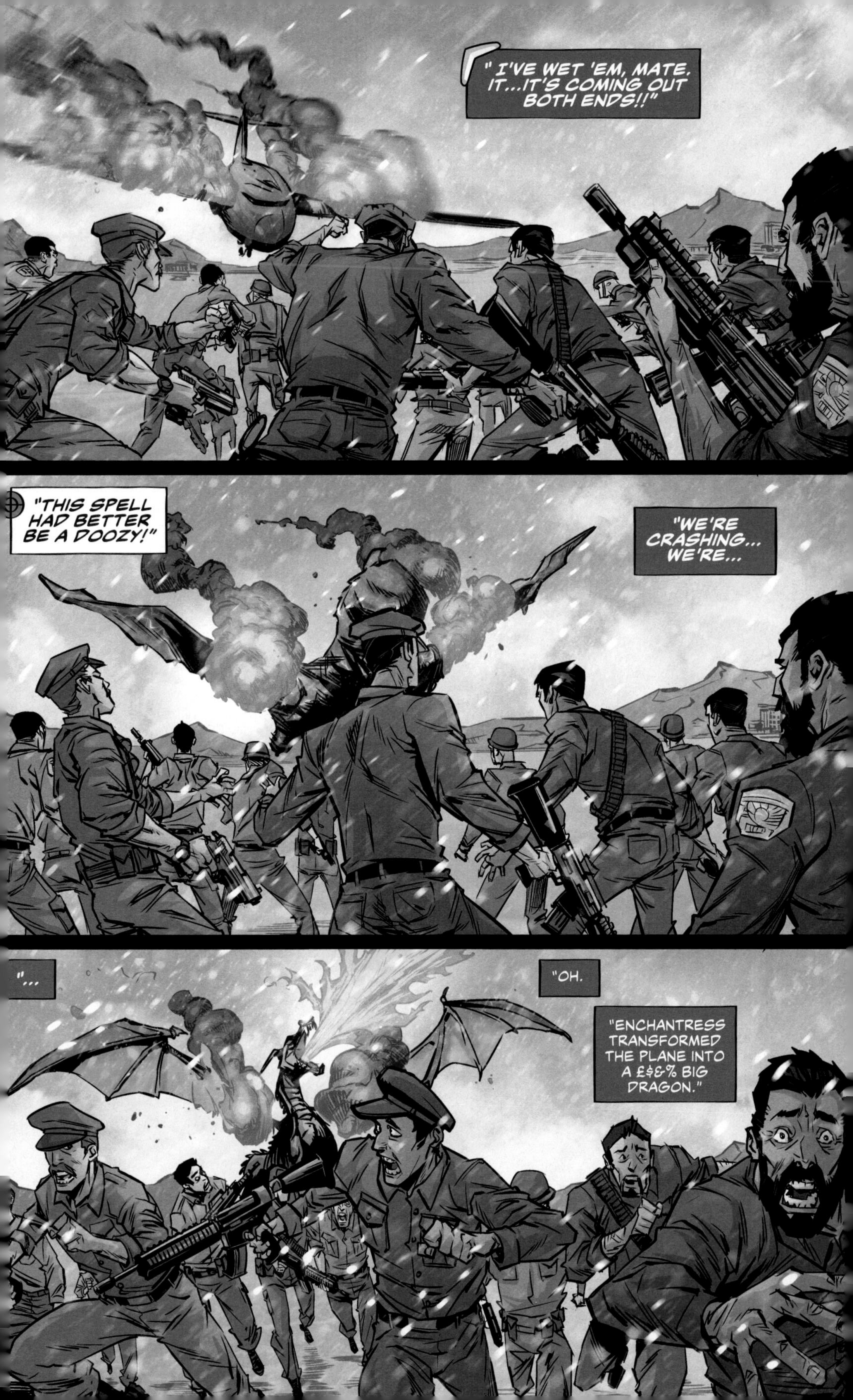
"I'VE WET 'EM, MATE. IT...IT'S COMING OUT BOTH ENDS!!"
"THIS SPELL HAD BETTER BE A DOOZY!"
"WE'RE CRASHING... WE'RE...
"...
"OH.
"ENCHANTRESS TRANSFORMED THE PLANE INTO A £$&% BIG DRAGON."

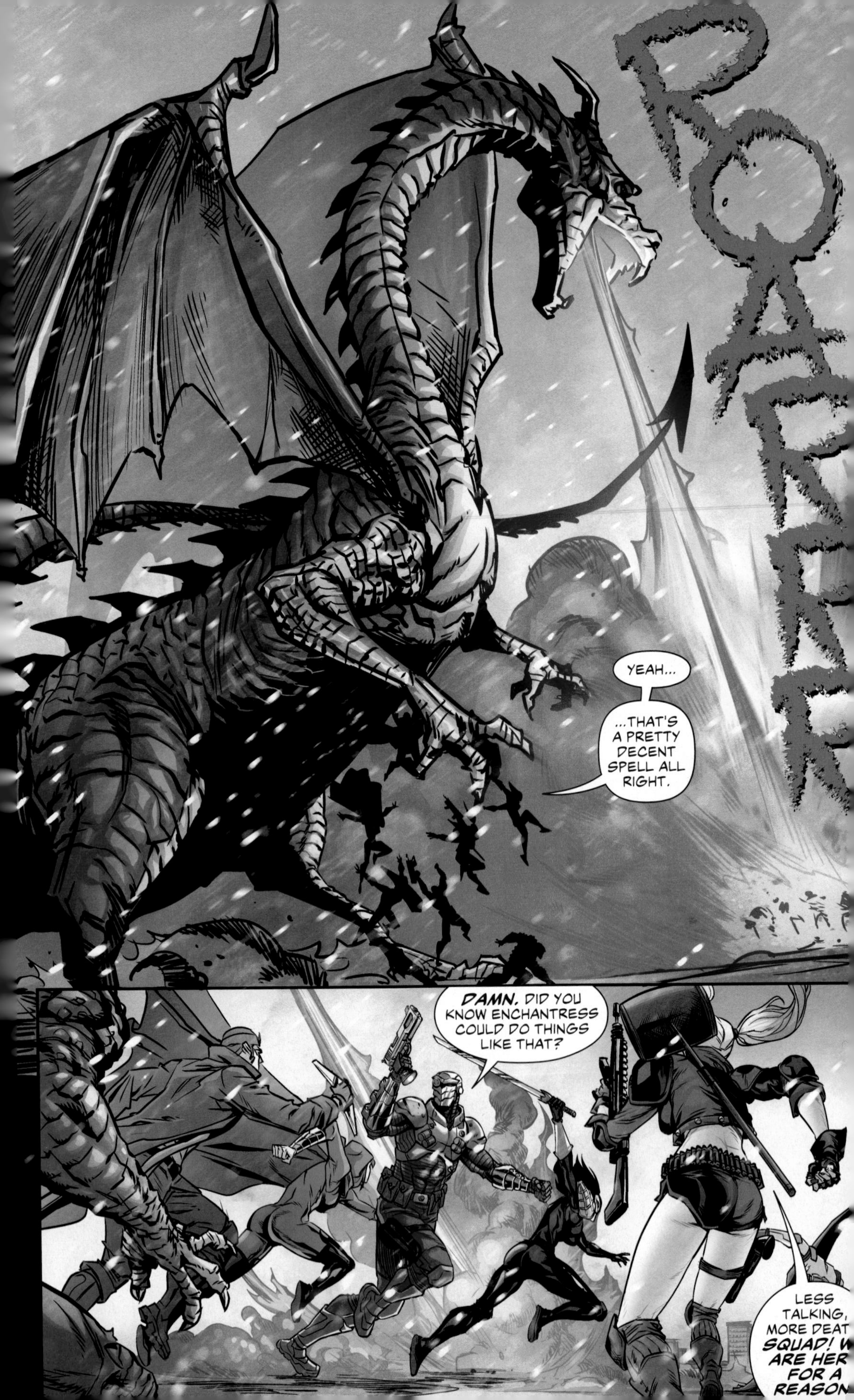
ROARRR
YEAH...
...THAT'S A PRETTY DECENT SPELL ALL RIGHT.
DAMN. DID YOU KNOW ENCHANTRESS COULD DO THINGS LIKE THAT?
LESS TALKING, MORE DEAT SQUAD! W ARE HER FOR A REASON

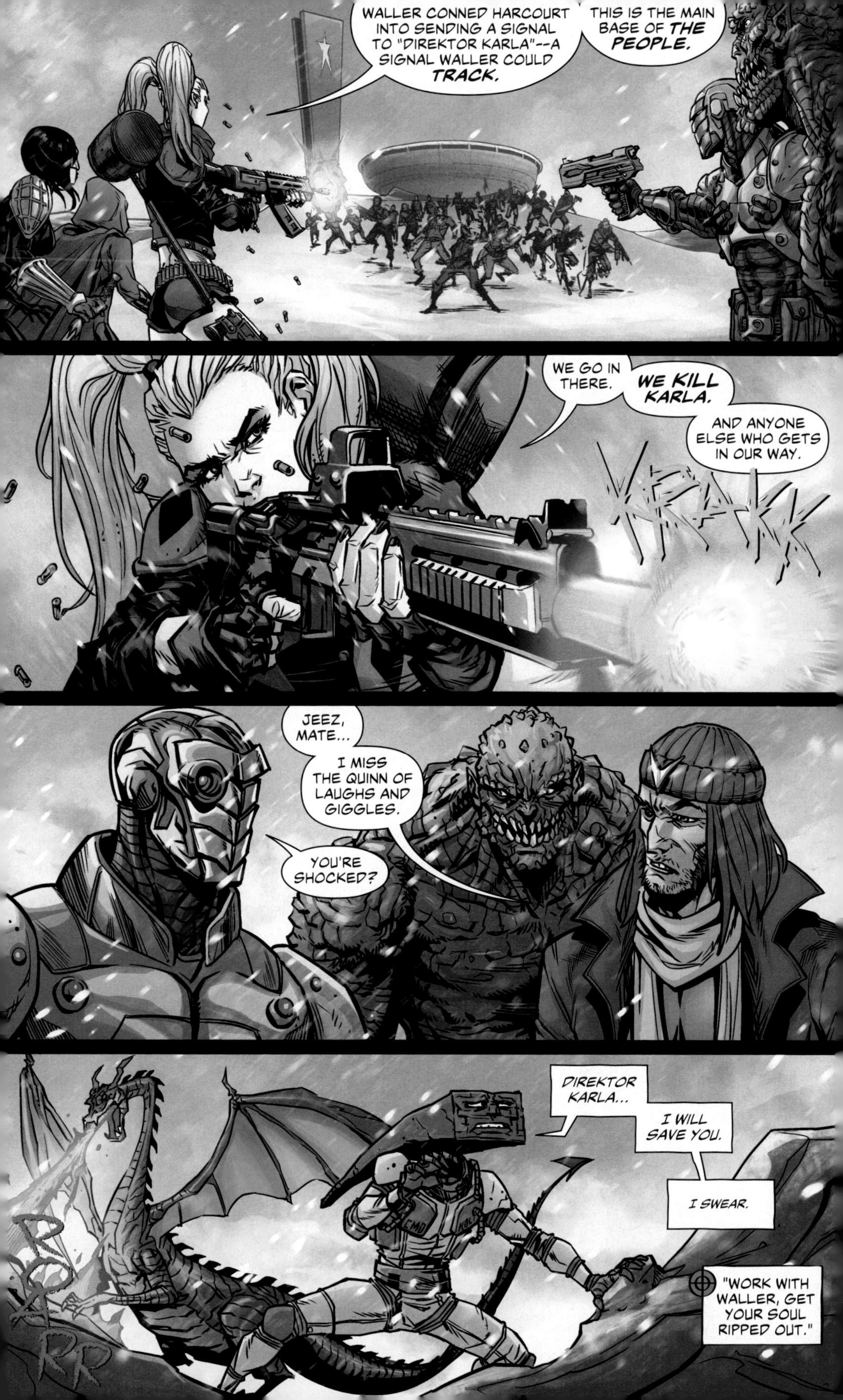

WALLER CONNED HARCOURT INTO SENDING A SIGNAL TO "DIREKTOR KARLA"--A SIGNAL WALLER COULD TRACK.
THIS IS THE MAIN BASE OF THE PEOPLE.
WE GO IN THERE.
WE KILL KARLA.
AND ANYONE ELSE WHO GETS IN OUR WAY.
KRAKK
JEEZ, MATE...
I MISS THE QUINN OF LAUGHS AND GIGGLES.
YOU'RE SHOCKED?
DIREKTOR KARLA...
I WILL SAVE YOU.
I SWEAR.
"WORK WITH WALLER, GET YOUR SOUL RIPPED OUT."

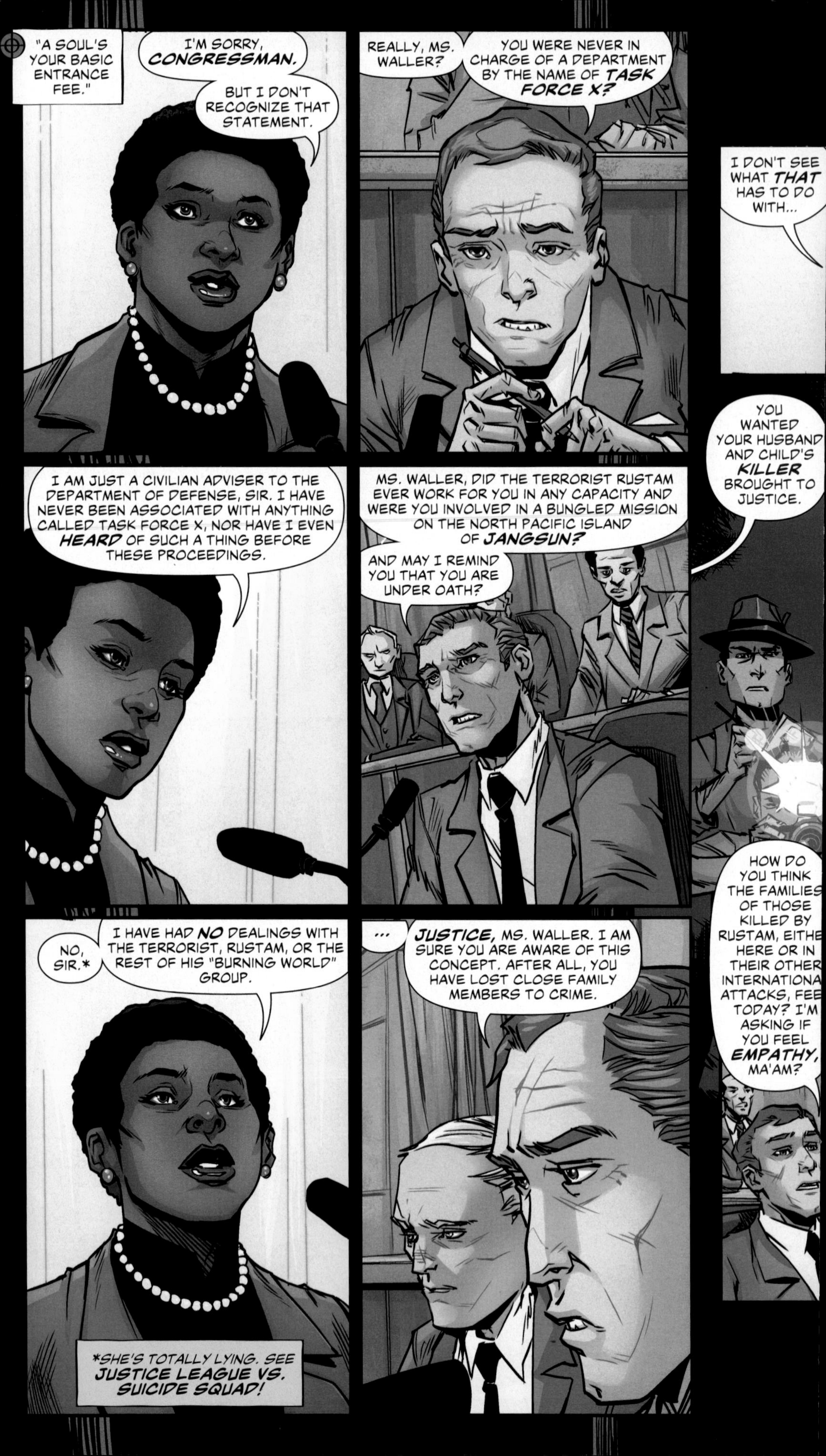

"A SOUL'S YOUR BASIC ENTRANCE FEE."
I'M SORRY, **CONGRESSMAN.**
BUT I DON'T RECOGNIZE THAT STATEMENT.
REALLY, MS. WALLER?
YOU WERE NEVER IN CHARGE OF A DEPARTMENT BY THE NAME OF **TASK FORCE X?**
I AM JUST A CIVILIAN ADVISER TO THE DEPARTMENT OF DEFENSE, SIR. I HAVE NEVER BEEN ASSOCIATED WITH ANYTHING CALLED TASK FORCE X, NOR HAVE I EVEN **HEARD** OF SUCH A THING BEFORE THESE PROCEEDINGS.
MS. WALLER, DID THE TERRORIST RUSTAM EVER WORK FOR YOU IN ANY CAPACITY AND WERE YOU INVOLVED IN A BUNGLED MISSION ON THE NORTH PACIFIC ISLAND OF **JANGSUN?**
AND MAY I REMIND YOU THAT YOU ARE UNDER OATH?
NO, SIR.*
I HAVE HAD **NO** DEALINGS WITH THE TERRORIST, RUSTAM, OR THE REST OF HIS "BURNING WORLD" GROUP.
*SHE'S TOTALLY LYING. SEE **JUSTICE LEAGUE VS. SUICIDE SQUAD!**
...
JUSTICE, MS. WALLER. I AM SURE YOU ARE AWARE OF THIS CONCEPT. AFTER ALL, YOU HAVE LOST CLOSE FAMILY MEMBERS TO CRIME.
I DON'T SEE WHAT **THAT** HAS TO DO WITH...
YOU WANTED YOUR HUSBAND AND CHILD'S **KILLER** BROUGHT TO JUSTICE.
HOW DO YOU THINK THE FAMILIES OF THOSE KILLED BY RUSTAM, EITHE HERE OR IN THEIR OTHER INTERNATIONA ATTACKS, FEE TODAY? I'M ASKING IF YOU FEEL **EMPATHY,** MA'AM?

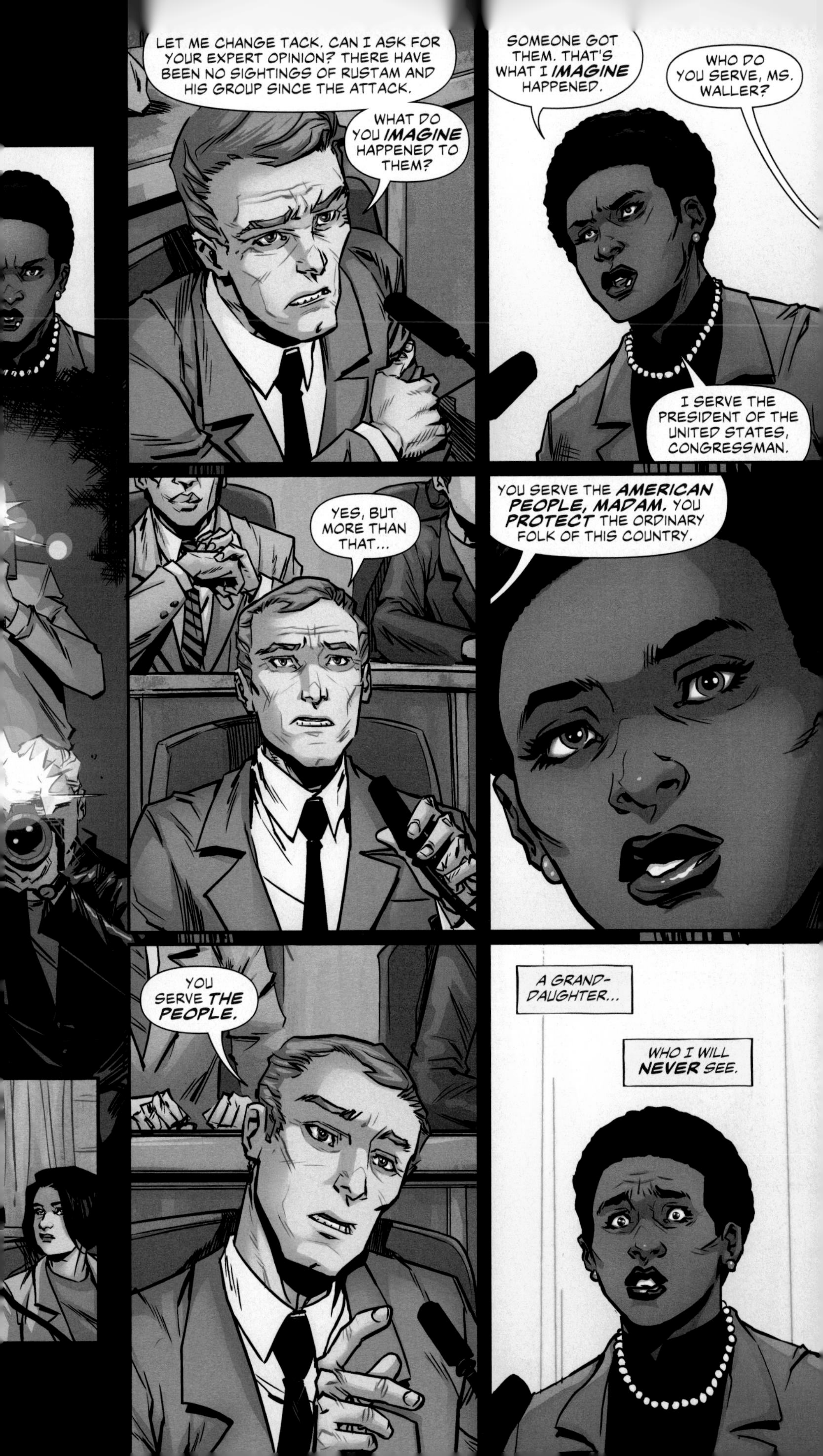
LET ME CHANGE TACK. CAN I ASK FOR YOUR EXPERT OPINION? THERE HAVE BEEN NO SIGHTINGS OF RUSTAM AND HIS GROUP SINCE THE ATTACK.
WHAT DO YOU IMAGINE HAPPENED TO THEM?
SOMEONE GOT THEM. THAT'S WHAT I IMAGINE HAPPENED.
WHO DO YOU SERVE, MS. WALLER?
I SERVE THE PRESIDENT OF THE UNITED STATES, CONGRESSMAN.
YES, BUT MORE THAN THAT...
YOU SERVE THE AMERICAN PEOPLE, MADAM. YOU PROTECT THE ORDINARY FOLK OF THIS COUNTRY.
YOU SERVE THE PEOPLE.
A GRAND-DAUGHTER...
WHO I WILL NEVER SEE.

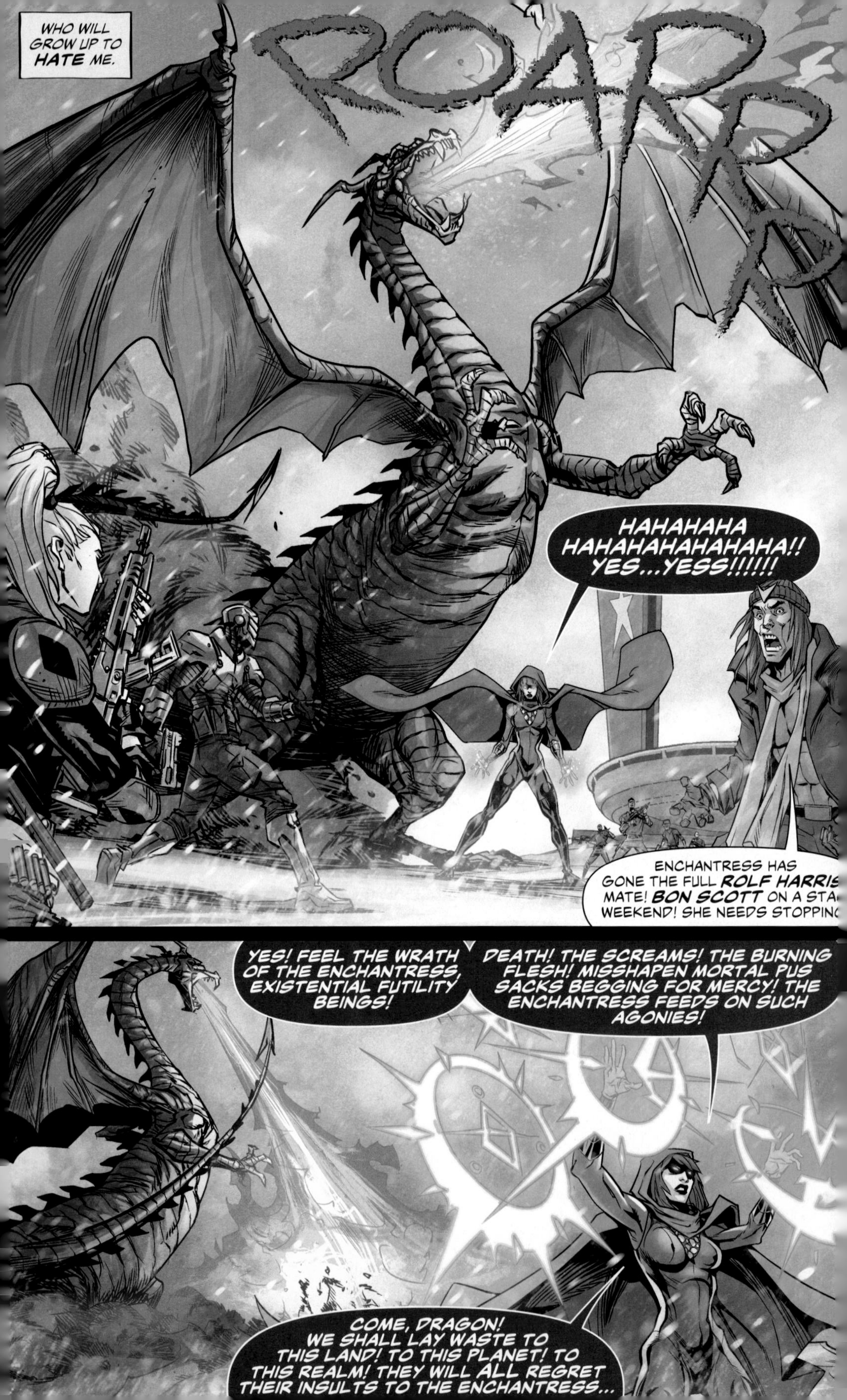
WHO WILL GROW UP TO HATE ME.
ROARRRR
HAHAHAHA HAHAHAHAHAHAHA!! YES...YESS!!!!!!
ENCHANTRESS HAS GONE THE FULL ROLF HARRIS MATE! BON SCOTT ON A STA WEEKEND! SHE NEEDS STOPPING
YES! FEEL THE WRATH OF THE ENCHANTRESS, EXISTENTIAL FUTILITY BEINGS!
DEATH! THE SCREAMS! THE BURNING FLESH! MISSHAPEN MORTAL PUS SACKS BEGGING FOR MERCY! THE ENCHANTRESS FEEDS ON SUCH AGONIES!
COME, DRAGON! WE SHALL LAY WASTE TO THIS LAND! TO THIS PLANET! TO THIS REALM! THEY WILL ALL REGRET THEIR INSULTS TO THE ENCHANTRESS...

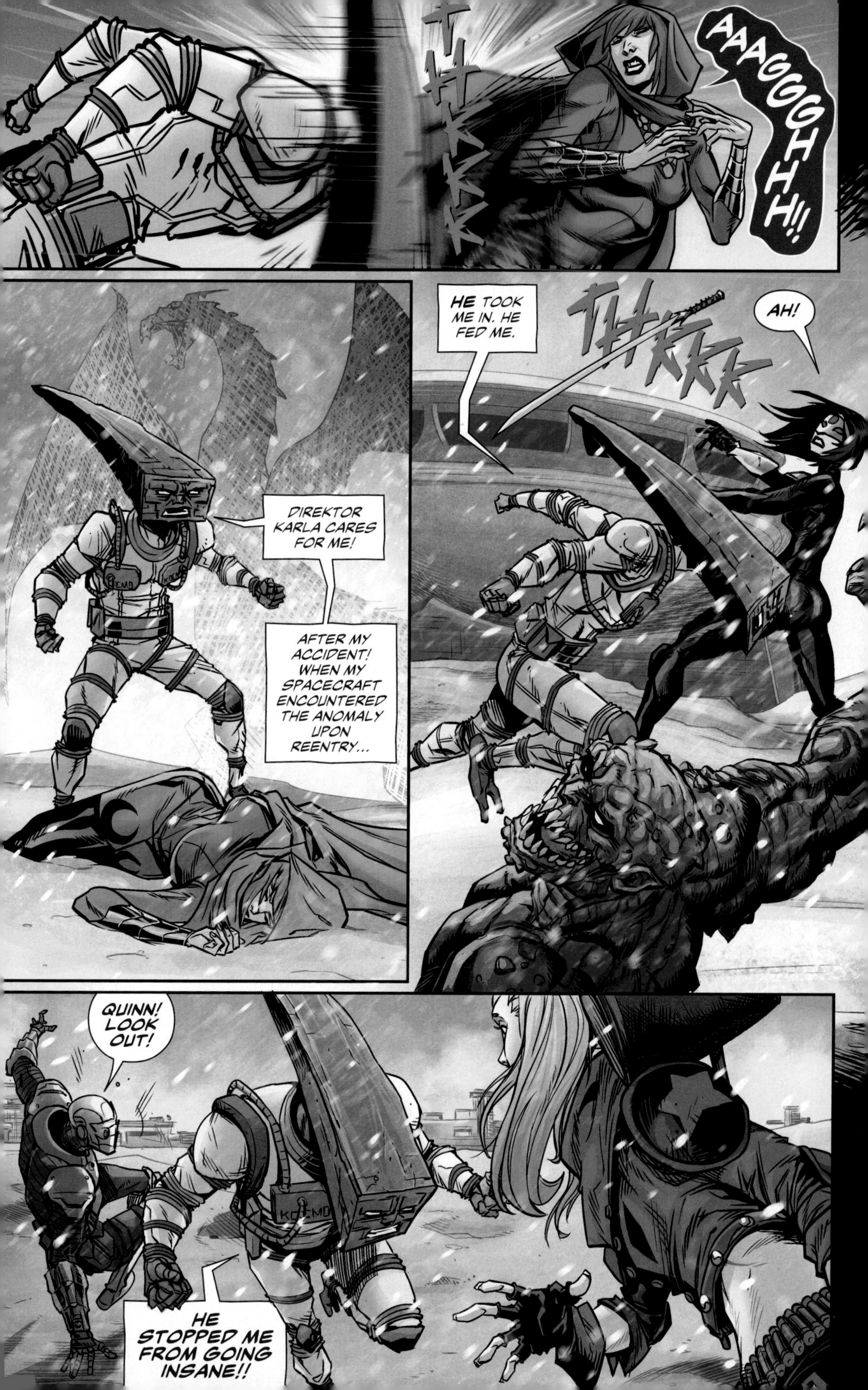
THHKKKK
AAAGGGHHH!!
DIREKTOR KARLA CARES FOR ME!
AFTER MY ACCIDENT! WHEN MY SPACECRAFT ENCOUNTERED THE ANOMALY UPON REENTRY...
HE TOOK ME IN. HE FED ME.
THHKKKK
AH!
QUINN! LOOK OUT!
HE STOPPED ME FROM GOING INSANE!!

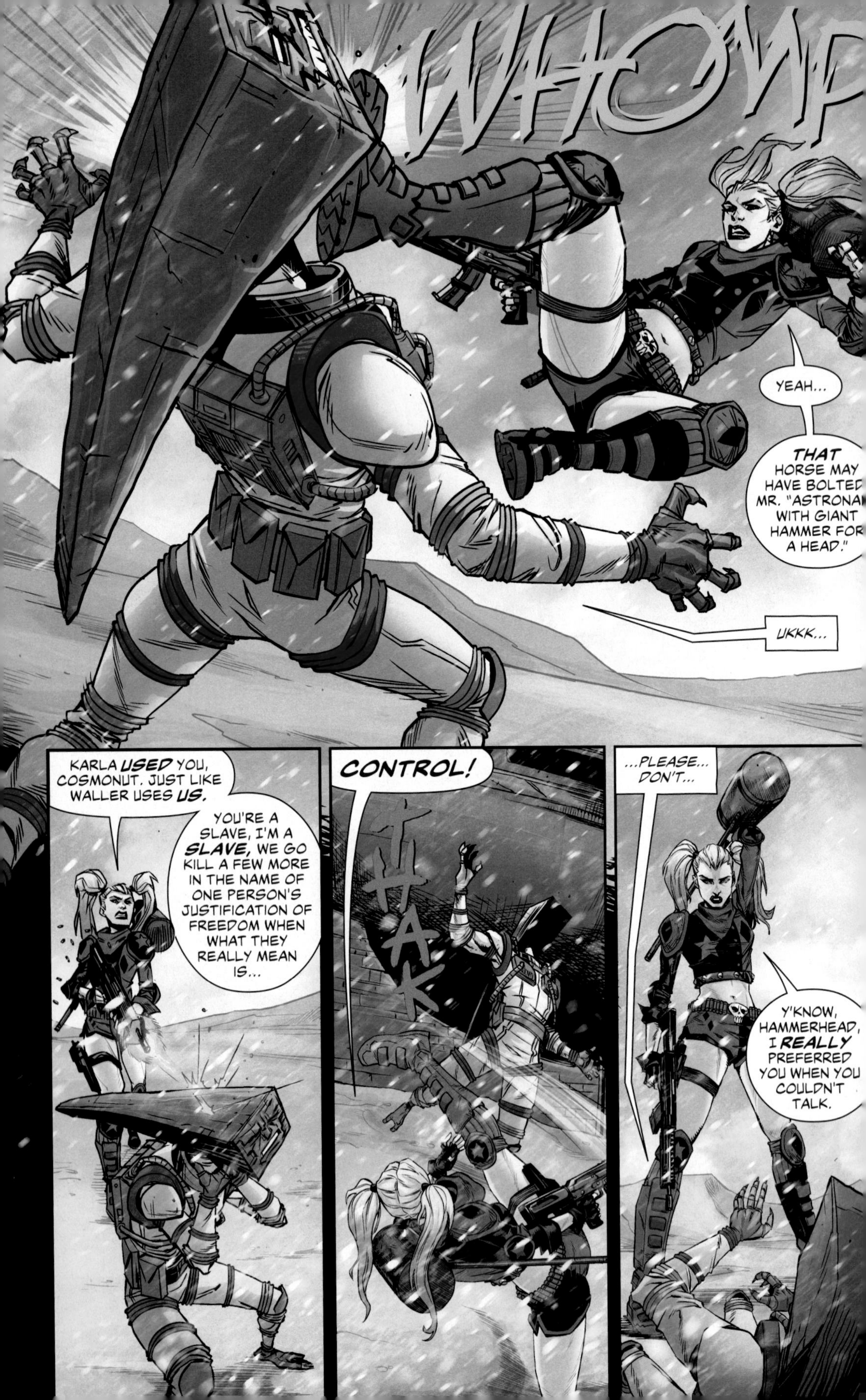
WHOMP
YEAH...
THAT HORSE MAY HAVE BOLTED MR. "ASTRONA WITH GIANT HAMMER FOR A HEAD."
UKKK...
KARLA USED YOU, COSMONUT. JUST LIKE WALLER USES US.
YOU'RE A SLAVE, I'M A SLAVE, WE GO KILL A FEW MORE IN THE NAME OF ONE PERSON'S JUSTIFICATION OF FREEDOM WHEN WHAT THEY REALLY MEAN IS...
CONTROL!
THAK
...PLEASE... DON'T...
Y'KNOW, HAMMERHEAD, I REALLY PREFERRED YOU WHEN YOU COULDN'T TALK.

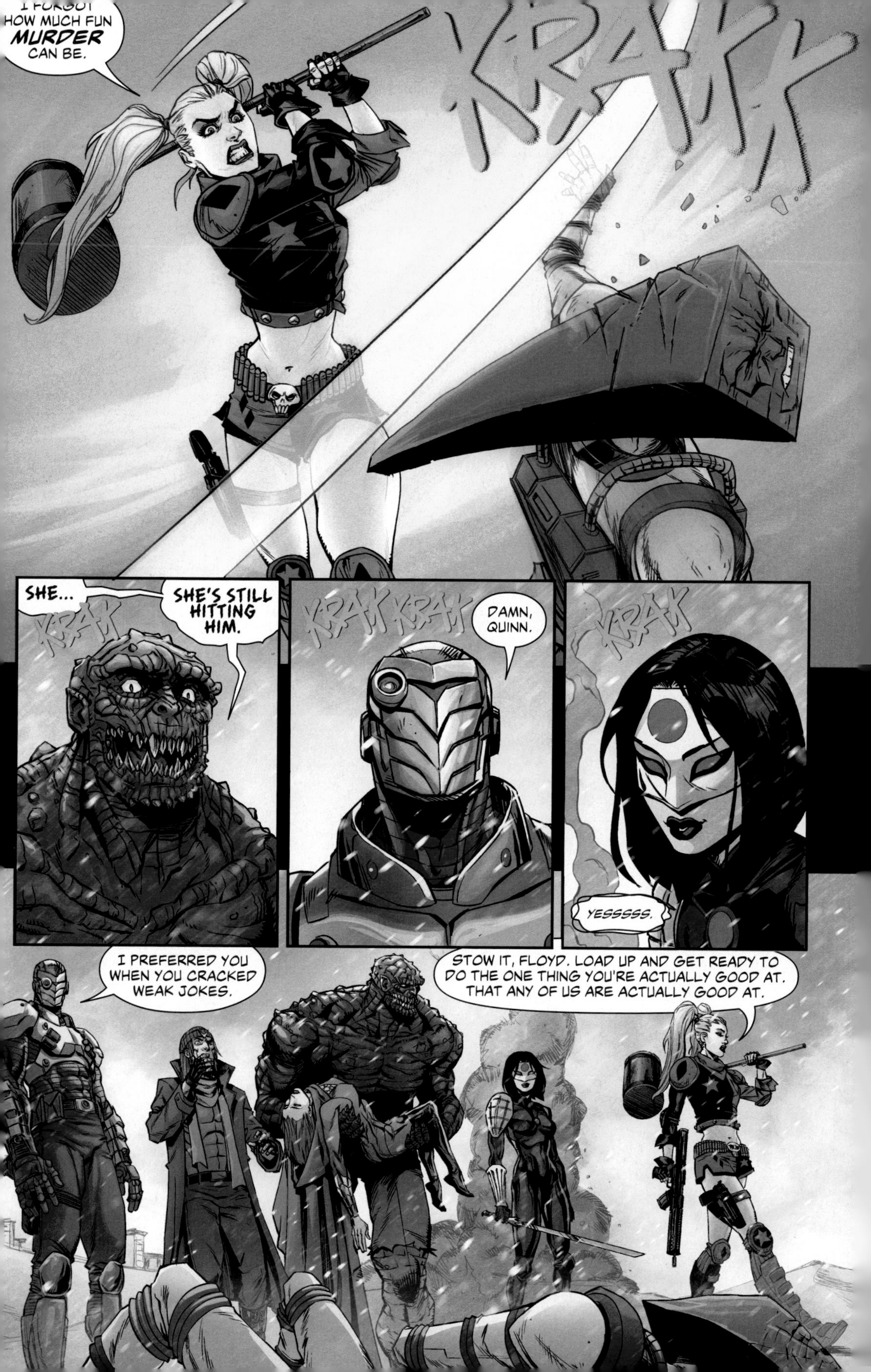

I FORGOT HOW MUCH FUN MURDER CAN BE.
KRAKK
SHE...
KRAK
SHE'S STILL HITTING HIM.
KRAK KRAK
DAMN, QUINN.
KRAK
YESSSSS.
I PREFERRED YOU WHEN YOU CRACKED WEAK JOKES.
STOW IT, FLOYD. LOAD UP AND GET READY TO DO THE ONE THING YOU'RE ACTUALLY GOOD AT. THAT ANY OF US ARE ACTUALLY GOOD AT.

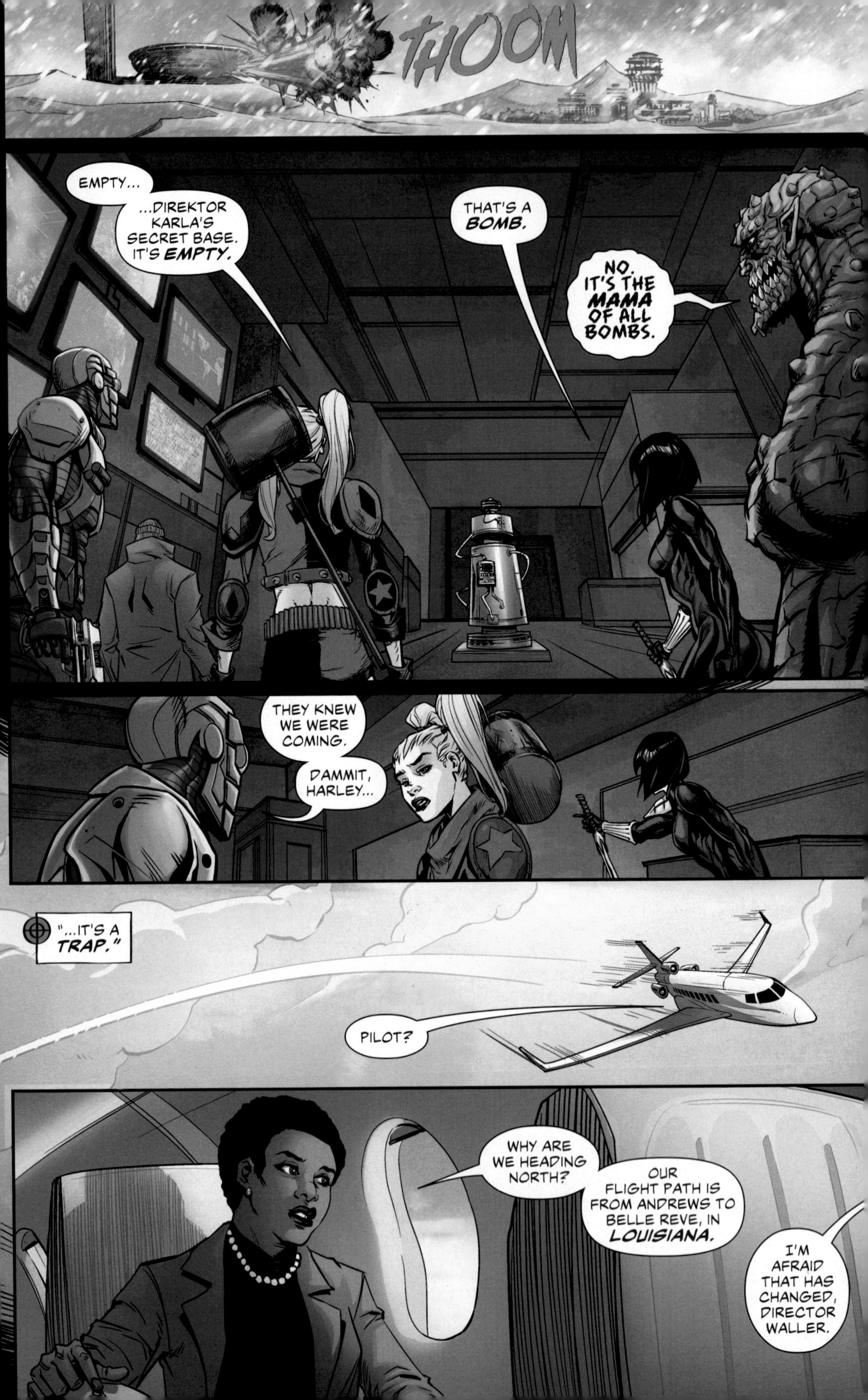
THOOM
EMPTY...
...DIREKTOR KARLA'S SECRET BASE. IT'S EMPTY.
THAT'S A BOMB.
NO. IT'S THE MAMA OF ALL BOMBS.
THEY KNEW WE WERE COMING.
DAMMIT, HARLEY...
"...IT'S A TRAP."
PILOT?
WHY ARE WE HEADING NORTH?
OUR FLIGHT PATH IS FROM ANDREWS TO BELLE REVE, IN LOUISIANA.
I'M AFRAID THAT HAS CHANGED, DIRECTOR WALLER.

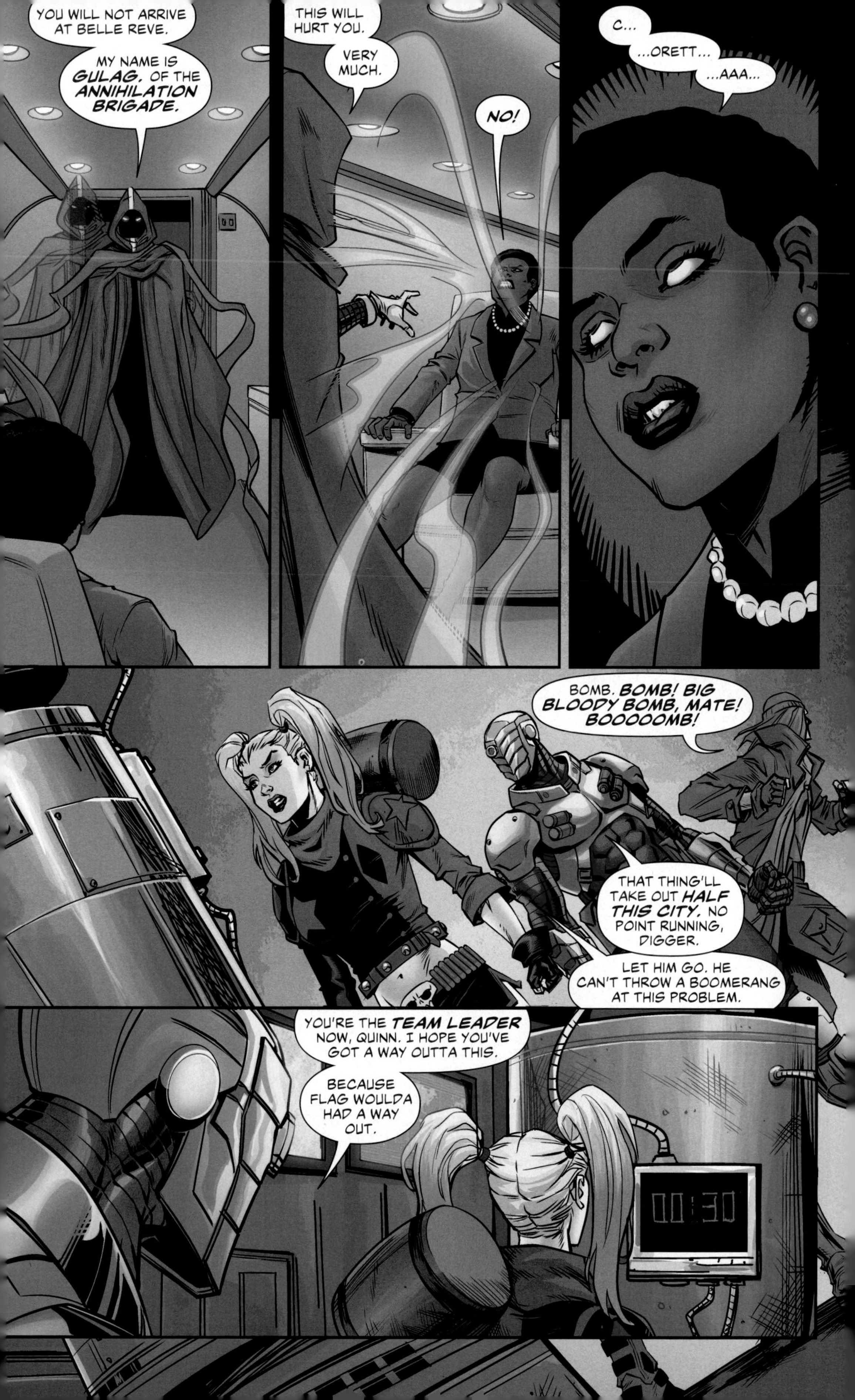
YOU WILL NOT ARRIVE AT BELLE REVE.
MY NAME IS GULAG, OF THE ANNIHILATION BRIGADE.
THIS WILL HURT YOU.
VERY MUCH.
NO!
C...
...ORETT...
...AAA...
BOMB. BOMB! BIG BLOODY BOMB, MATE! BOOOOOMB!
THAT THING'LL TAKE OUT HALF THIS CITY. NO POINT RUNNING, DIGGER.
LET HIM GO. HE CAN'T THROW A BOOMERANG AT THIS PROBLEM.
YOU'RE THE TEAM LEADER NOW, QUINN. I HOPE YOU'VE GOT A WAY OUTTA THIS.
BECAUSE FLAG WOULDA HAD A WAY OUT.
00:30

WAKE ENCHANTRESS UP.

CAN'T. JUNE IS *HURT.* UNCONSCIOUS.

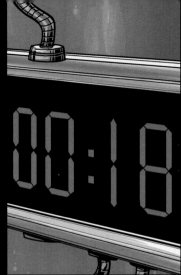

WAKE HER...

DON'T. TOUCH. HER.

I LOVE HER.

YEAH... AND SHE LOVES *YOU.*

DEADSHOT. SHOOT CROC IN THE HEAD.

OKAY. YOU'RE THE BOSS.

WHAT?

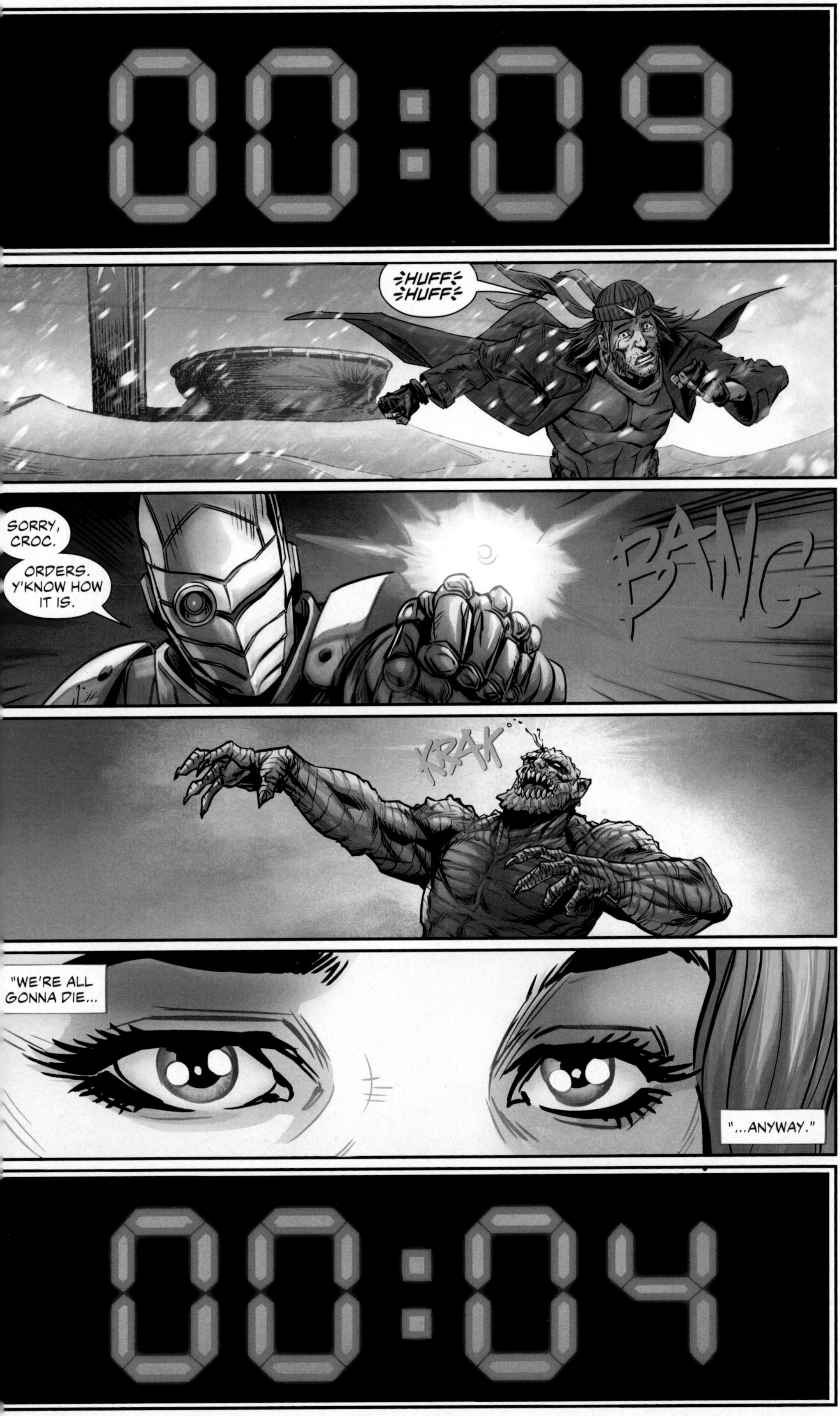
00:09
HUFF HUFF
SORRY, CROC.
ORDERS. Y'KNOW HOW IT IS.
BANG
KRAK
"WE'RE ALL GONNA DIE...
"...ANYWAY."
00:04

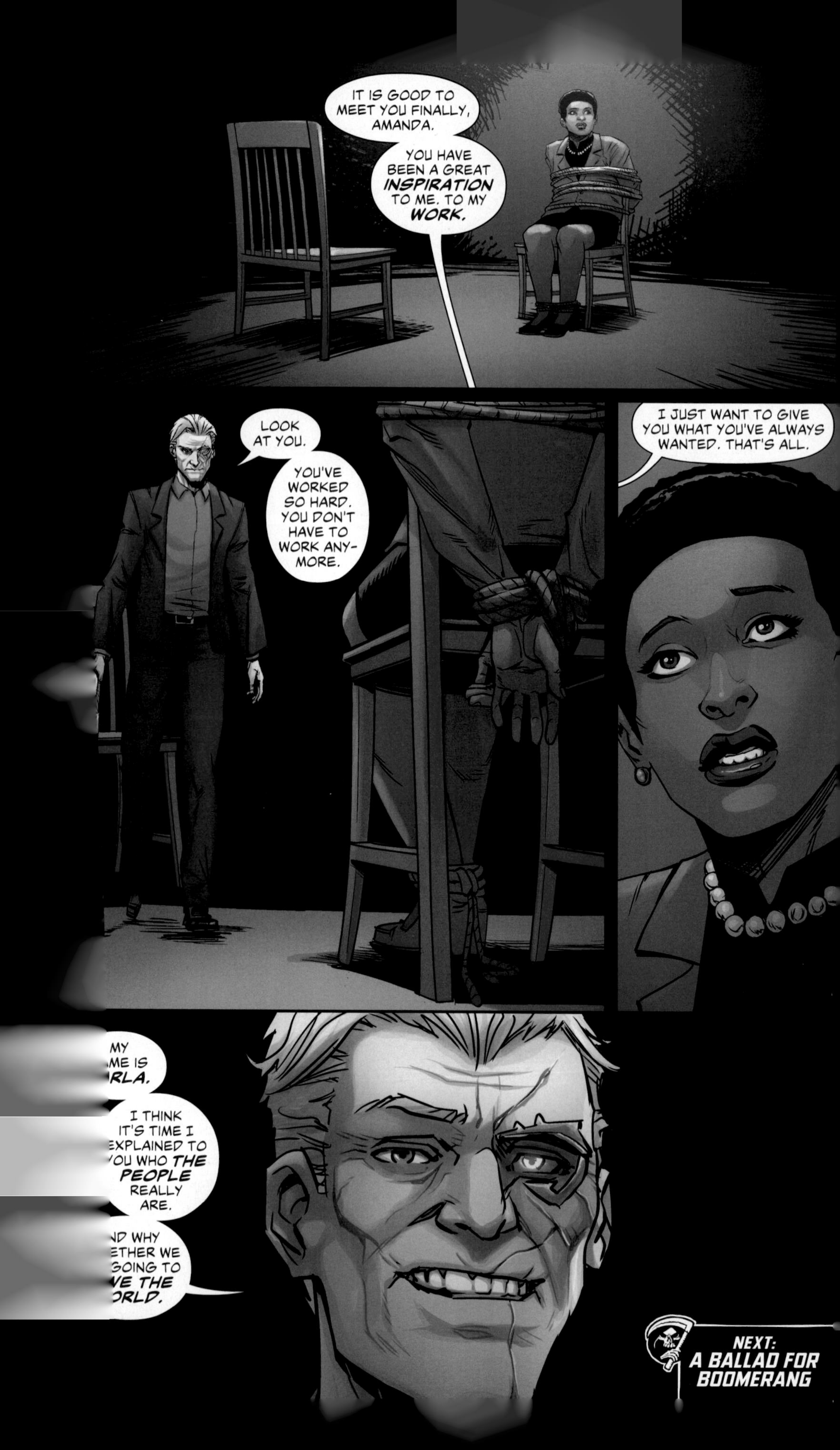

IT IS GOOD TO MEET YOU FINALLY, AMANDA.
YOU HAVE BEEN A GREAT INSPIRATION TO ME. TO MY WORK.
LOOK AT YOU.
YOU'VE WORKED SO HARD. YOU DON'T HAVE TO WORK ANY-MORE.
I JUST WANT TO GIVE YOU WHAT YOU'VE ALWAYS WANTED. THAT'S ALL.
MY
ME IS
RLA.
I THINK IT'S TIME I
XPLAINED TO
OU WHO THE PEOPLE REALLY ARE.
D WHY
ETHER WE
GOING TO
VE THE
RLD.
NEXT: A BALLAD FOR BOOMERANG

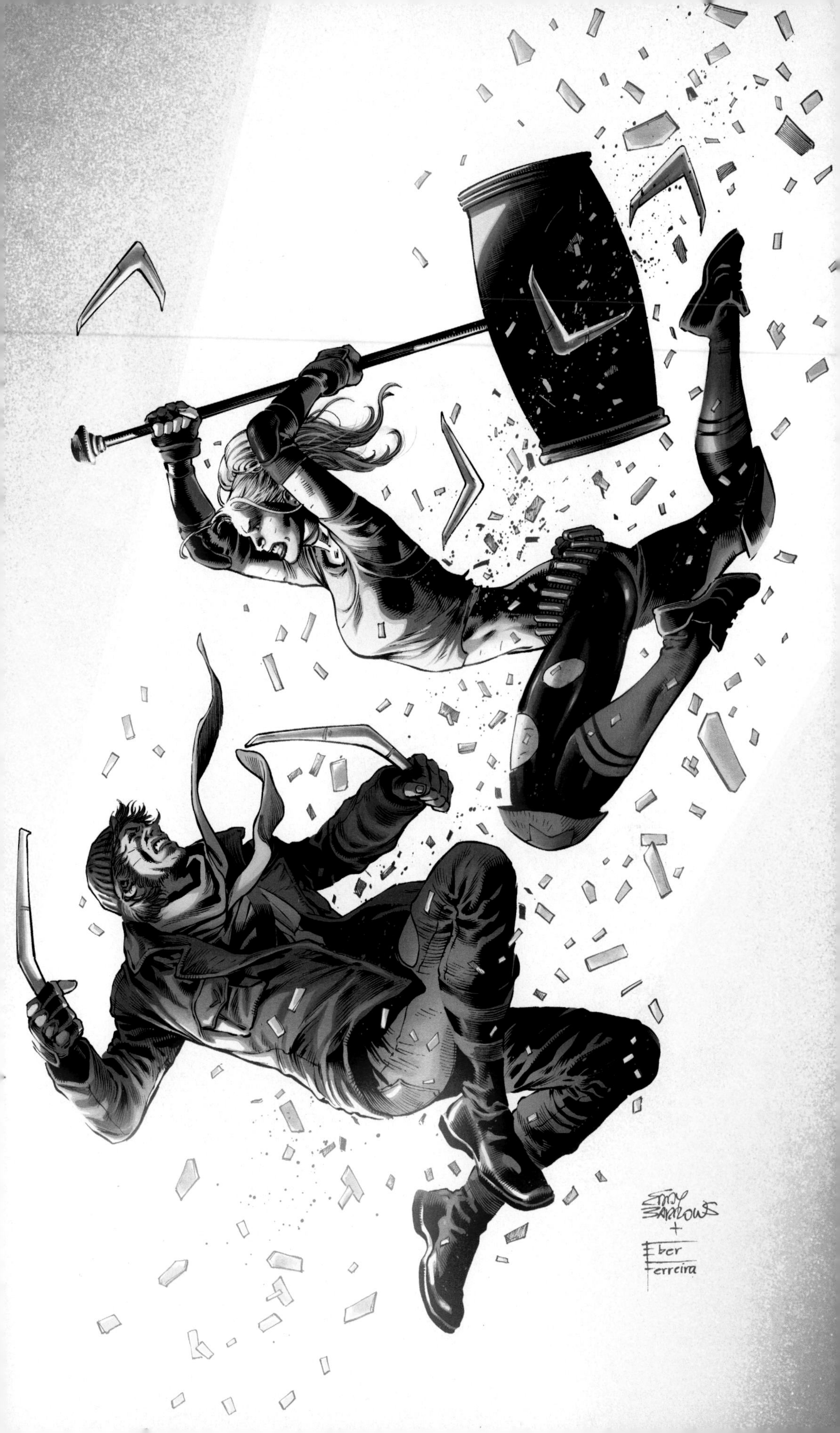
Eddy Barrows
+
Eber Ferreira

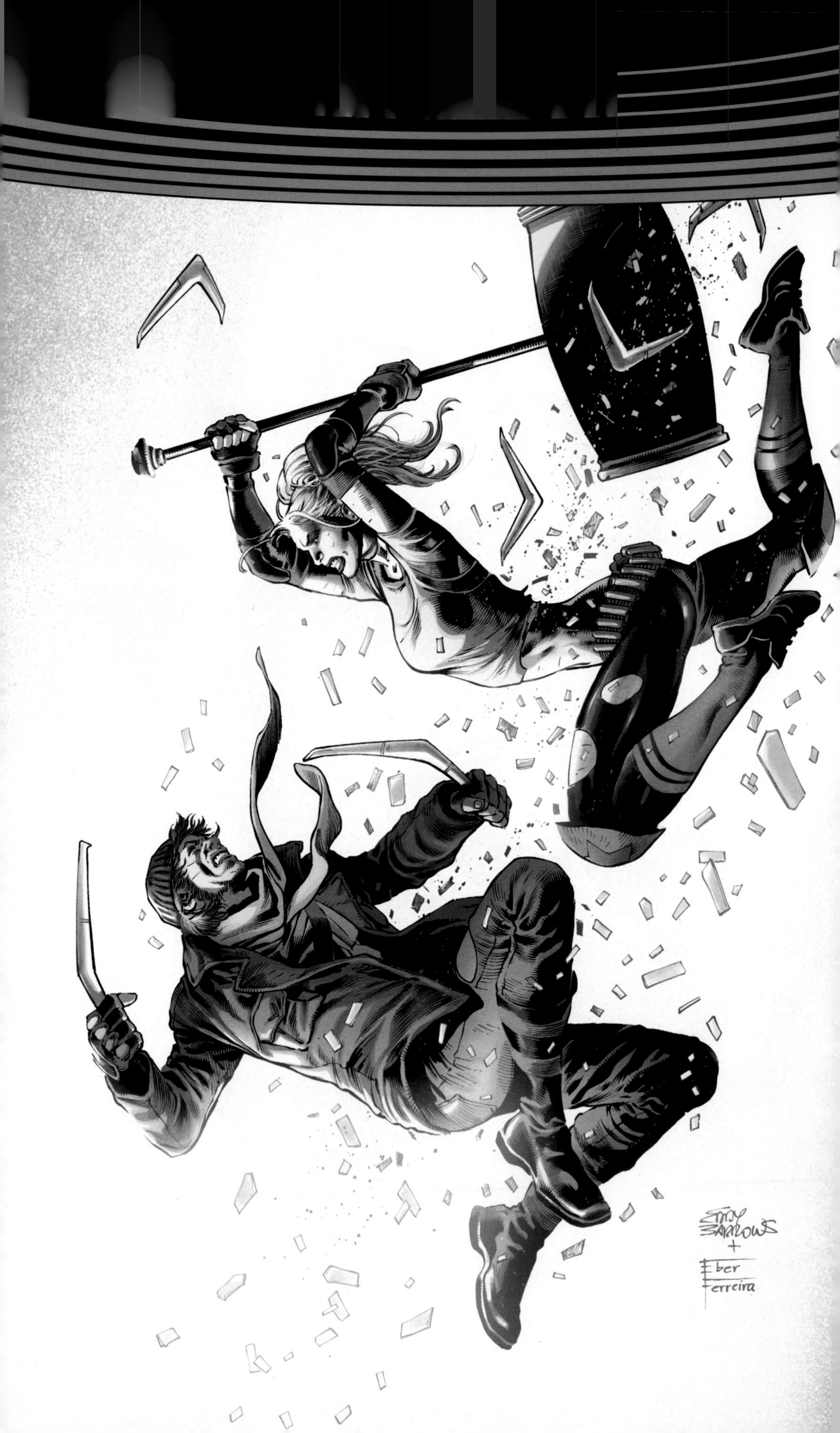
Eber
Ferreira

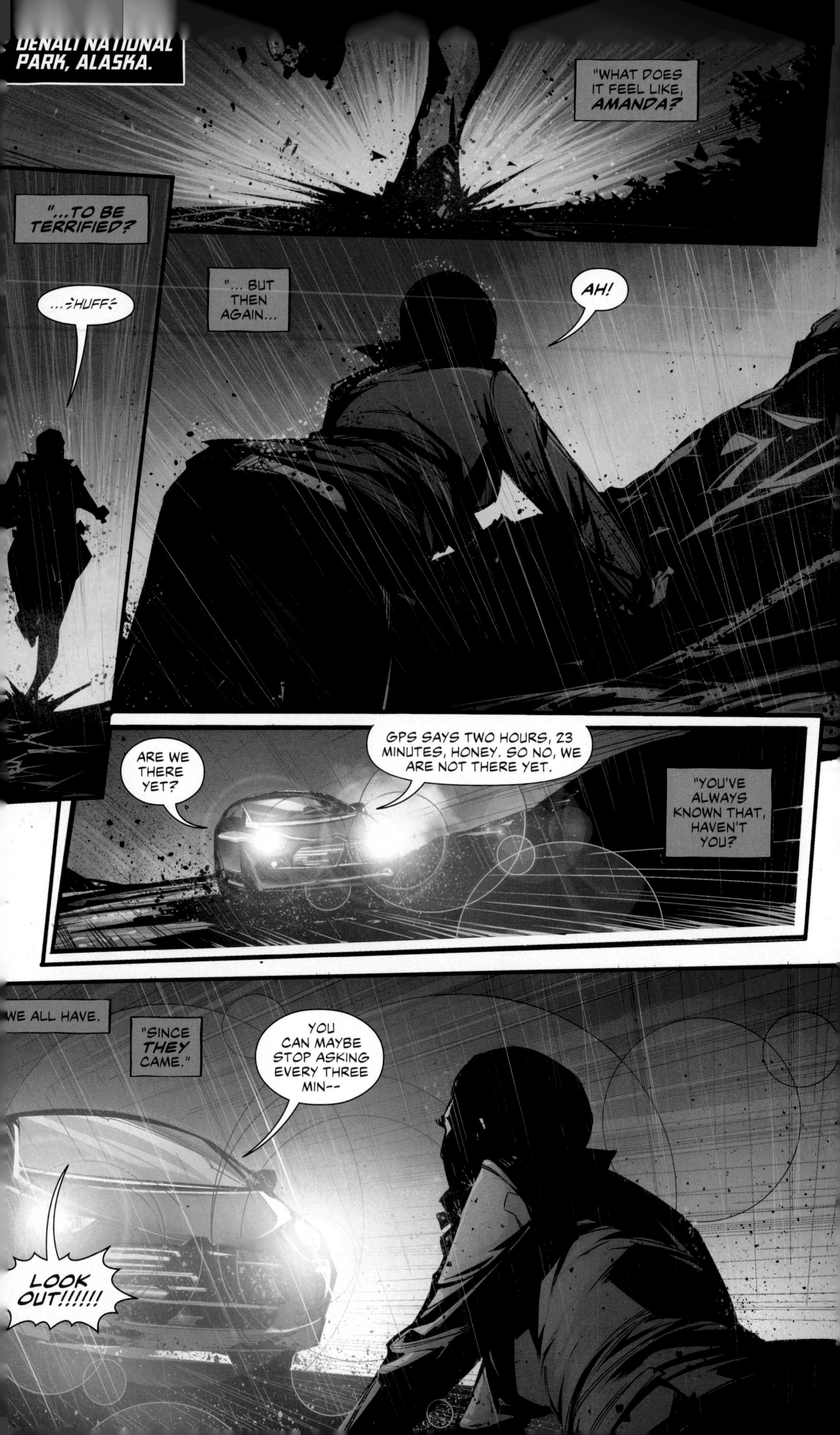
DENALI NATIONAL PARK, ALASKA.
"WHAT DOES IT FEEL LIKE, AMANDA?
"...TO BE TERRIFIED?
...HUFF
"... BUT THEN AGAIN...
AH!
ARE WE THERE YET?
GPS SAYS TWO HOURS, 23 MINUTES, HONEY. SO NO, WE ARE NOT THERE YET.
"YOU'VE ALWAYS KNOWN THAT, HAVEN'T YOU?
WE ALL HAVE.
"SINCE THEY CAME."
YOU CAN MAYBE STOP ASKING EVERY THREE MIN--
LOOK OUT!!!!!!

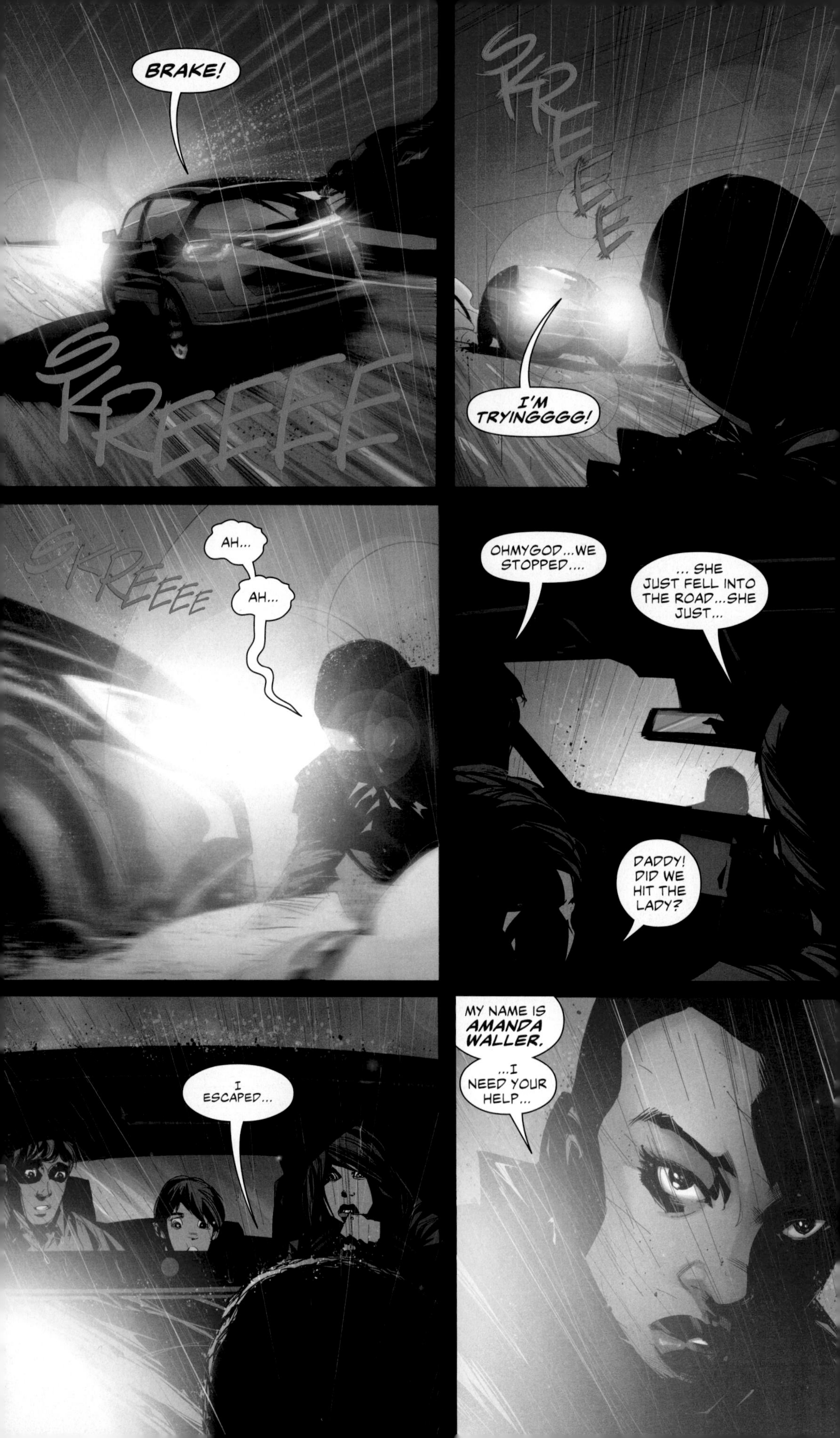
BRAKE!
SKREEEE
SKREEEE
I'M TRYINGGGG!
SKREEEE
AH...
AH...
OHMYGOD...WE STOPPED....
... SHE JUST FELL INTO THE ROAD...SHE JUST...
DADDY! DID WE HIT THE LADY?
I ESCAPED...
MY NAME IS ***AMANDA WALLER.***
...I NEED YOUR HELP...

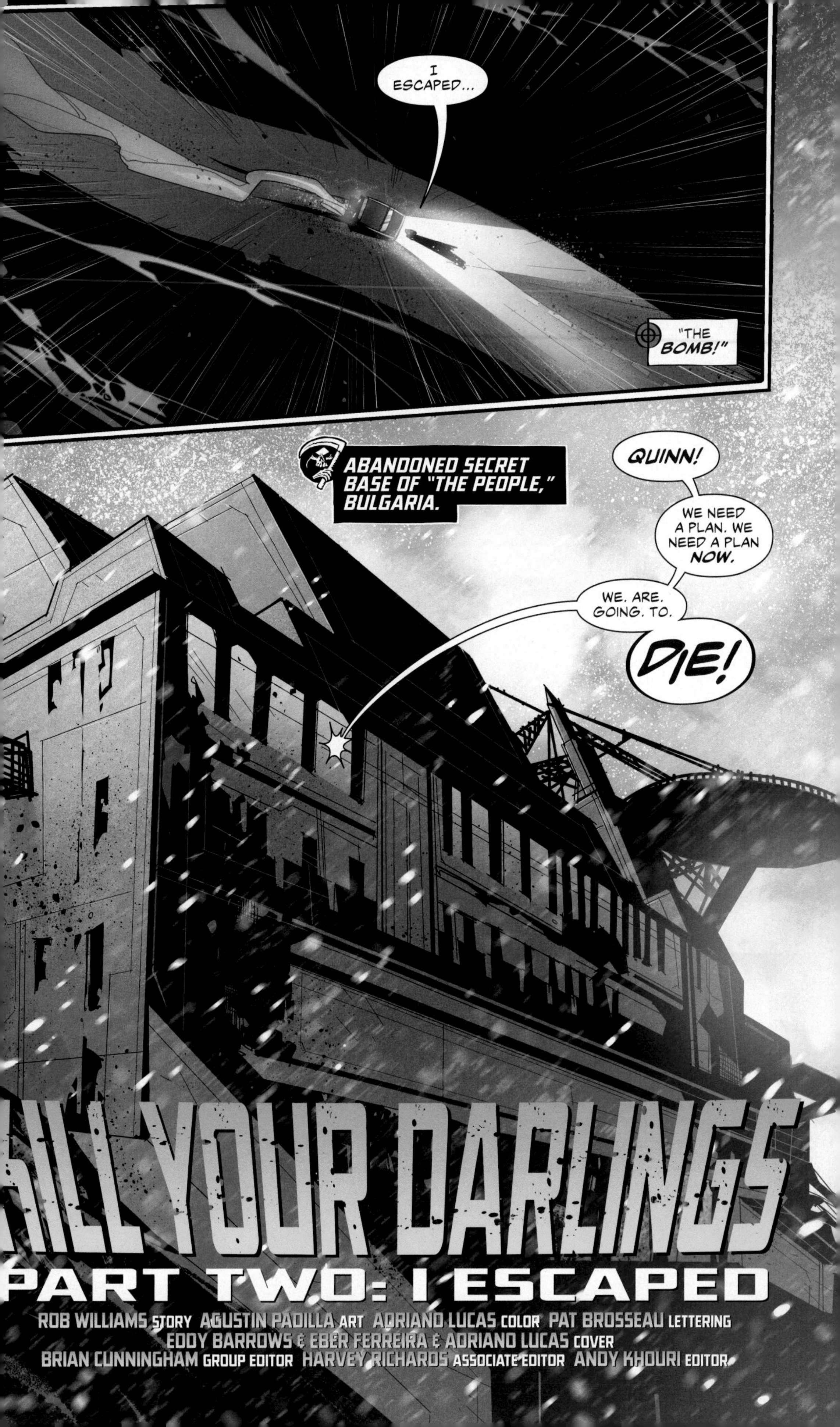

I ESCAPED...
"THE BOMB!"
ABANDONED SECRET BASE OF "THE PEOPLE," BULGARIA.
QUINN!
WE NEED A PLAN. WE NEED A PLAN NOW.
WE. ARE. GOING. TO.
DIE!
KILL YOUR DARLINGS
PART TWO: I ESCAPED
ROB WILLIAMS STORY AGUSTIN PADILLA ART ADRIANO LUCAS COLOR PAT BROSSEAU LETTERING
EDDY BARROWS & EBER FERREIRA & ADRIANO LUCAS COVER
BRIAN CUNNINGHAM GROUP EDITOR HARVEY RICHARDS ASSOCIATE EDITOR ANDY KHOURI EDITOR

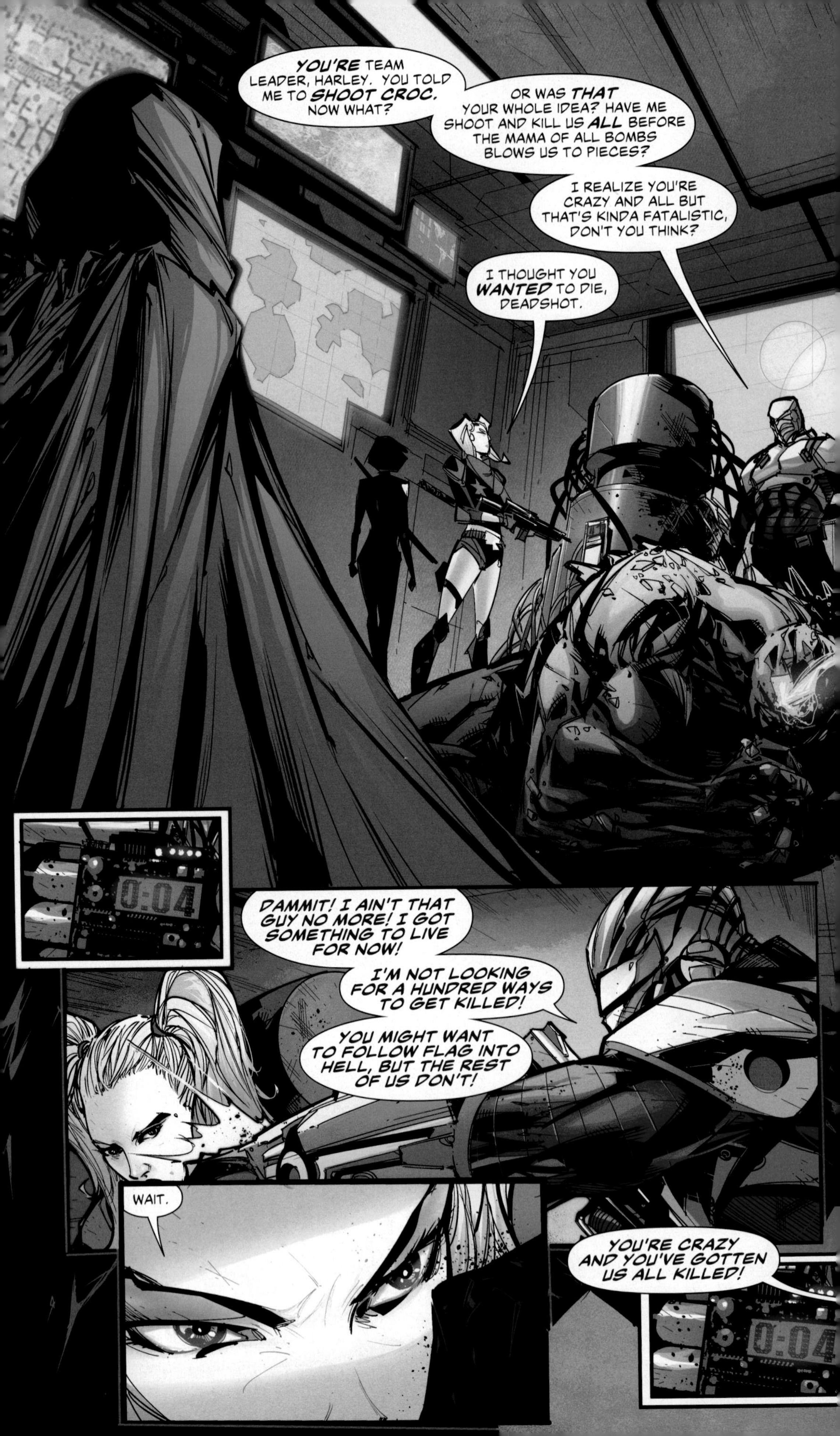

YOU'RE TEAM LEADER, HARLEY. YOU TOLD ME TO SHOOT CROC. NOW WHAT?
OR WAS THAT YOUR WHOLE IDEA? HAVE ME SHOOT AND KILL US ALL BEFORE THE MAMA OF ALL BOMBS BLOWS US TO PIECES?
I REALIZE YOU'RE CRAZY AND ALL BUT THAT'S KINDA FATALISTIC, DON'T YOU THINK?
I THOUGHT YOU WANTED TO DIE, DEADSHOT.
0:04
DAMMIT! I AIN'T THAT GUY NO MORE! I GOT SOMETHING TO LIVE FOR NOW!
I'M NOT LOOKING FOR A HUNDRED WAYS TO GET KILLED!
YOU MIGHT WANT TO FOLLOW FLAG INTO HELL, BUT THE REST OF US DON'T!
WAIT.
YOU'RE CRAZY AND YOU'VE GOTTEN US ALL KILLED!
0:04

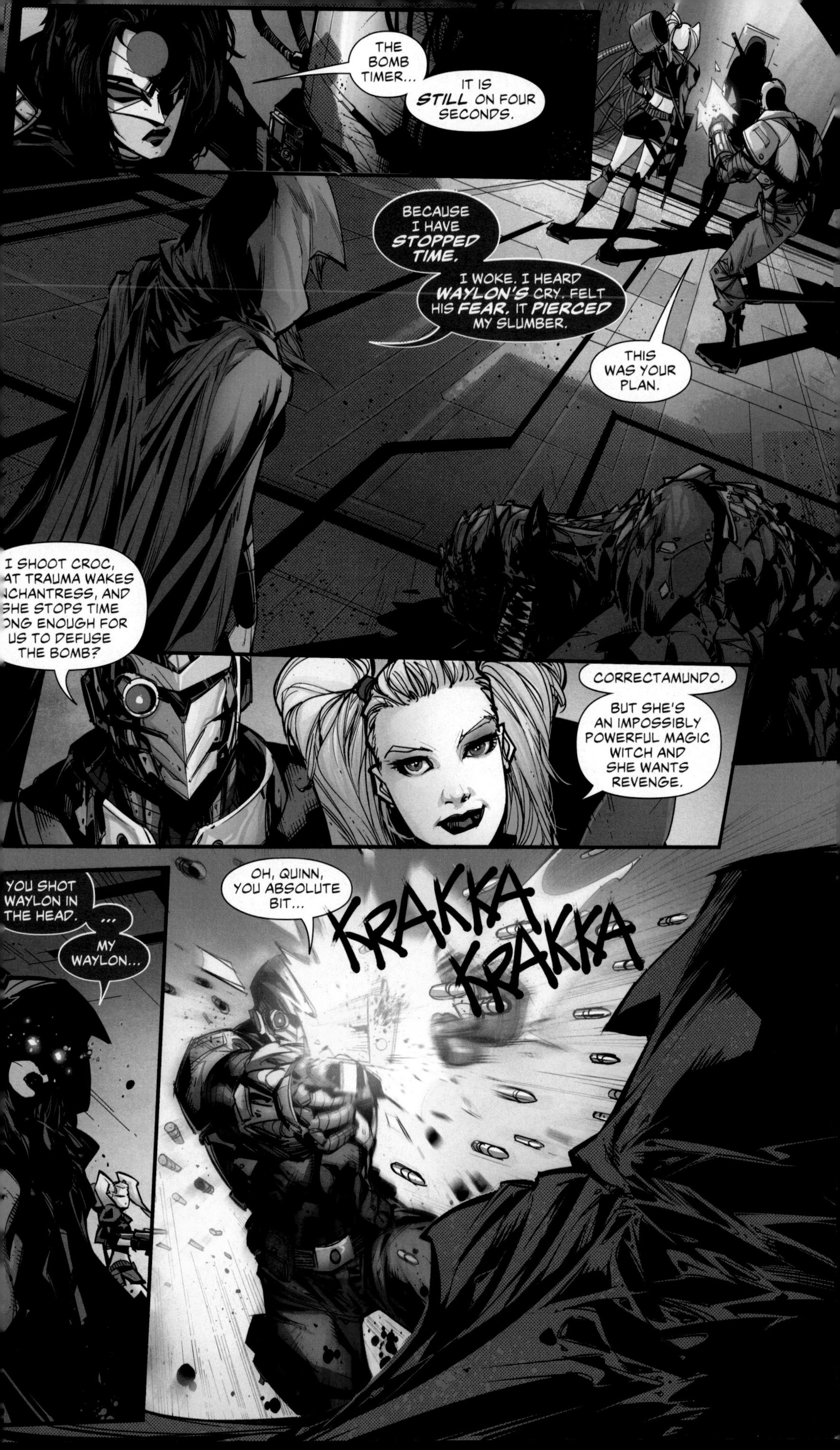
THE BOMB TIMER...
IT IS STILL ON FOUR SECONDS.
BECAUSE I HAVE STOPPED TIME.
I WOKE. I HEARD WAYLON'S CRY. FELT HIS FEAR. IT PIERCED MY SLUMBER.
THIS WAS YOUR PLAN.
I SHOOT CROC, AT TRAUMA WAKES NCHANTRESS, AND SHE STOPS TIME ONG ENOUGH FOR US TO DEFUSE THE BOMB?
CORRECTAMUNDO.
BUT SHE'S AN IMPOSSIBLY POWERFUL MAGIC WITCH AND SHE WANTS REVENGE.
YOU SHOT WAYLON IN THE HEAD.
...
MY WAYLON...
OH, QUINN, YOU ABSOLUTE BIT...
KRAKKA KRAKKA

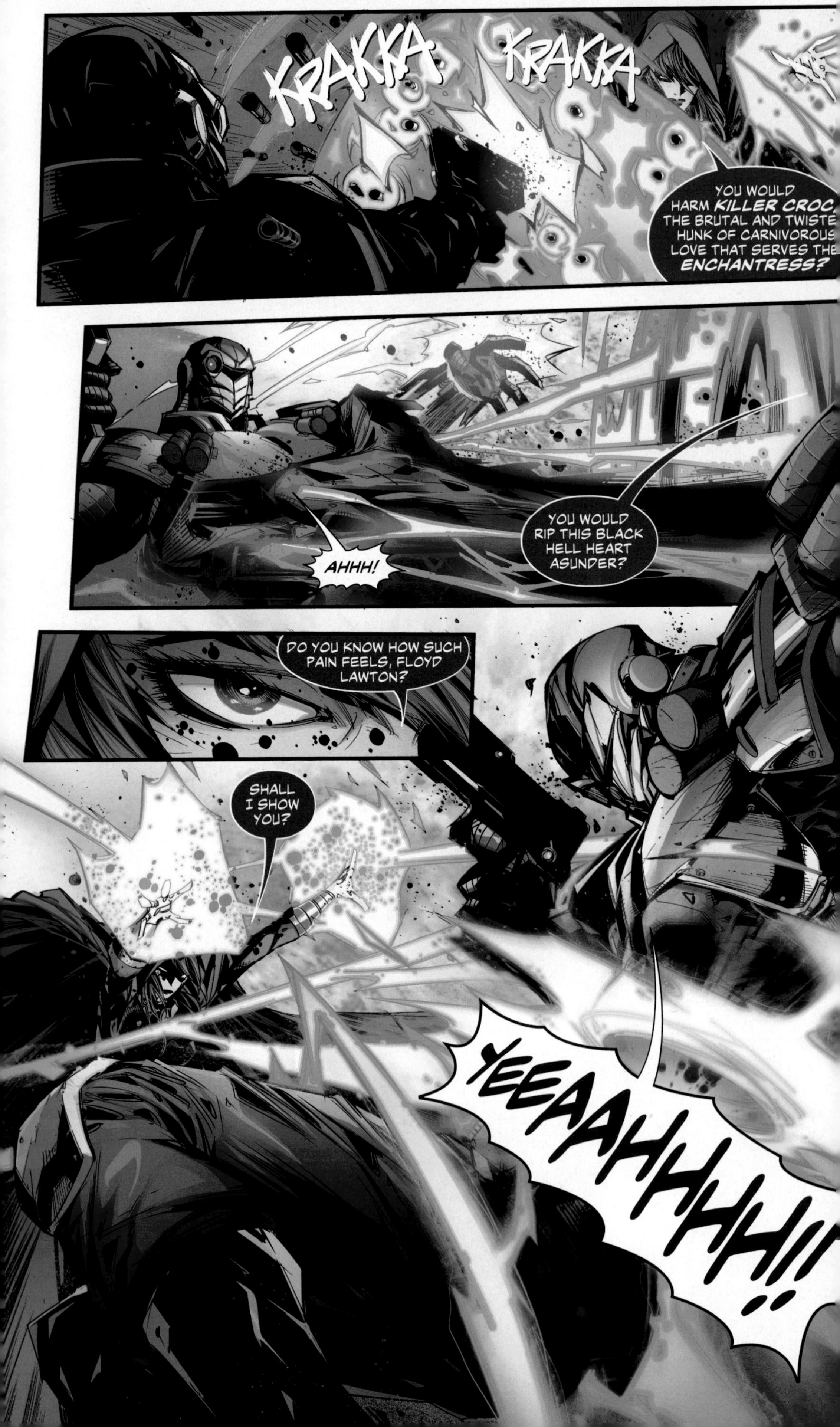
KRAKKA KRAKKA
YOU WOULD HARM KILLER CROC, THE BRUTAL AND TWISTED HUNK OF CARNIVOROUS LOVE THAT SERVES THE ENCHANTRESS?
YOU WOULD RIP THIS BLACK HELL HEART ASUNDER?
AHHH!
DO YOU KNOW HOW SUCH PAIN FEELS, FLOYD LAWTON?
SHALL I SHOW YOU?
YEEAAHHHHH!!

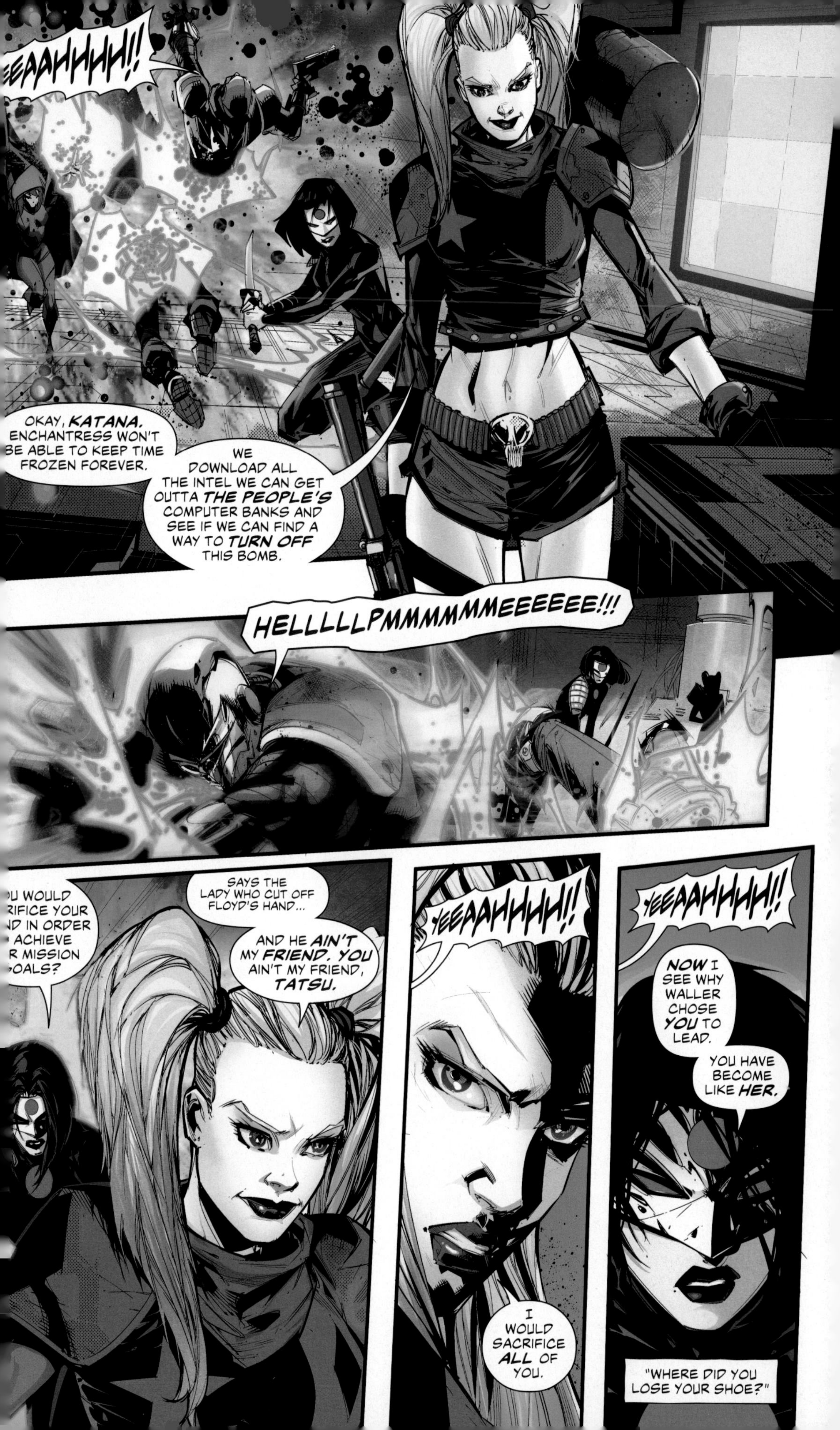

EEAAHHHH!!
OKAY, KATANA. ENCHANTRESS WON'T BE ABLE TO KEEP TIME FROZEN FOREVER.
WE DOWNLOAD ALL THE INTEL WE CAN GET OUTTA THE PEOPLE'S COMPUTER BANKS AND SEE IF WE CAN FIND A WAY TO TURN OFF THIS BOMB.
HELLLLLPMMMMMEEEEEE!!!
OU WOULD RIFICE YOUR ND IN ORDER ACHIEVE R MISSION OALS?
SAYS THE LADY WHO CUT OFF FLOYD'S HAND...
AND HE AIN'T MY FRIEND. YOU AIN'T MY FRIEND, TATSU.
YEEAAHHHH!!
I WOULD SACRIFICE ALL OF YOU.
YEEAAHHHH!!
NOW I SEE WHY WALLER CHOSE YOU TO LEAD.
YOU HAVE BECOME LIKE HER.
"WHERE DID YOU LOSE YOUR SHOE?"

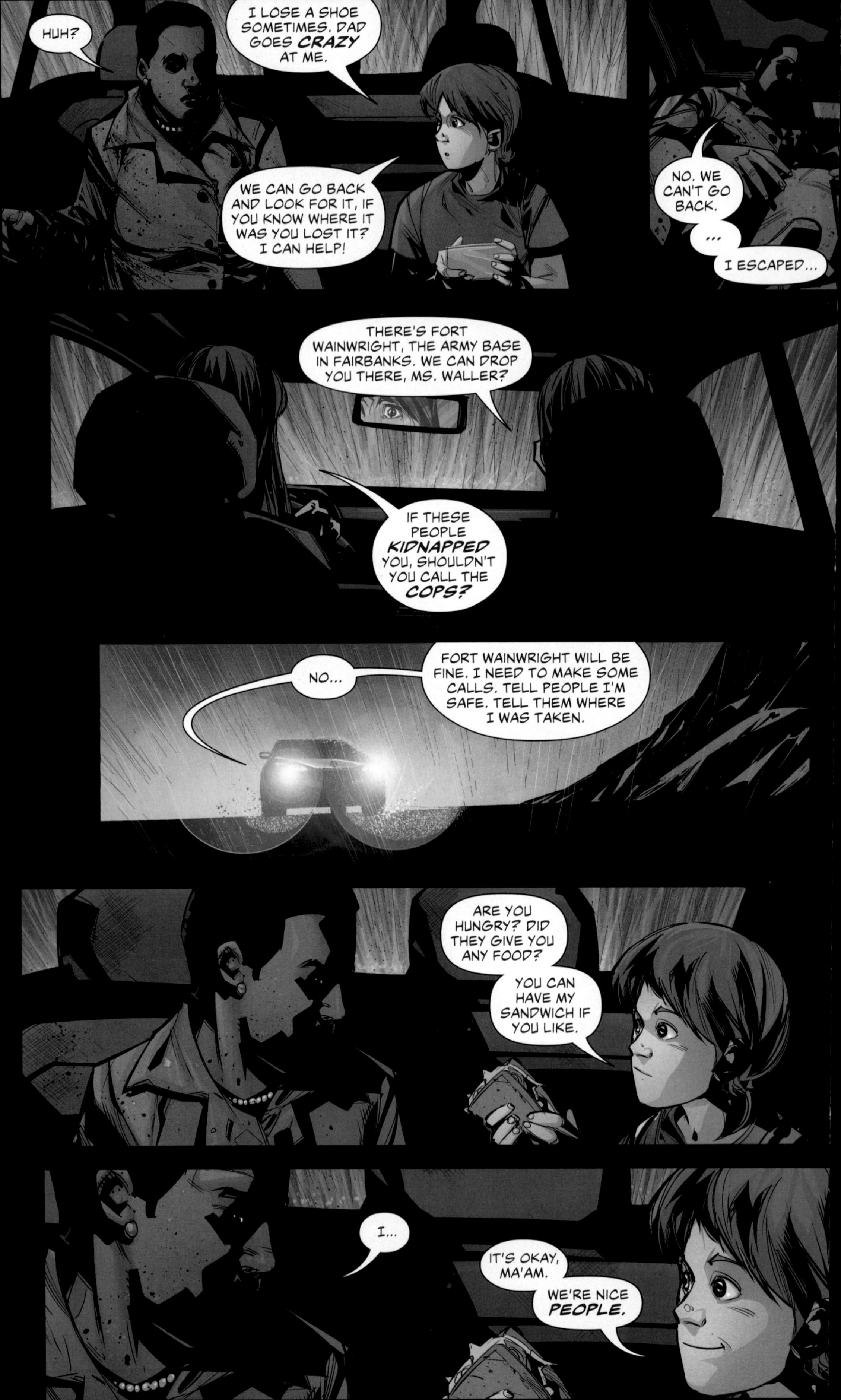
HUH?
I LOSE A SHOE SOMETIMES. DAD GOES CRAZY AT ME.
WE CAN GO BACK AND LOOK FOR IT, IF YOU KNOW WHERE IT WAS YOU LOST IT? I CAN HELP!
NO. WE CAN'T GO BACK.
...
I ESCAPED...
THERE'S FORT WAINWRIGHT, THE ARMY BASE IN FAIRBANKS. WE CAN DROP YOU THERE, MS. WALLER?
IF THESE PEOPLE KIDNAPPED YOU, SHOULDN'T YOU CALL THE COPS?
NO...
FORT WAINWRIGHT WILL BE FINE. I NEED TO MAKE SOME CALLS. TELL PEOPLE I'M SAFE. TELL THEM WHERE I WAS TAKEN.
ARE YOU HUNGRY? DID THEY GIVE YOU ANY FOOD?
YOU CAN HAVE MY SANDWICH IF YOU LIKE.
I...
IT'S OKAY, MA'AM.
WE'RE NICE PEOPLE.

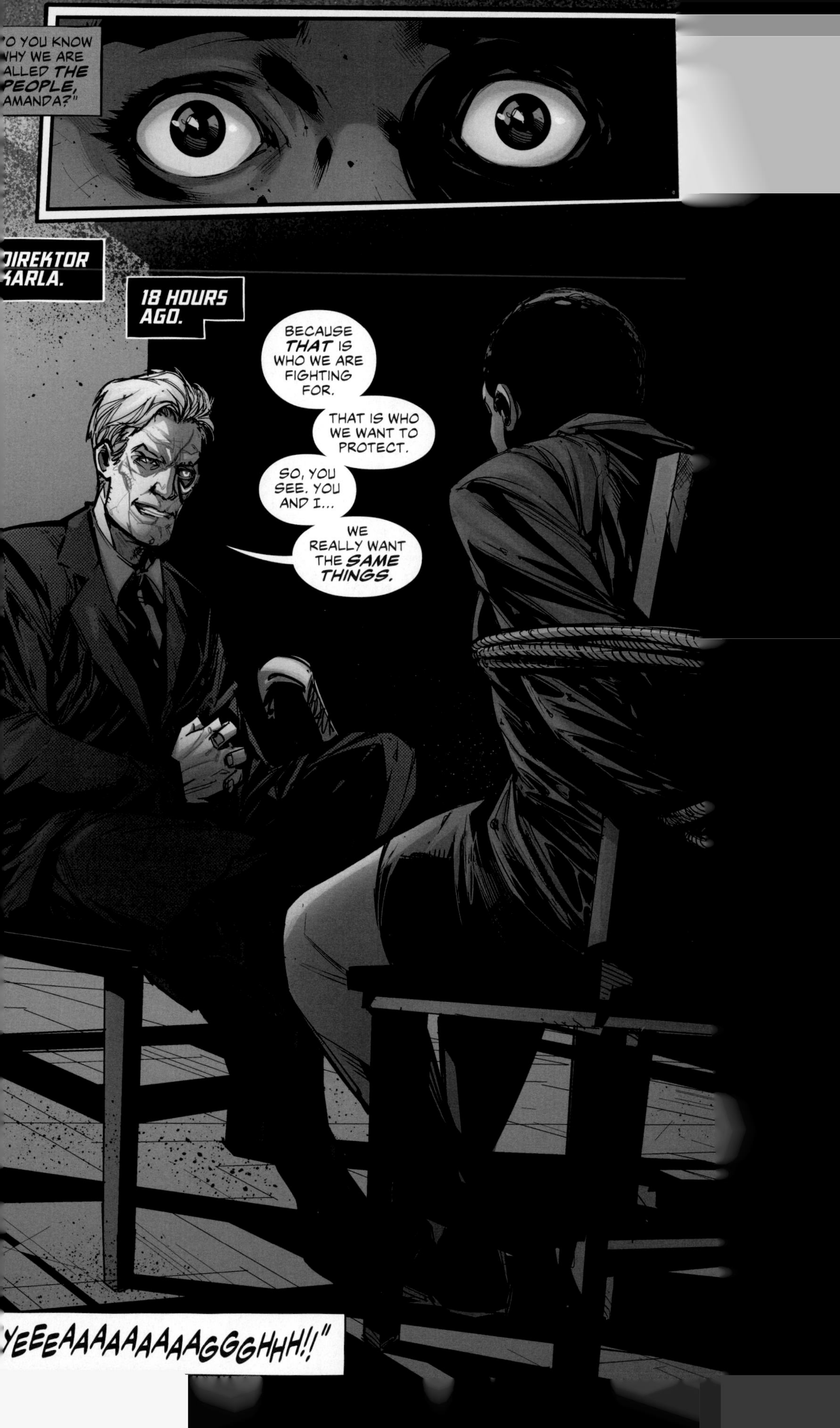
"O YOU KNOW
WHY WE ARE
ALLED THE
PEOPLE,
AMANDA?"
DIREKTOR
KARLA.
18 HOURS
AGO.
BECAUSE THAT IS WHO WE ARE FIGHTING FOR.
THAT IS WHO WE WANT TO PROTECT.
SO, YOU SEE. YOU AND I...
WE REALLY WANT THE SAME THINGS.
YEEEAAAAAAAAAGGGHHH!!"

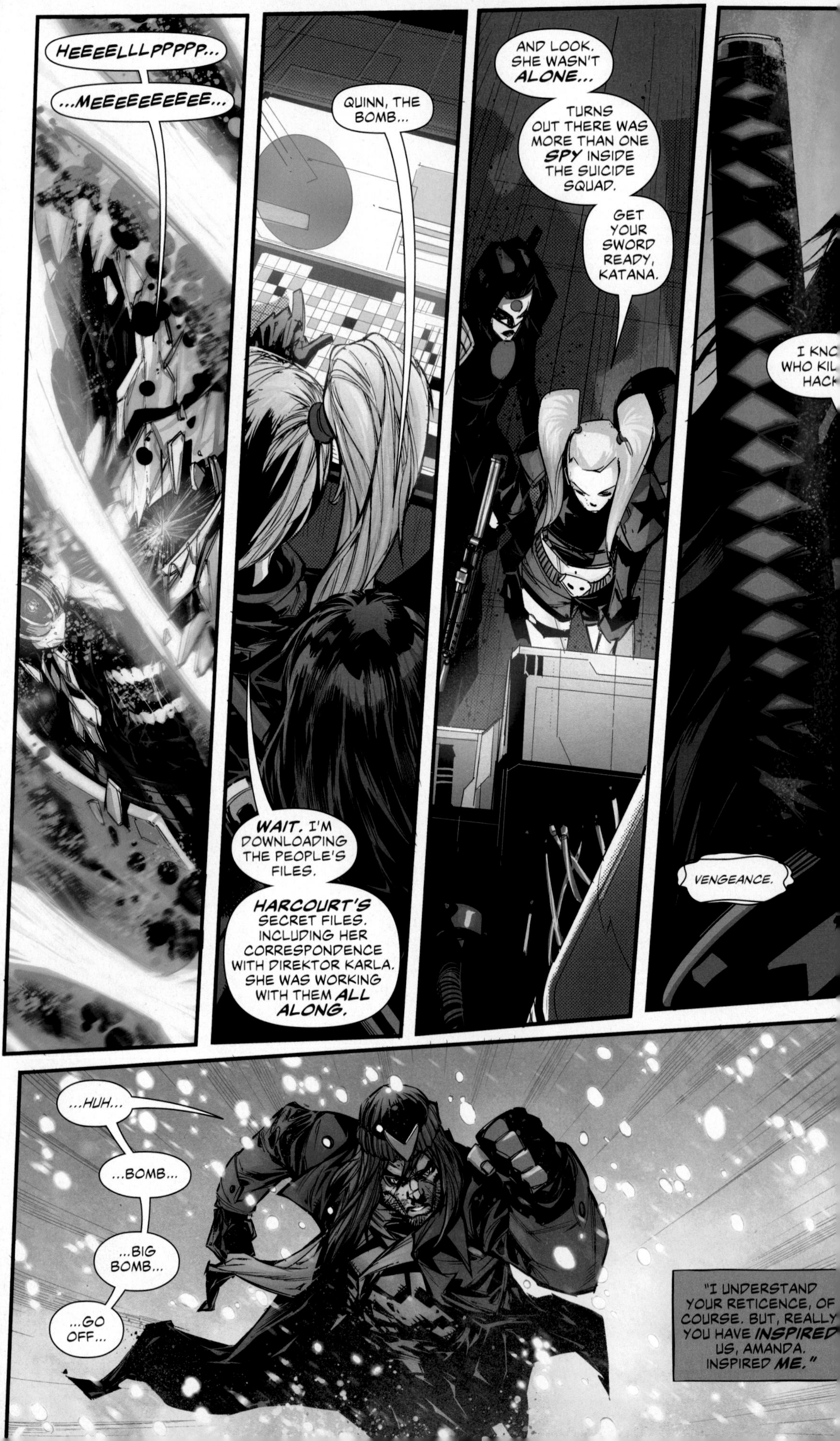
HEEEELLLPPPPP...
...MEEEEEEEEEE...
QUINN, THE BOMB...
WAIT. I'M DOWNLOADING THE PEOPLE'S FILES.
HARCOURT'S SECRET FILES. INCLUDING HER CORRESPONDENCE WITH DIREKTOR KARLA. SHE WAS WORKING WITH THEM ALL ALONG.
AND LOOK. SHE WASN'T ALONE...
TURNS OUT THERE WAS MORE THAN ONE SPY INSIDE THE SUICIDE SQUAD.
GET YOUR SWORD READY, KATANA.
VENGEANCE.
...HUH...
...BOMB...
...BIG BOMB...
...GO OFF...
"I UNDERSTAND YOUR RETICENCE, OF COURSE. BUT, REALLY YOU HAVE INSPIRED US, AMANDA. INSPIRED ME."

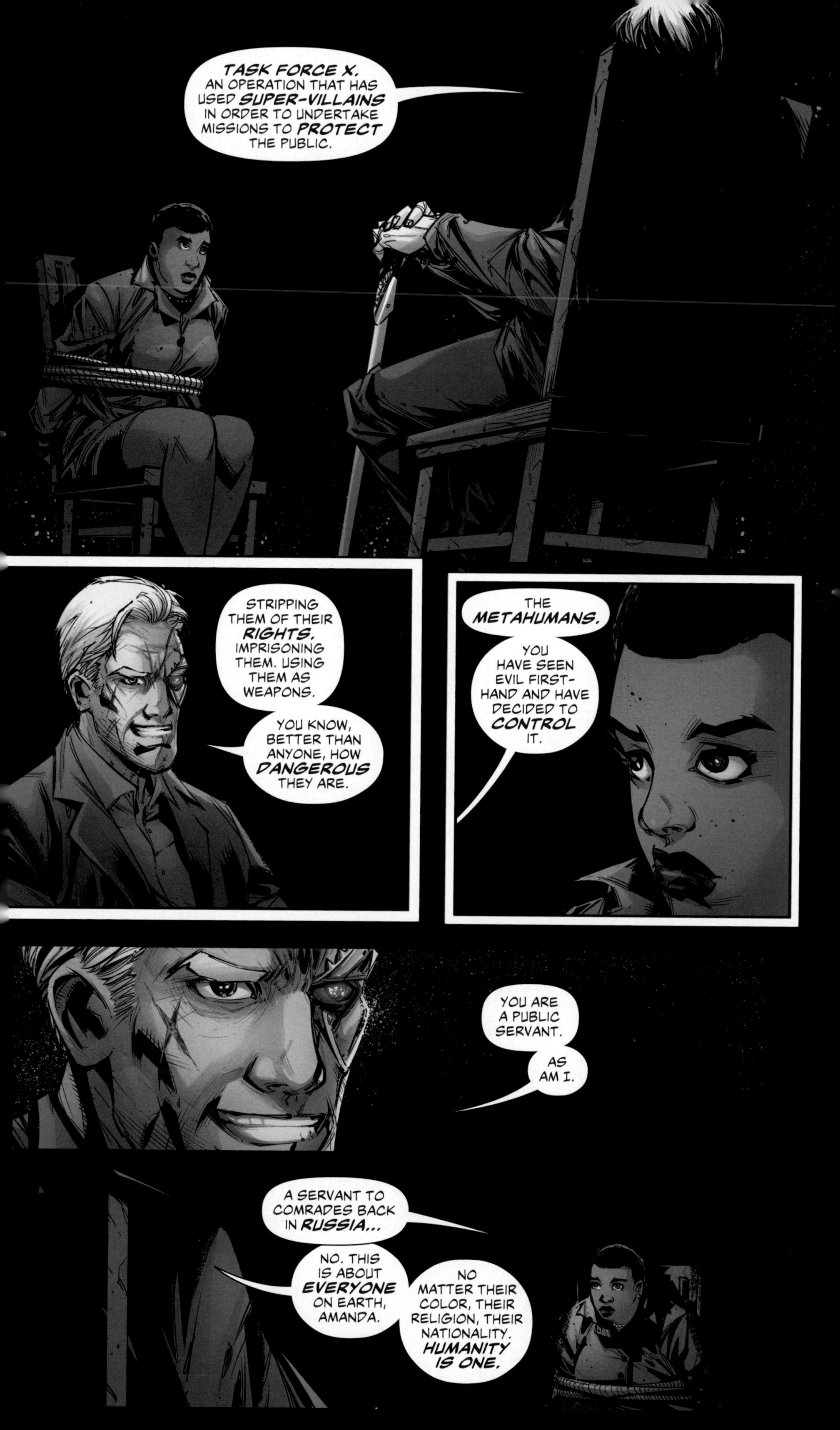
TASK FORCE X. AN OPERATION THAT HAS USED SUPER-VILLAINS IN ORDER TO UNDERTAKE MISSIONS TO PROTECT THE PUBLIC.
STRIPPING THEM OF THEIR RIGHTS. IMPRISONING THEM. USING THEM AS WEAPONS.
YOU KNOW, BETTER THAN ANYONE, HOW DANGEROUS THEY ARE.
THE METAHUMANS.
YOU HAVE SEEN EVIL FIRST-HAND AND HAVE DECIDED TO CONTROL IT.
YOU ARE A PUBLIC SERVANT.
AS AM I.
A SERVANT TO COMRADES BACK IN RUSSIA...
NO. THIS IS ABOUT EVERYONE ON EARTH, AMANDA.
NO MATTER THEIR COLOR, THEIR RELIGION, THEIR NATIONALITY. HUMANITY IS ONE.

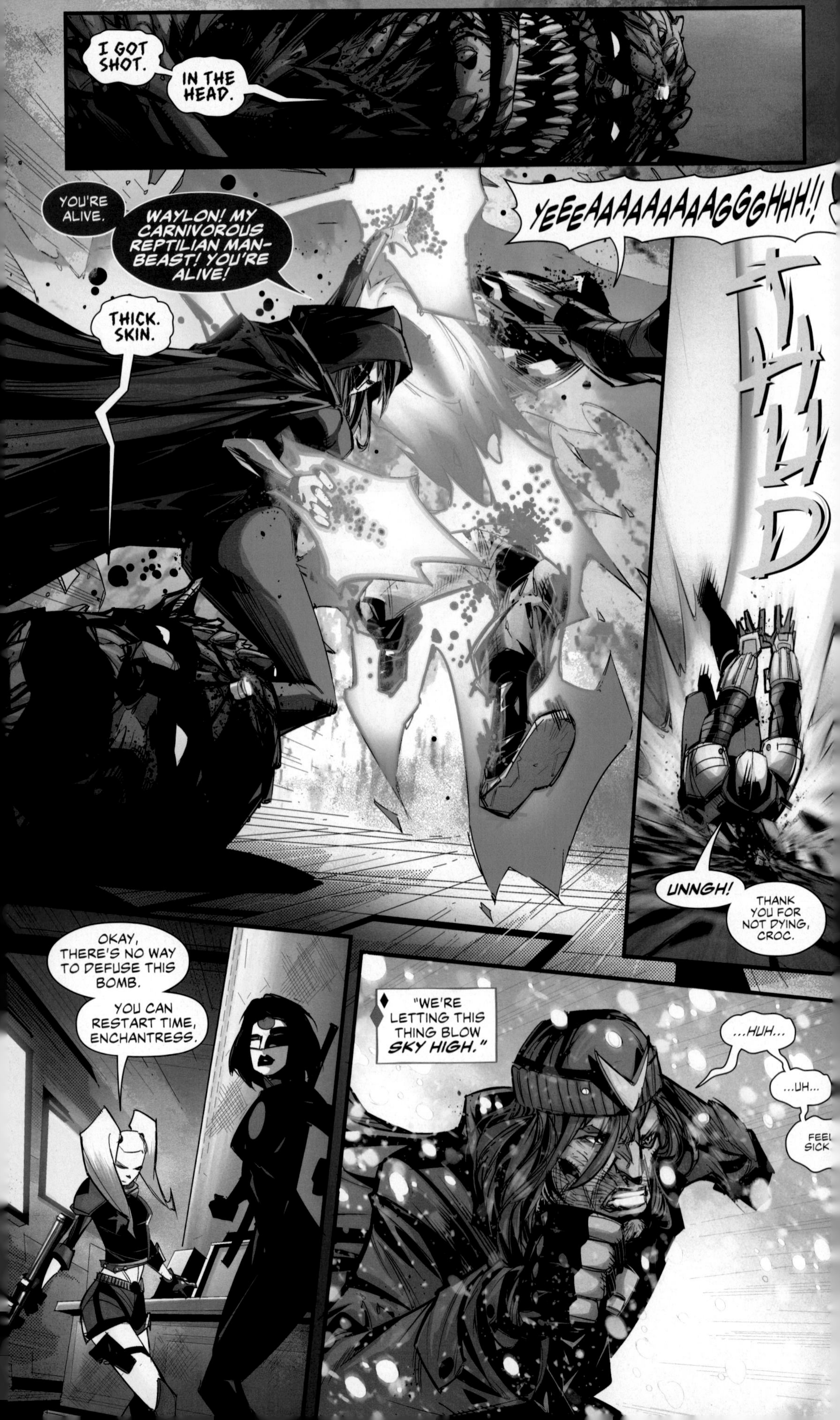
I GOT SHOT.
IN THE HEAD.
YOU'RE ALIVE.
WAYLON! MY CARNIVOROUS REPTILIAN MAN-BEAST! YOU'RE ALIVE!
YEEEAAAAAAAAAGGGHHH!!
THICK. SKIN.
THUD
UNNGH!
THANK YOU FOR NOT DYING, CROC.
OKAY, THERE'S NO WAY TO DEFUSE THIS BOMB.
YOU CAN RESTART TIME, ENCHANTRESS.
"WE'RE LETTING THIS THING BLOW SKY HIGH."
...HUH...
...UH...

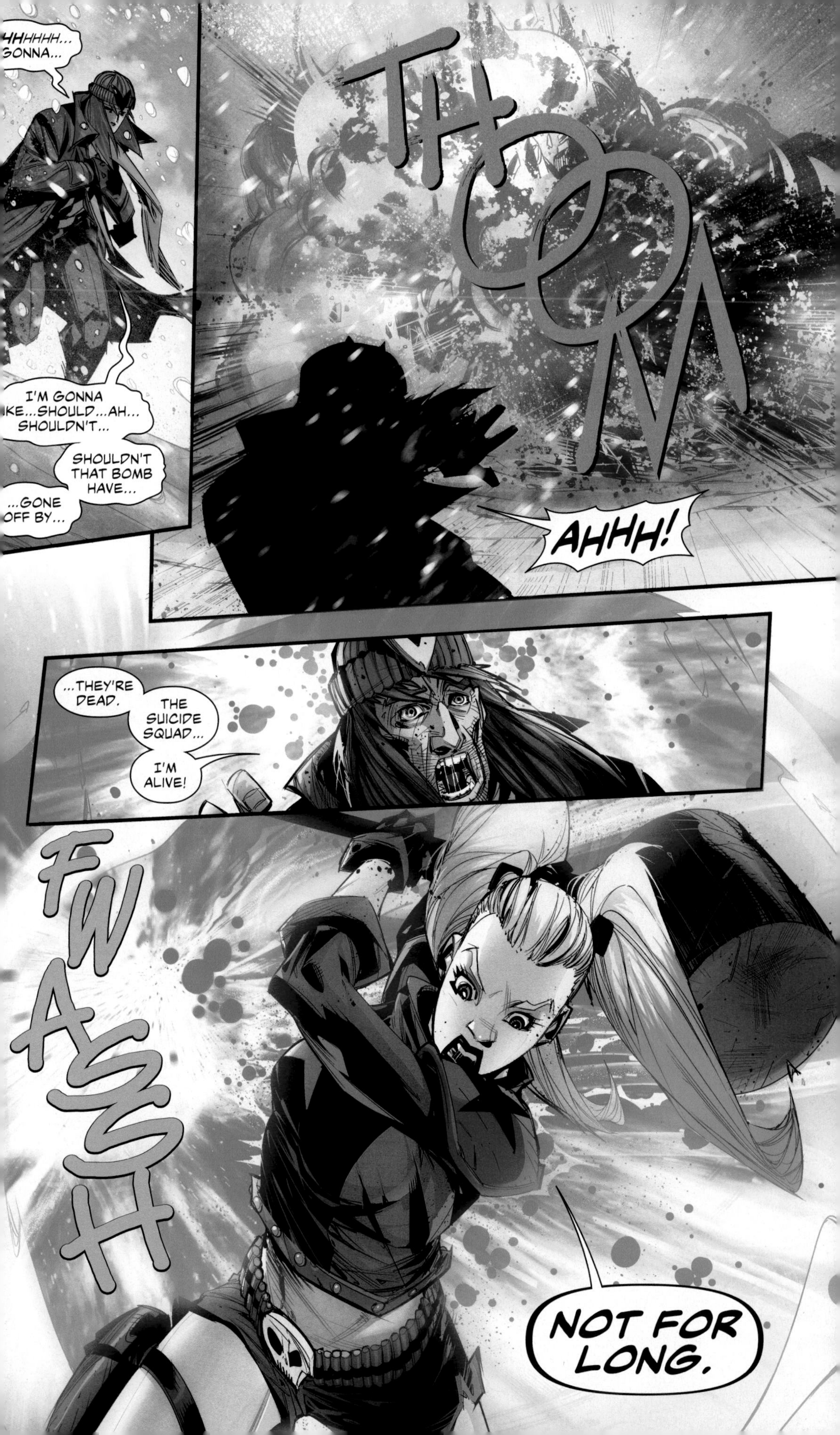
HHHHH... GONNA...
I'M GONNA KE...SHOULD...AH... SHOULDN'T...
SHOULDN'T THAT BOMB HAVE...
...GONE OFF BY...
THOOM
AHHH!
...THEY'RE DEAD.
THE SUICIDE SQUAD...
I'M ALIVE!
FWASH
NOT FOR LONG.

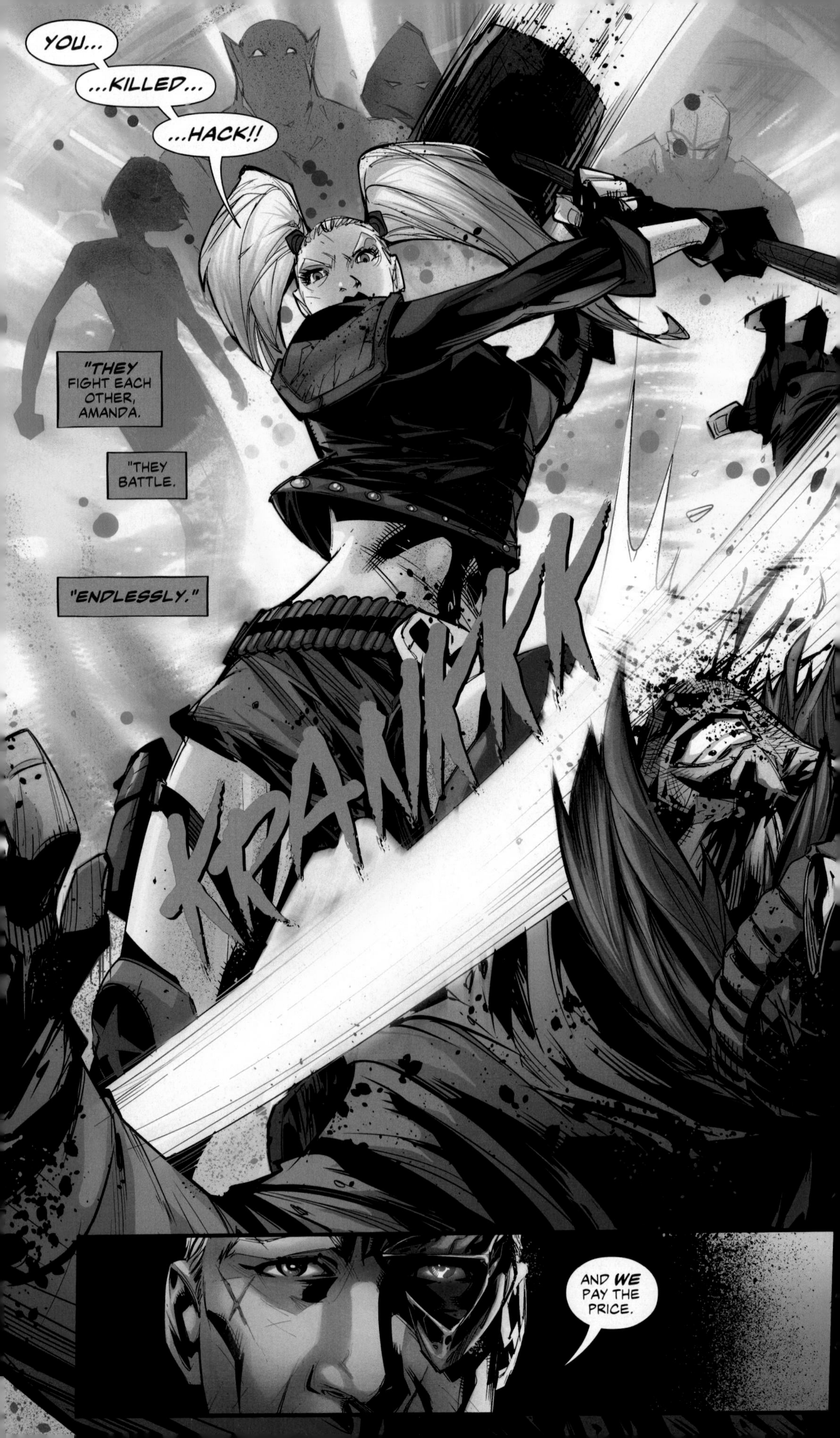
YOU...
...KILLED...
...HACK!!
"THEY FIGHT EACH OTHER, AMANDA.
"THEY BATTLE.
"ENDLESSLY."
KRANKKK
AND WE PAY THE PRICE.

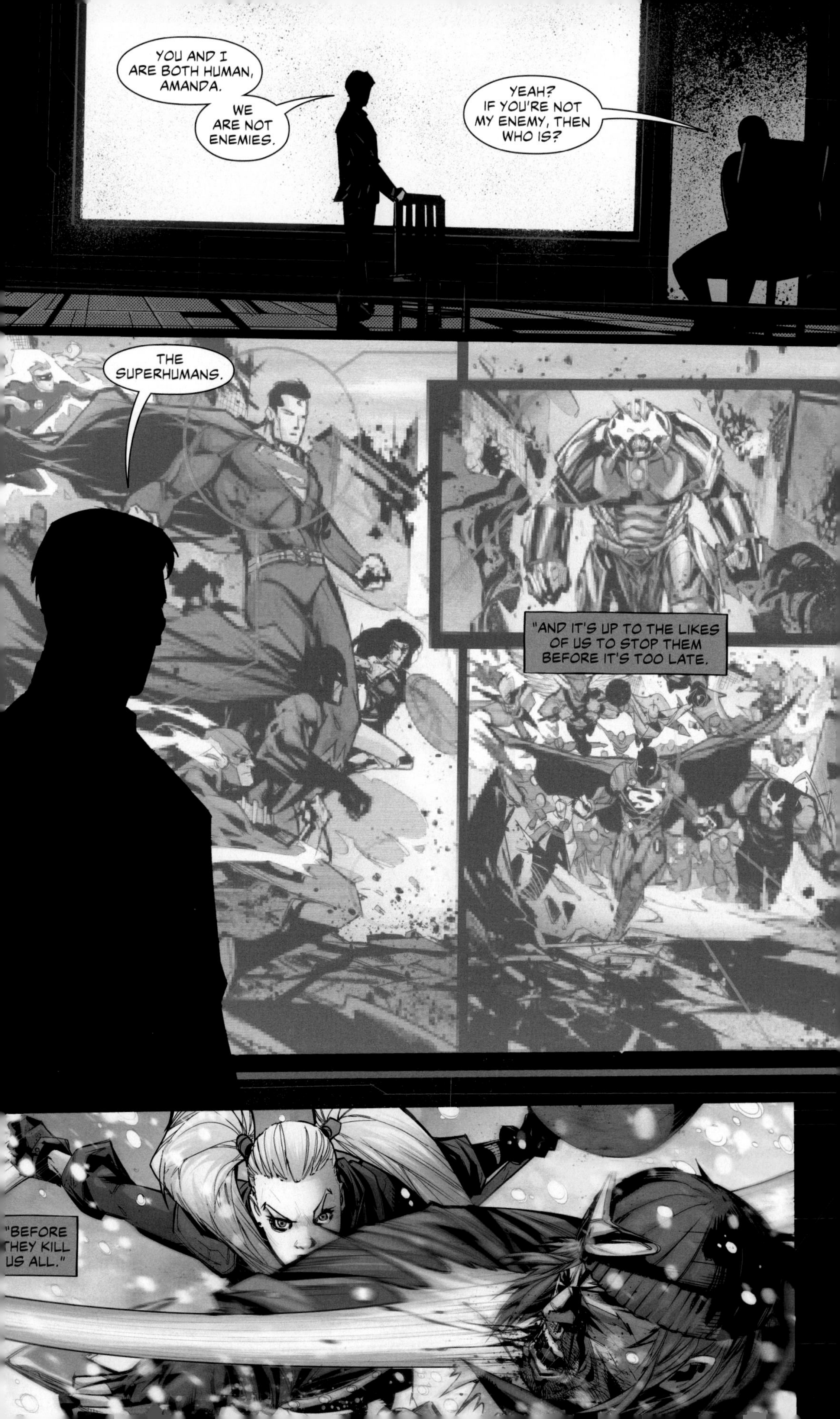
YOU AND I ARE BOTH HUMAN, AMANDA.
WE ARE NOT ENEMIES.
YEAH? IF YOU'RE NOT MY ENEMY, THEN WHO IS?
THE SUPERHUMANS.
"AND IT'S UP TO THE LIKES OF US TO STOP THEM BEFORE IT'S TOO LATE.
"BEFORE THEY KILL US ALL."

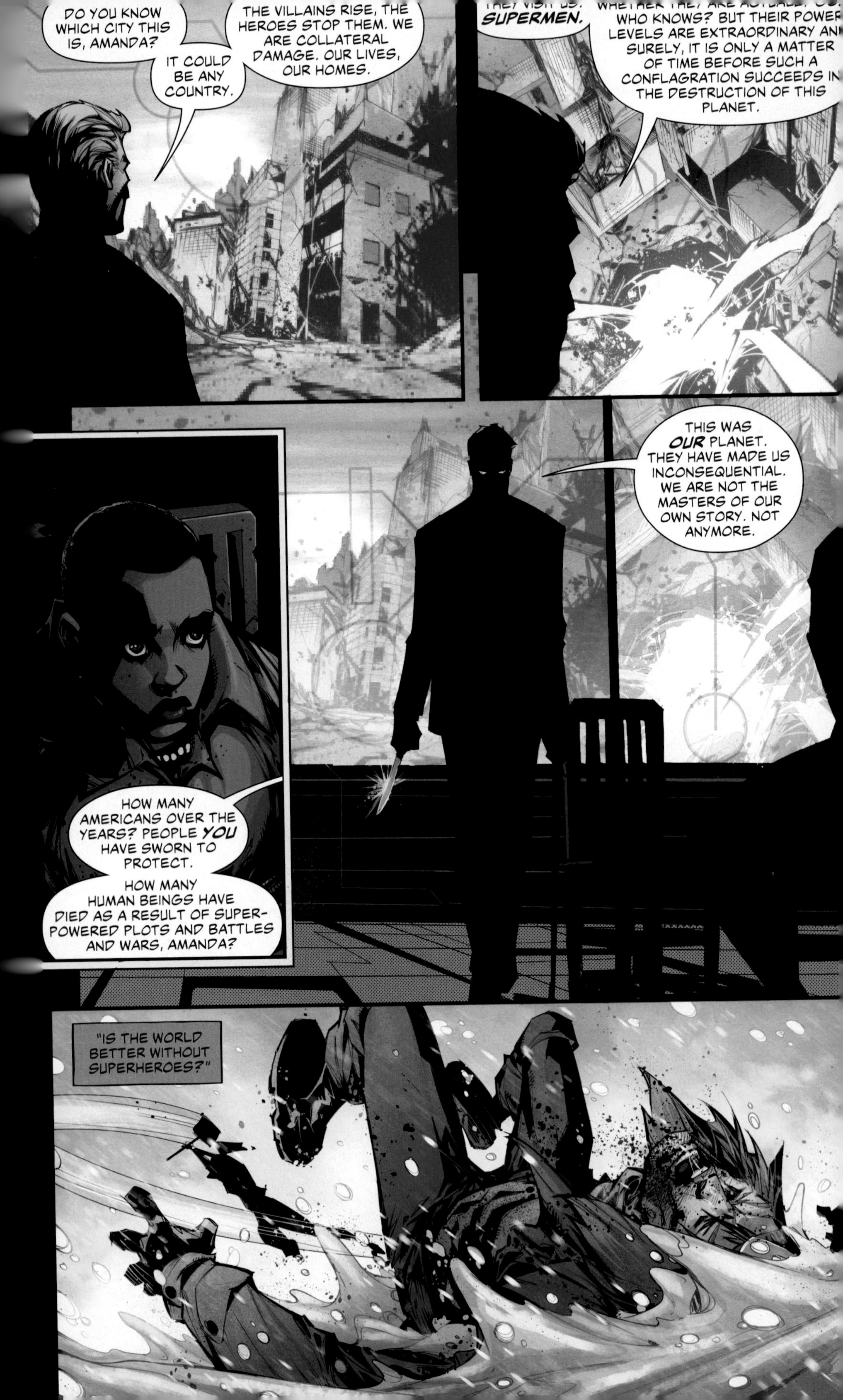
DO YOU KNOW WHICH CITY THIS IS, AMANDA?
IT COULD BE ANY COUNTRY.
THE VILLAINS RISE, THE HEROES STOP THEM. WE ARE COLLATERAL DAMAGE. OUR LIVES, OUR HOMES.
SUPERMEN.
WHO KNOWS? BUT THEIR POWER LEVELS ARE EXTRAORDINARY AN SURELY, IT IS ONLY A MATTER OF TIME BEFORE SUCH A CONFLAGRATION SUCCEEDS IN THE DESTRUCTION OF THIS PLANET.
THIS WAS OUR PLANET. THEY HAVE MADE US INCONSEQUENTIAL. WE ARE NOT THE MASTERS OF OUR OWN STORY. NOT ANYMORE.
HOW MANY AMERICANS OVER THE YEARS? PEOPLE YOU HAVE SWORN TO PROTECT.
HOW MANY HUMAN BEINGS HAVE DIED AS A RESULT OF SUPER-POWERED PLOTS AND BATTLES AND WARS, AMANDA?
"IS THE WORLD BETTER WITHOUT SUPERHEROES?"

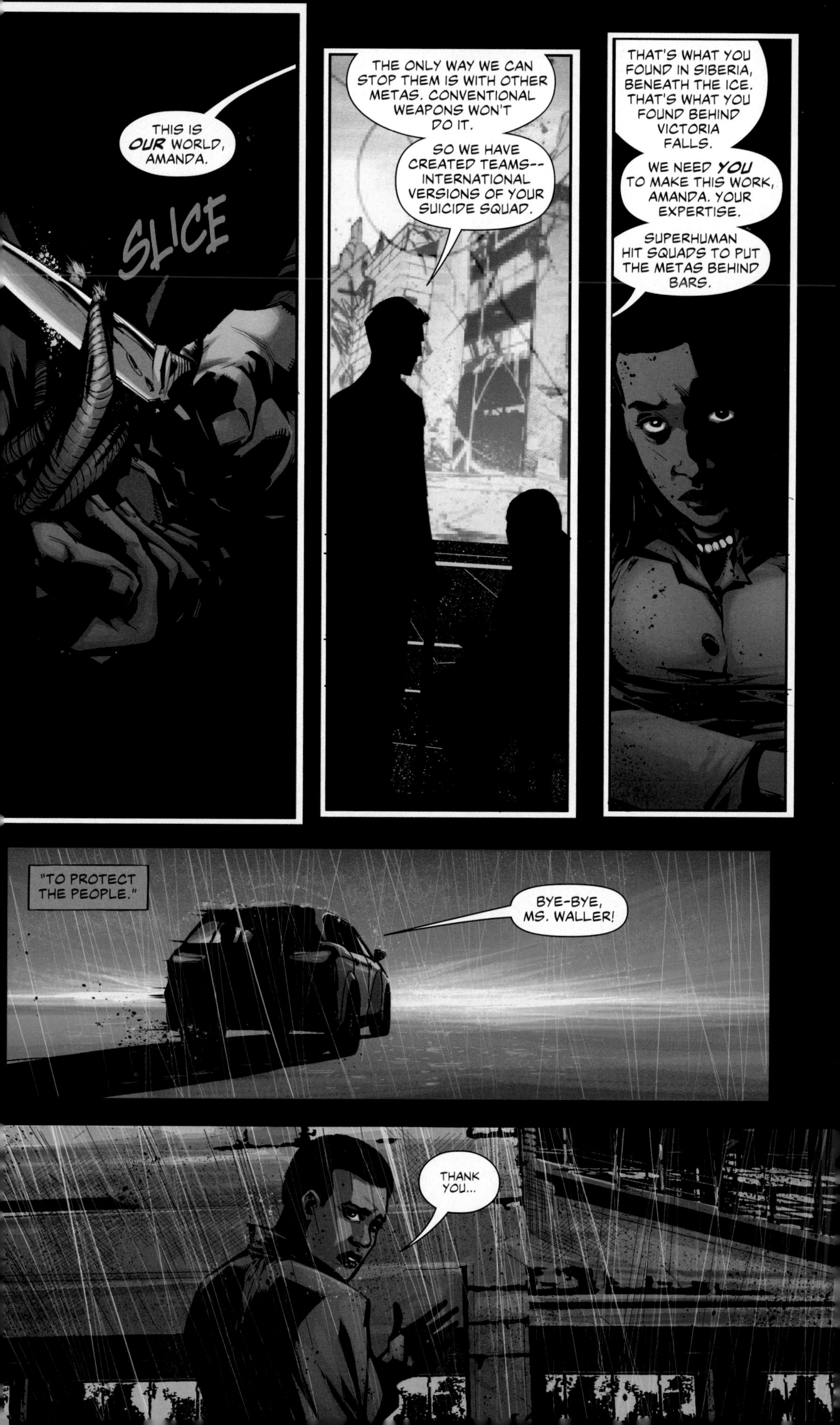
THIS IS OUR WORLD, AMANDA.
SLICE
THE ONLY WAY WE CAN STOP THEM IS WITH OTHER METAS. CONVENTIONAL WEAPONS WON'T DO IT.
SO WE HAVE CREATED TEAMS--INTERNATIONAL VERSIONS OF YOUR SUICIDE SQUAD.
THAT'S WHAT YOU FOUND IN SIBERIA, BENEATH THE ICE. THAT'S WHAT YOU FOUND BEHIND VICTORIA FALLS.
WE NEED YOU TO MAKE THIS WORK, AMANDA. YOUR EXPERTISE.
SUPERHUMAN HIT SQUADS TO PUT THE METAS BEHIND BARS.
"TO PROTECT THE PEOPLE."
BYE-BYE, MS. WALLER!
THANK YOU...

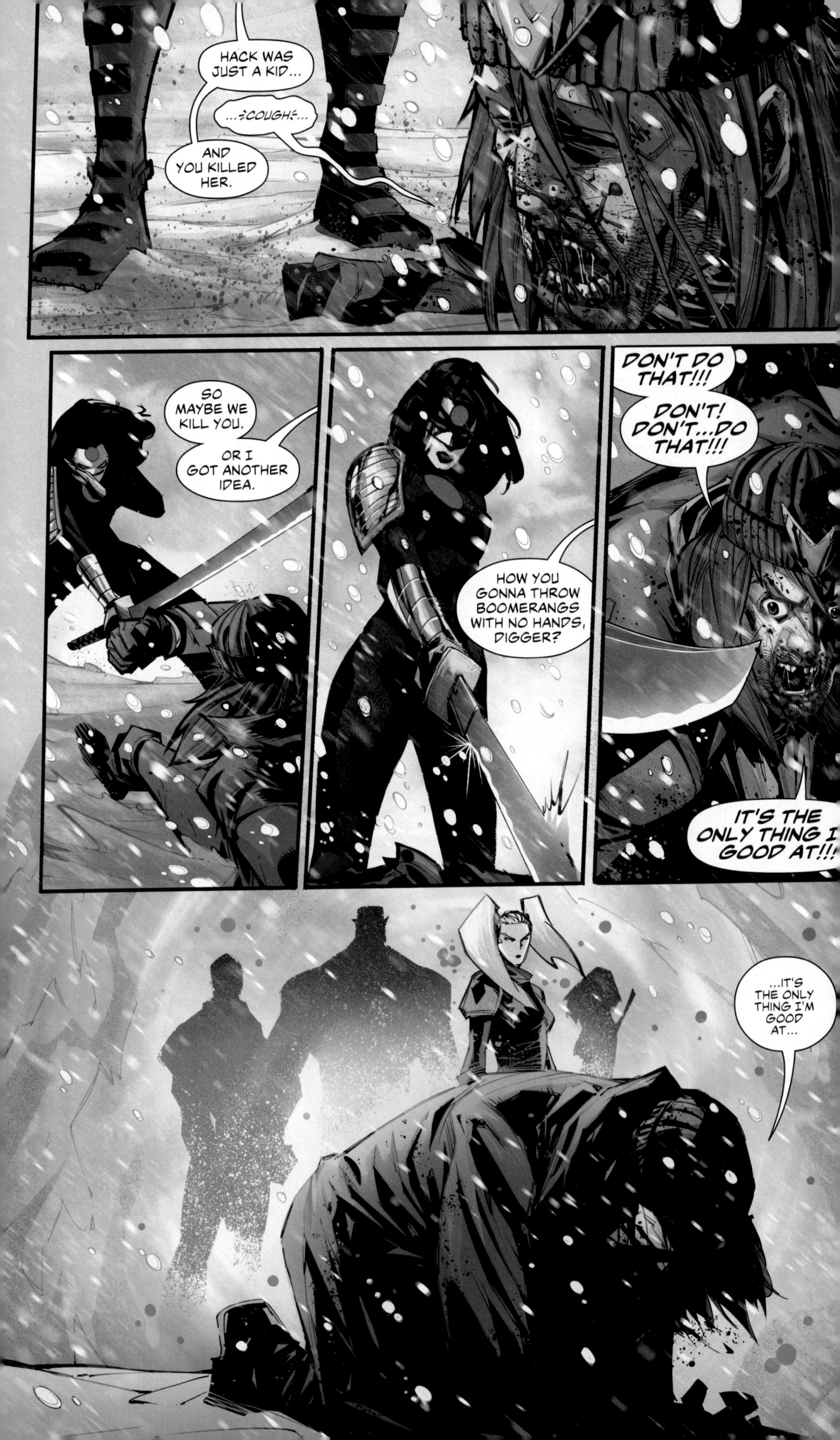
HACK WAS JUST A KID...
...COUGH...
AND YOU KILLED HER.
SO MAYBE WE KILL YOU.
OR I GOT ANOTHER IDEA.
HOW YOU GONNA THROW BOOMERANGS WITH NO HANDS, DIGGER?
DON'T DO THAT!!!
DON'T! DON'T...DO THAT!!!
IT'S THE ONLY THING I GOOD AT!!!
...IT'S THE ONLY THING I'M GOOD AT...

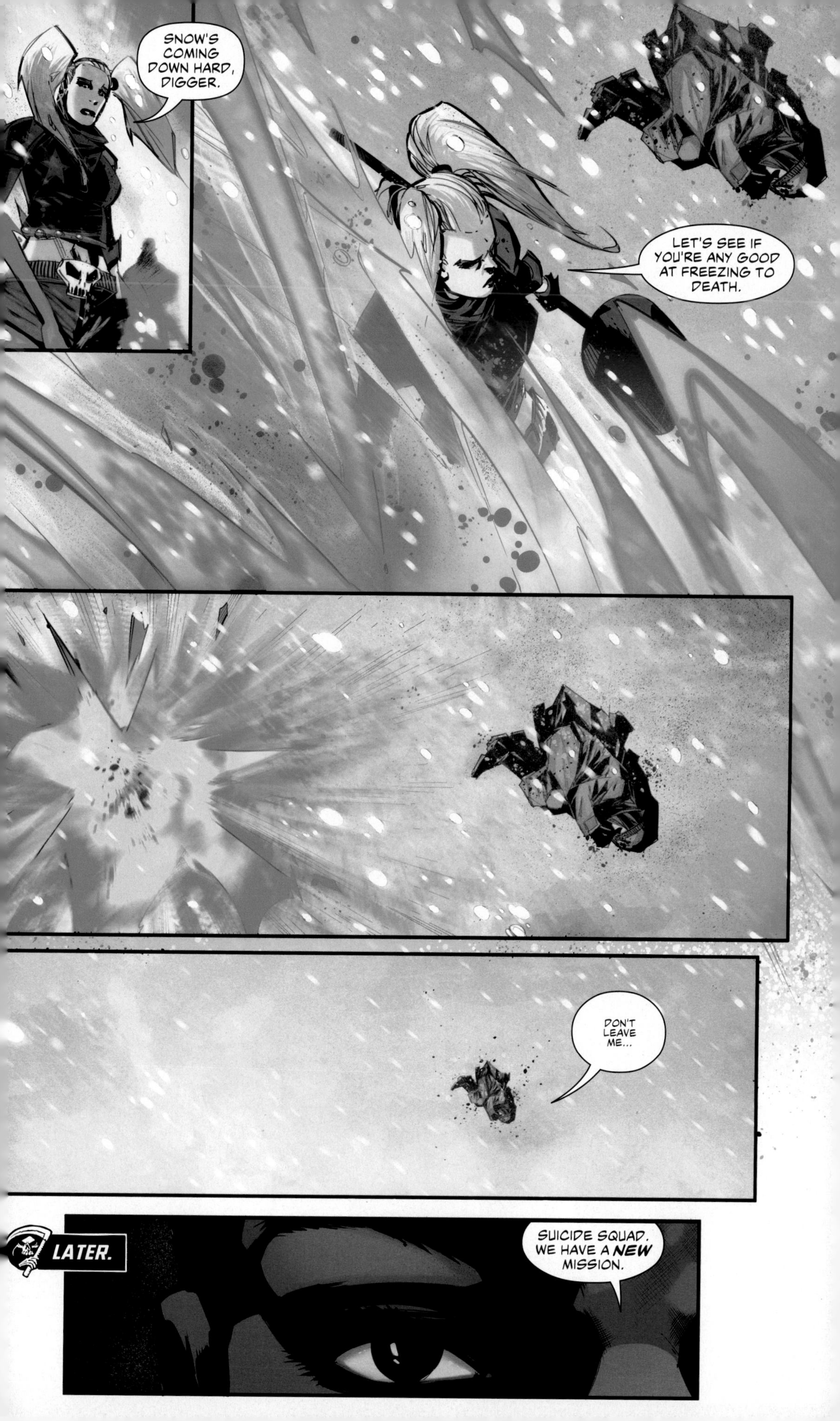
SNOW'S COMING DOWN HARD, DIGGER.
LET'S SEE IF YOU'RE ANY GOOD AT FREEZING TO DEATH.
DON'T LEAVE ME...
LATER.
SUICIDE SQUAD. WE HAVE A NEW MISSION.

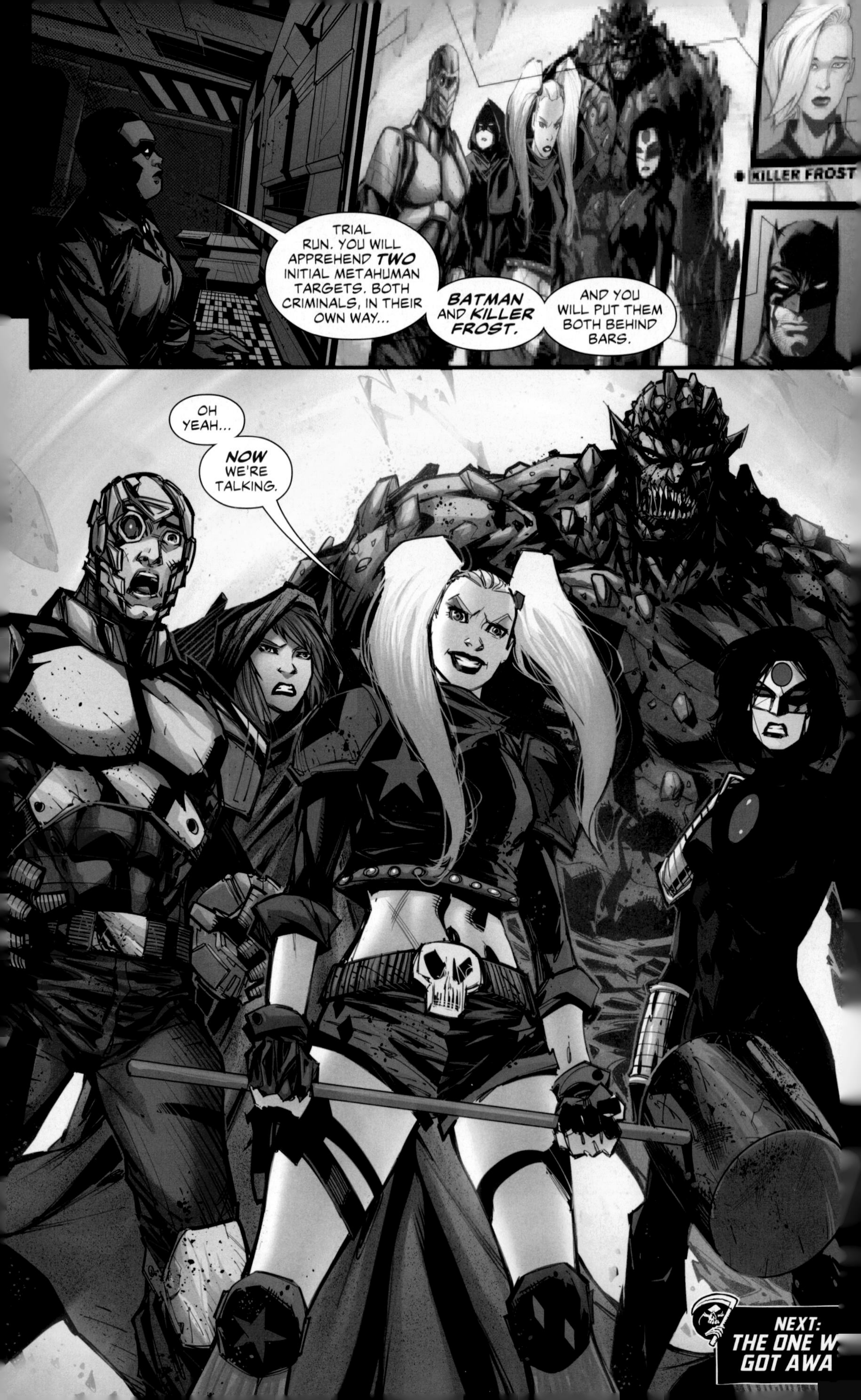
KILLER FROST
TRIAL RUN. YOU WILL APPREHEND **TWO** INITIAL METAHUMAN TARGETS. BOTH CRIMINALS, IN THEIR OWN WAY...
BATMAN AND ***KILLER FROST.***
AND YOU WILL PUT THEM BOTH BEHIND BARS.
OH YEAH...
NOW WE'RE TALKING.
NEXT: THE ONE W GOT AWA

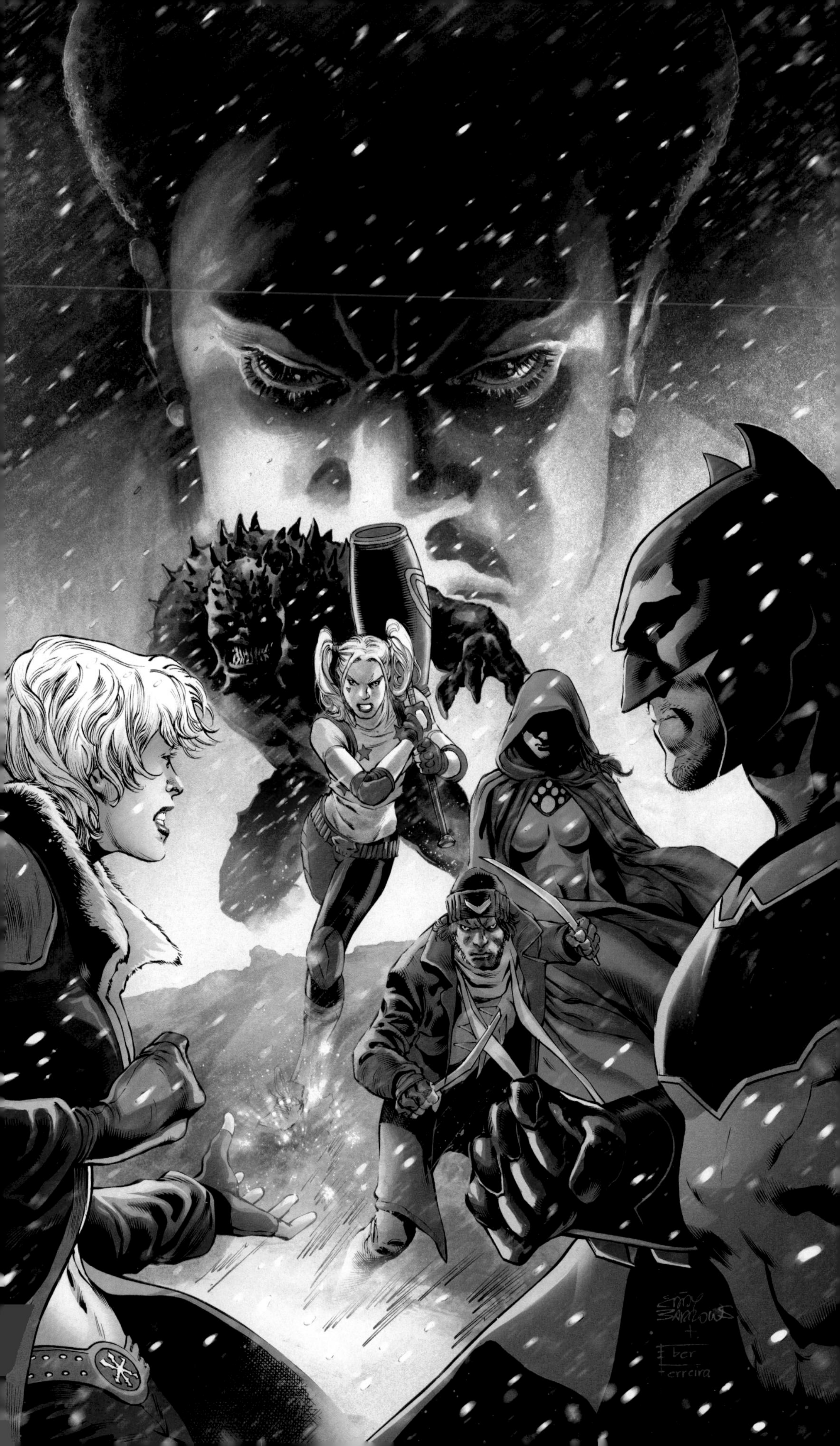

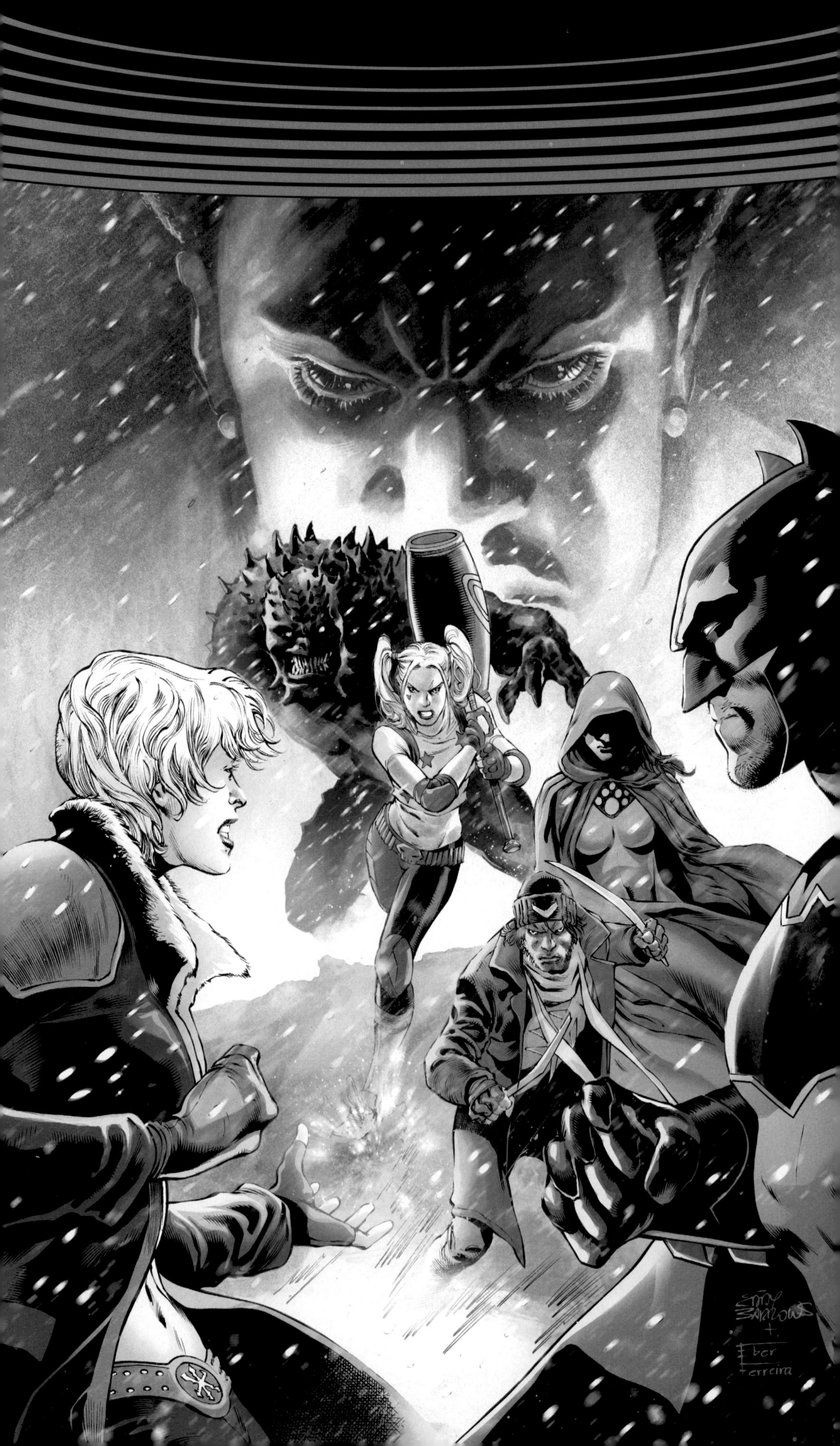

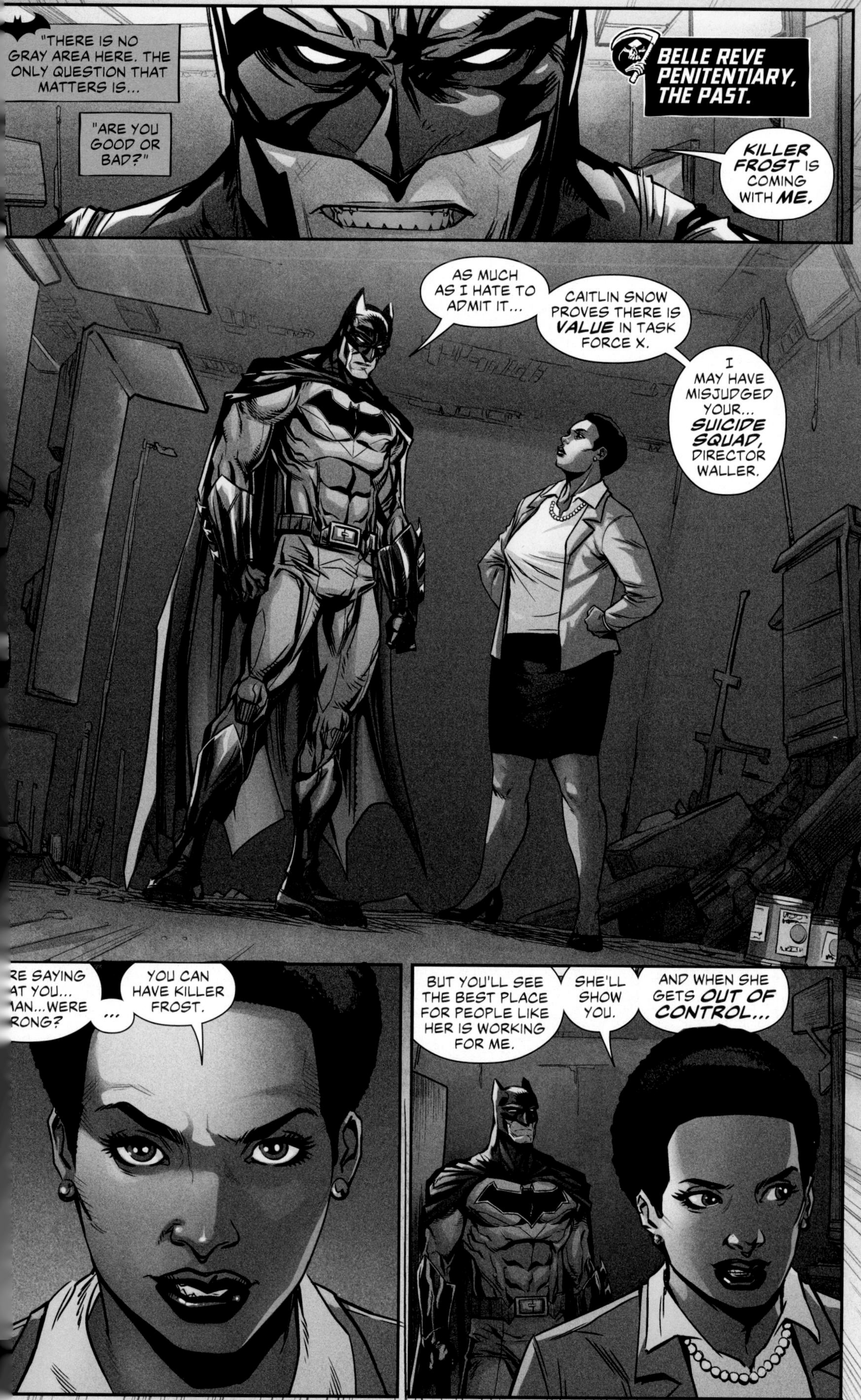
"THERE IS NO GRAY AREA HERE. THE ONLY QUESTION THAT MATTERS IS...
"ARE YOU GOOD OR BAD?"
BELLE REVE PENITENTIARY, THE PAST.
KILLER FROST IS COMING WITH ME.
AS MUCH AS I HATE TO ADMIT IT...
CAITLIN SNOW PROVES THERE IS VALUE IN TASK FORCE X.
I MAY HAVE MISJUDGED YOUR... SUICIDE SQUAD, DIRECTOR WALLER.
...
YOU CAN HAVE KILLER FROST.
BUT YOU'LL SEE THE BEST PLACE FOR PEOPLE LIKE HER IS WORKING FOR ME.
SHE'LL SHOW YOU.
AND WHEN SHE GETS OUT OF CONTROL...

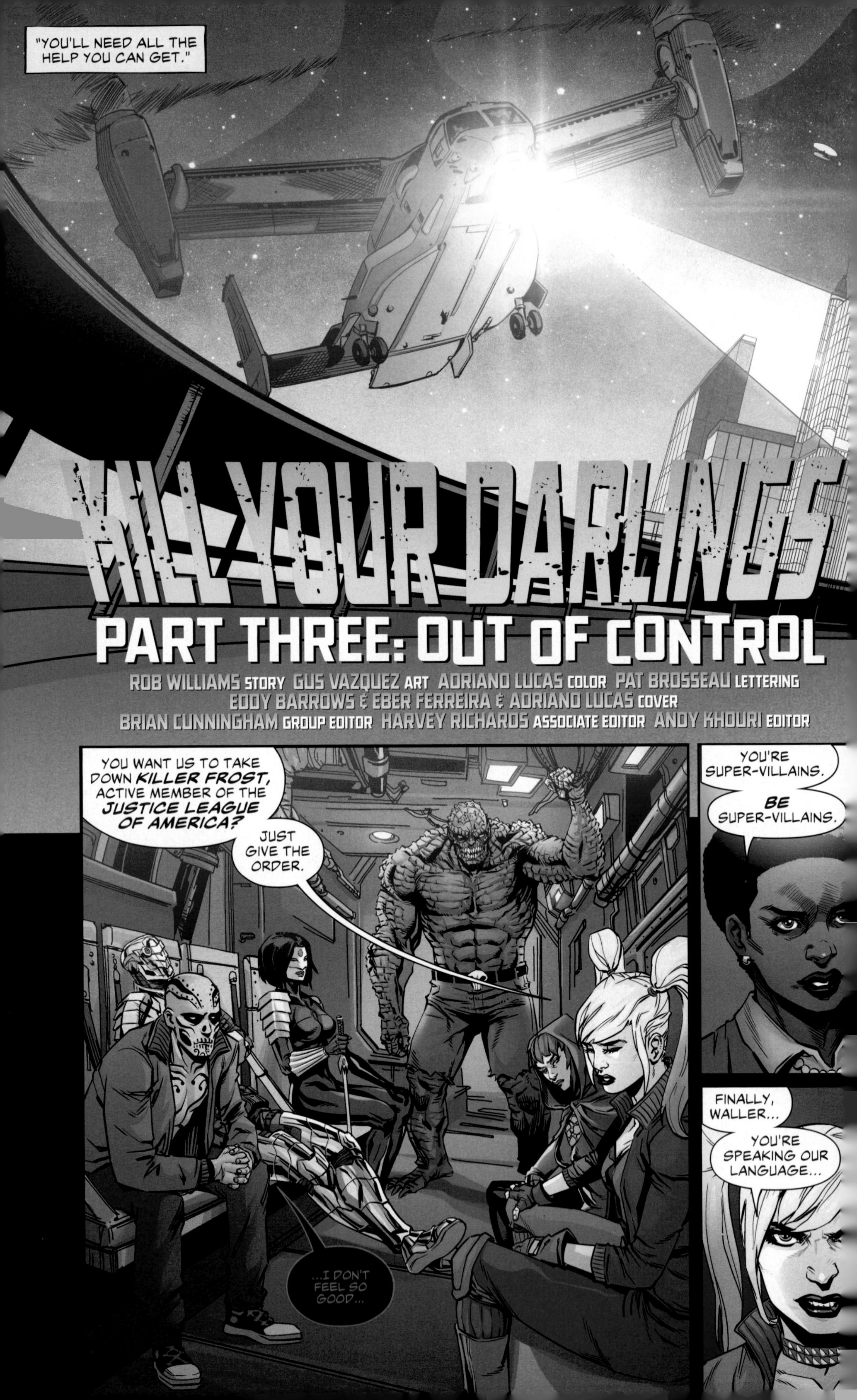
"YOU'LL NEED ALL THE HELP YOU CAN GET."
KILL YOUR DARLINGS
PART THREE: OUT OF CONTROL
ROB WILLIAMS STORY GUS VAZQUEZ ART ADRIANO LUCAS COLOR PAT BROSSEAU LETTERING
EDDY BARROWS & EBER FERREIRA & ADRIANO LUCAS COVER
BRIAN CUNNINGHAM GROUP EDITOR HARVEY RICHARDS ASSOCIATE EDITOR ANDY KHOURI EDITOR
YOU WANT US TO TAKE DOWN KILLER FROST, ACTIVE MEMBER OF THE JUSTICE LEAGUE OF AMERICA?
JUST GIVE THE ORDER.
...I DON'T FEEL SO GOOD...
YOU'RE SUPER-VILLAINS.
BE SUPER-VILLAINS.
FINALLY, WALLER...
YOU'RE SPEAKING OUR LANGUAGE...

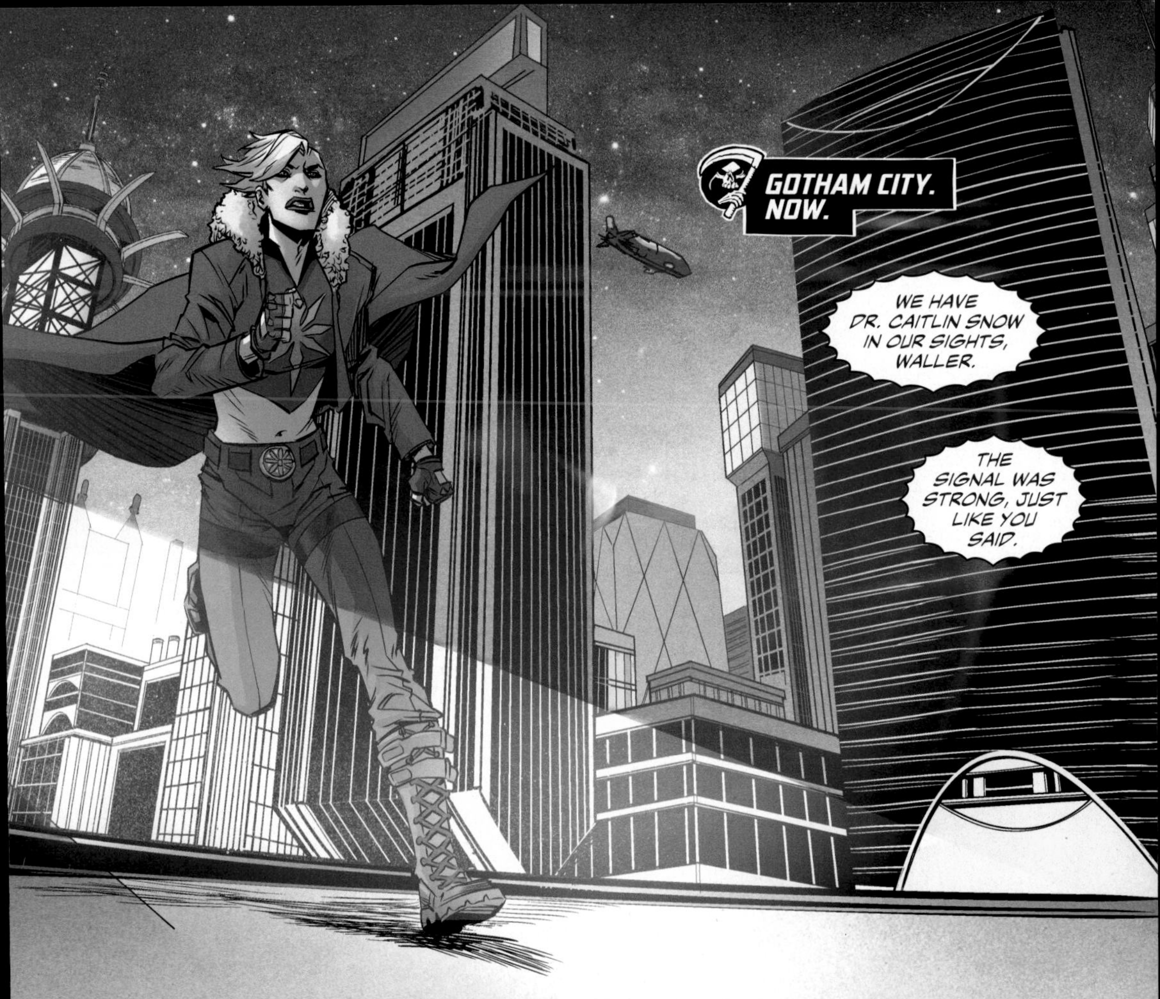
GOTHAM CITY. NOW.
WE HAVE DR. CAITLIN SNOW IN OUR SIGHTS, WALLER.
THE SIGNAL WAS STRONG, JUST LIKE YOU SAID.

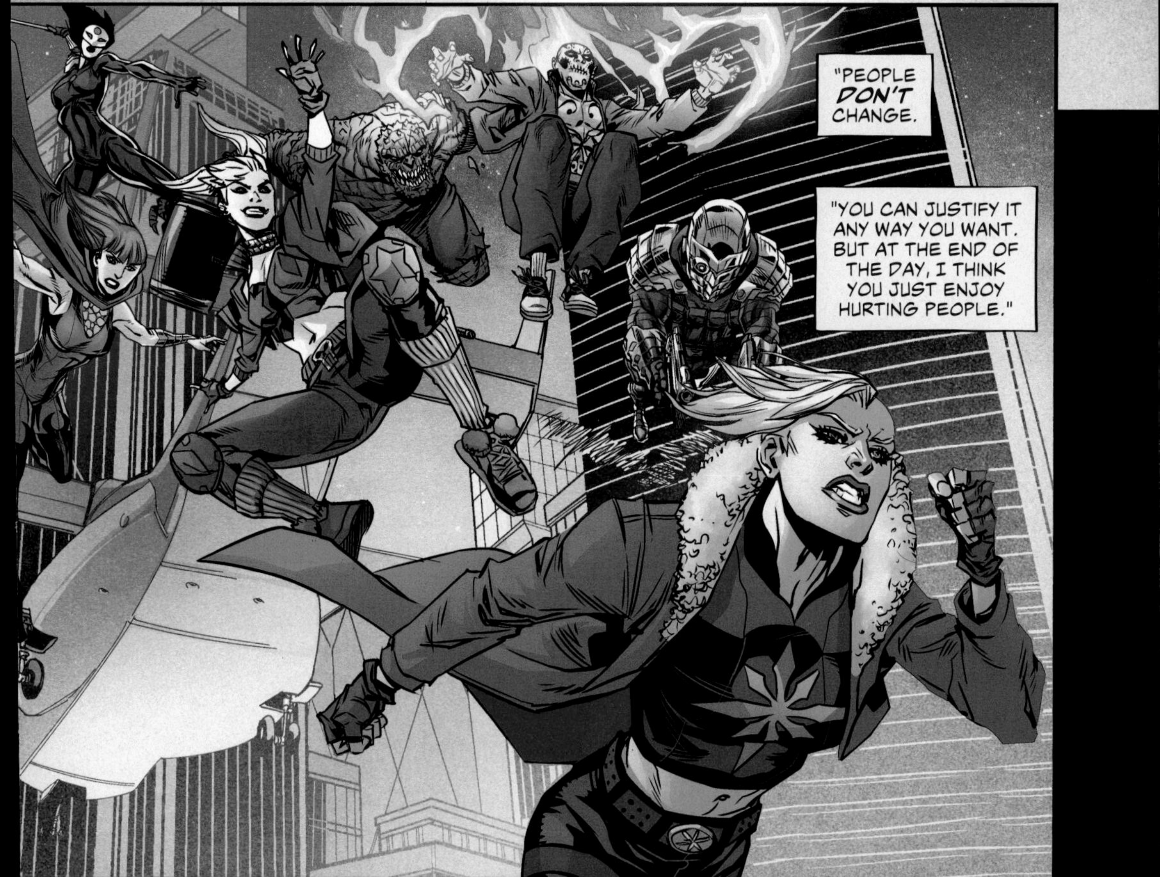
"PEOPLE DON'T CHANGE.
"YOU CAN JUSTIFY IT ANY WAY YOU WANT. BUT AT THE END OF THE DAY, I THINK YOU JUST ENJOY HURTING PEOPLE."

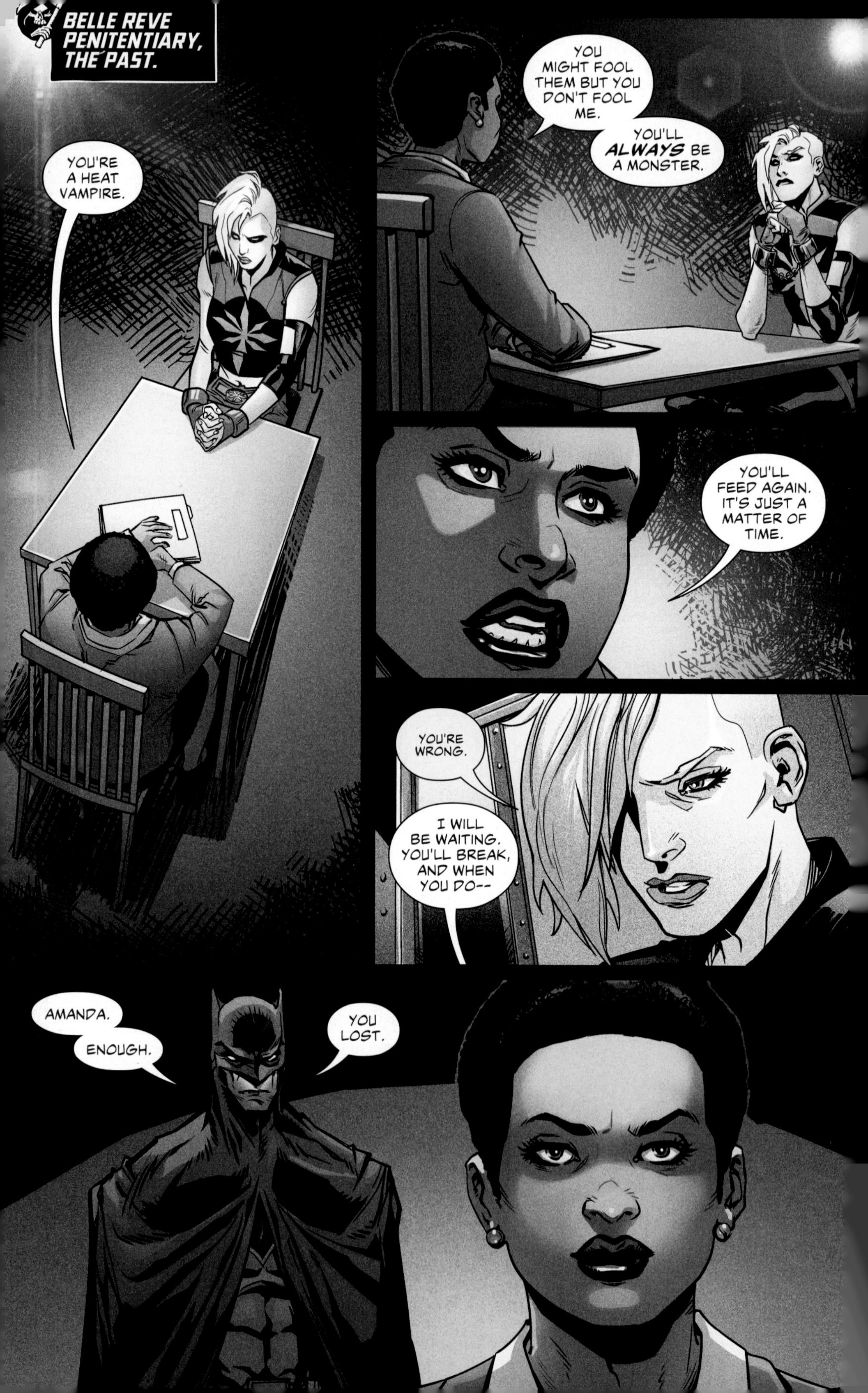
BELLE REVE PENITENTIARY, THE PAST.
YOU'RE A HEAT VAMPIRE.
YOU MIGHT FOOL THEM BUT YOU DON'T FOOL ME.
YOU'LL ALWAYS BE A MONSTER.
YOU'LL FEED AGAIN. IT'S JUST A MATTER OF TIME.
YOU'RE WRONG.
I WILL BE WAITING. YOU'LL BREAK, AND WHEN YOU DO--
AMANDA.
ENOUGH.
YOU LOST.

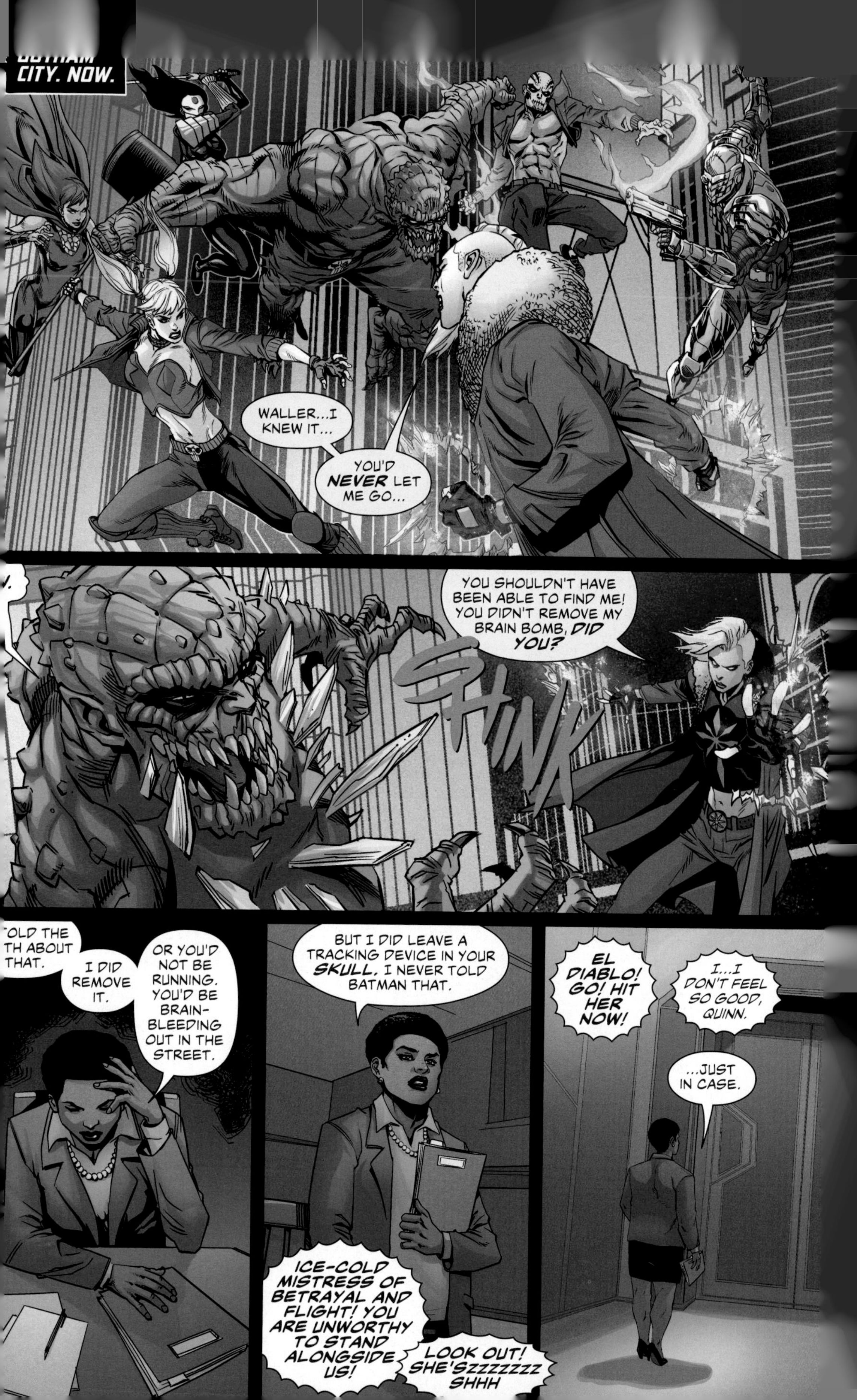
CITY. NOW.
WALLER...I KNEW IT...
YOU'D NEVER LET ME GO...
YOU SHOULDN'T HAVE BEEN ABLE TO FIND ME! YOU DIDN'T REMOVE MY BRAIN BOMB, DID YOU?
SHHHNK
I DID REMOVE IT.
OR YOU'D NOT BE RUNNING. YOU'D BE BRAIN-BLEEDING OUT IN THE STREET.
BUT I DID LEAVE A TRACKING DEVICE IN YOUR SKULL. I NEVER TOLD BATMAN THAT.
ICE-COLD MISTRESS OF BETRAYAL AND FLIGHT! YOU ARE UNWORTHY TO STAND ALONGSIDE US!
LOOK OUT! SHE'SZZZZZZZ SHHH
EL DIABLO! GO! HIT HER NOW!
I...I DON'T FEEL SO GOOD, QUINN.
...JUST IN CASE.

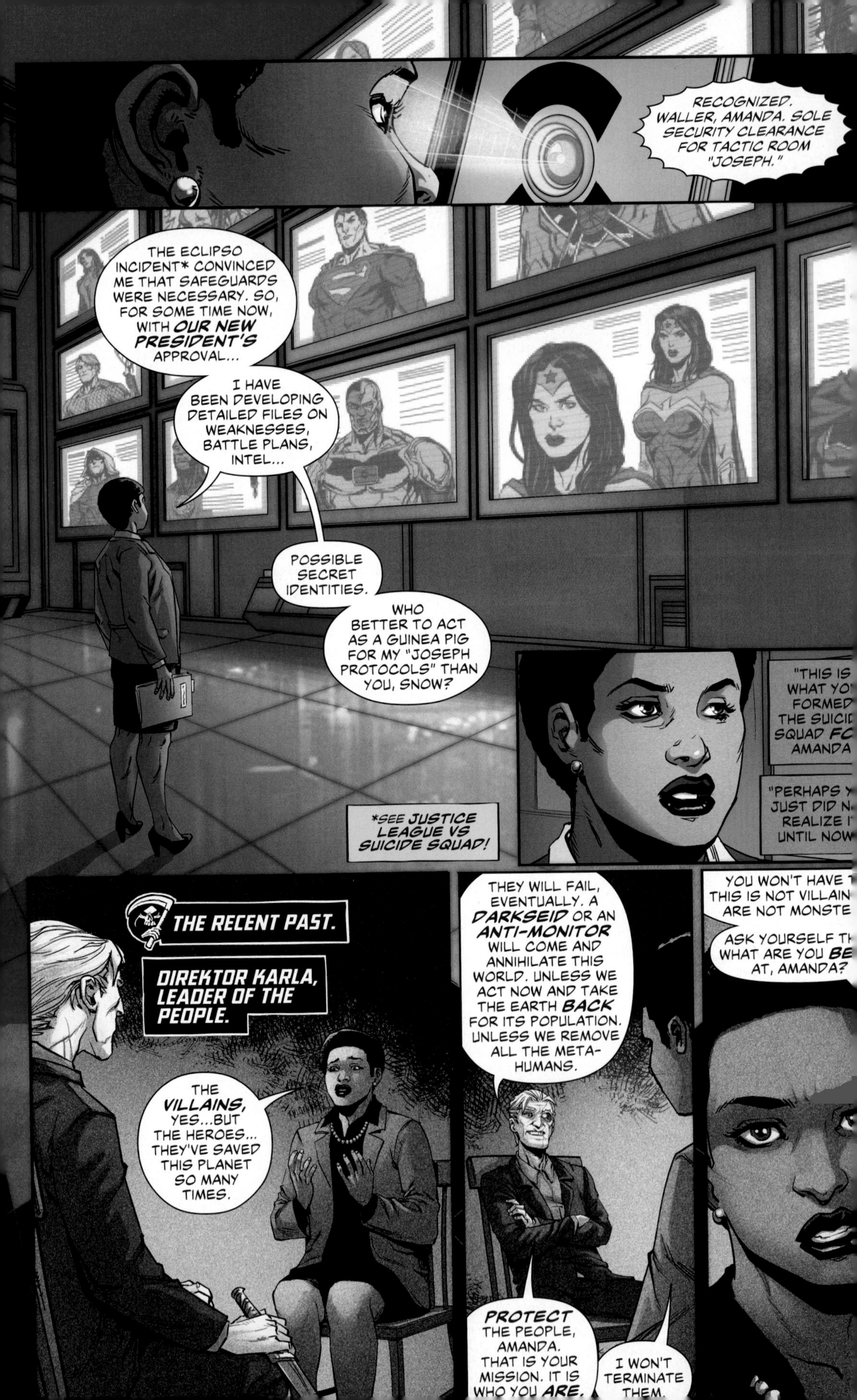

RECOGNIZED. WALLER, AMANDA. SOLE SECURITY CLEARANCE FOR TACTIC ROOM "JOSEPH."
THE ECLIPSO INCIDENT* CONVINCED ME THAT SAFEGUARDS WERE NECESSARY. SO, FOR SOME TIME NOW, WITH OUR NEW PRESIDENT'S APPROVAL...
I HAVE BEEN DEVELOPING DETAILED FILES ON WEAKNESSES, BATTLE PLANS, INTEL...
POSSIBLE SECRET IDENTITIES.
WHO BETTER TO ACT AS A GUINEA PIG FOR MY "JOSEPH PROTOCOLS" THAN YOU, SNOW?
*SEE JUSTICE LEAGUE VS SUICIDE SQUAD!
"THIS IS WHAT YO FORMED THE SUICID SQUAD FO AMANDA
"PERHAPS Y JUST DID N REALIZE I UNTIL NOW
THE RECENT PAST.
DIREKTOR KARLA, LEADER OF THE PEOPLE.
THE VILLAINS, YES...BUT THE HEROES... THEY'VE SAVED THIS PLANET SO MANY TIMES.
THEY WILL FAIL, EVENTUALLY. A DARKSEID OR AN ANTI-MONITOR WILL COME AND ANNIHILATE THIS WORLD. UNLESS WE ACT NOW AND TAKE THE EARTH BACK FOR ITS POPULATION. UNLESS WE REMOVE ALL THE META-HUMANS.
PROTECT THE PEOPLE, AMANDA. THAT IS YOUR MISSION. IT IS WHO YOU ARE.
I WON'T TERMINATE THEM.
YOU WON'T HAVE THIS IS NOT VILLAIN ARE NOT MONSTE
ASK YOURSELF TH WHAT ARE YOU BE AT, AMANDA?

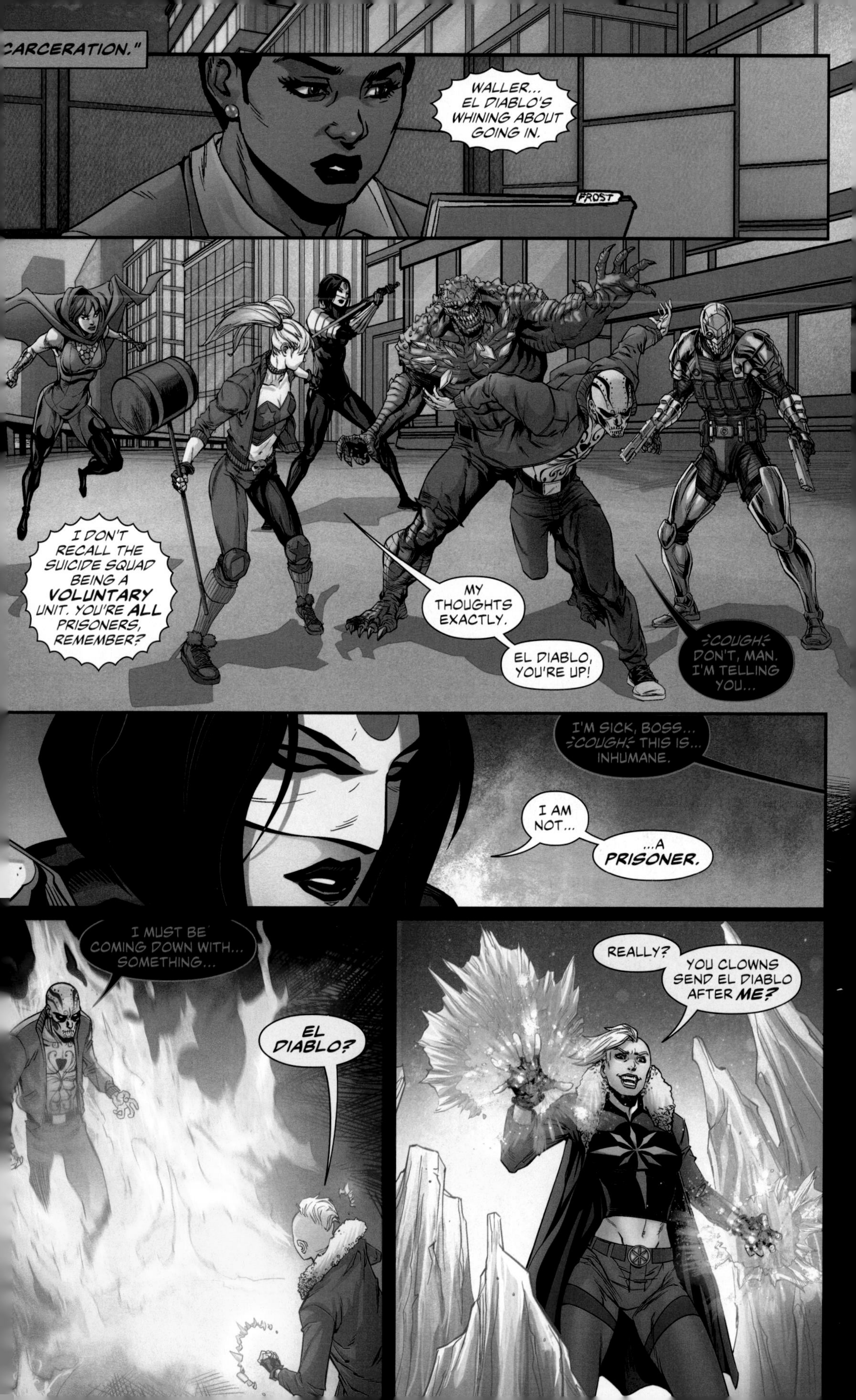
...CARCERATION."
WALLER... EL DIABLO'S WHINING ABOUT GOING IN.
FROST
I DON'T RECALL THE SUICIDE SQUAD BEING A VOLUNTARY UNIT. YOU'RE ALL PRISONERS, REMEMBER?
MY THOUGHTS EXACTLY.
EL DIABLO, YOU'RE UP!
COUGH DON'T, MAN. I'M TELLING YOU...
I'M SICK, BOSS... *COUGH* THIS IS... INHUMANE.
I AM NOT...
...A PRISONER.
I MUST BE COMING DOWN WITH... SOMETHING...
EL DIABLO?
REALLY?
YOU CLOWNS SEND EL DIABLO AFTER ME?

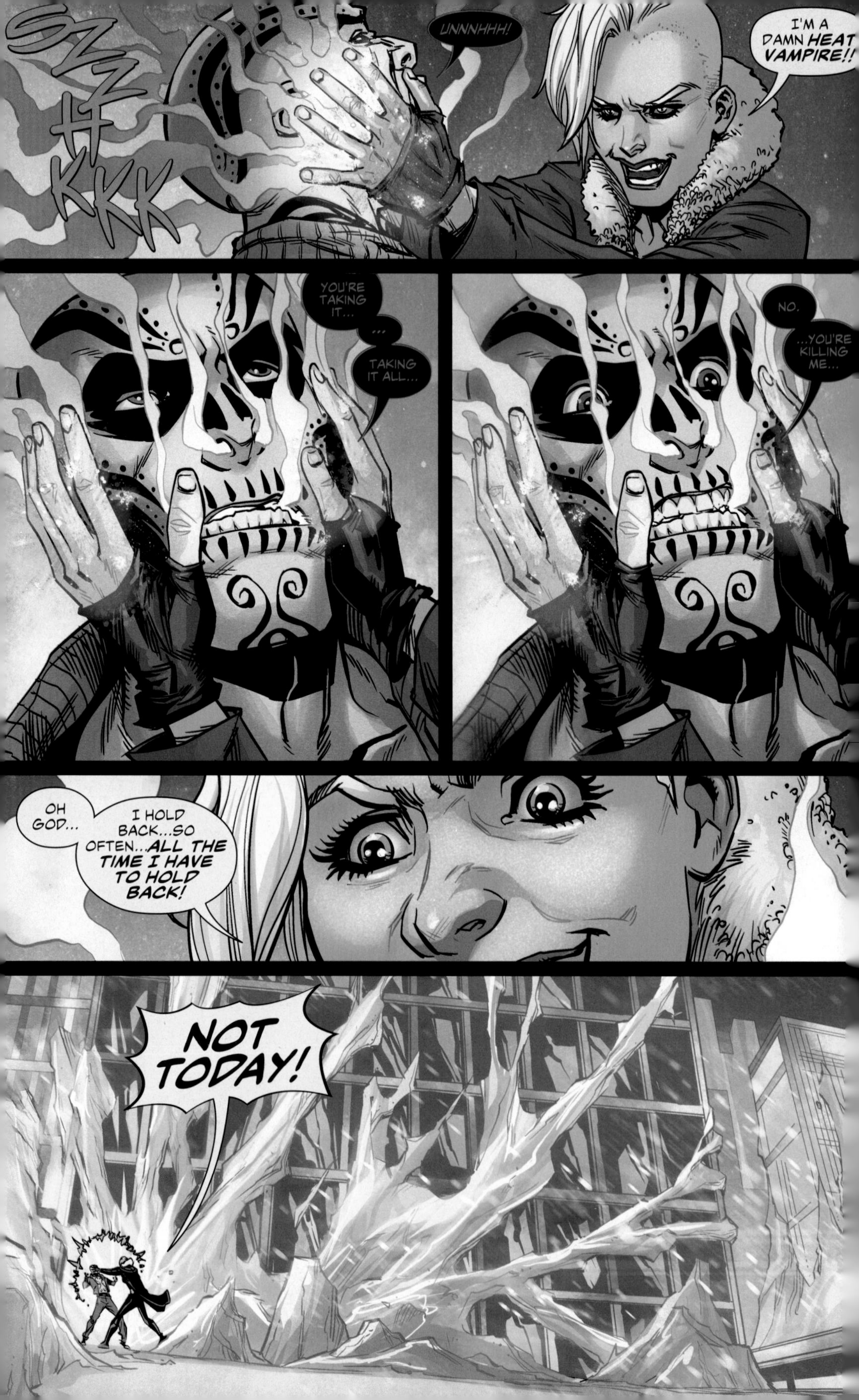
SZZZHHKKK
UNNNHHH!
I'M A DAMN HEAT VAMPIRE!!
YOU'RE TAKING IT...
...
TAKING IT ALL...
NO.
...YOU'RE KILLING ME...
OH GOD...
I HOLD BACK...SO OFTEN...ALL THE TIME I HAVE TO HOLD BACK!
NOT TODAY!

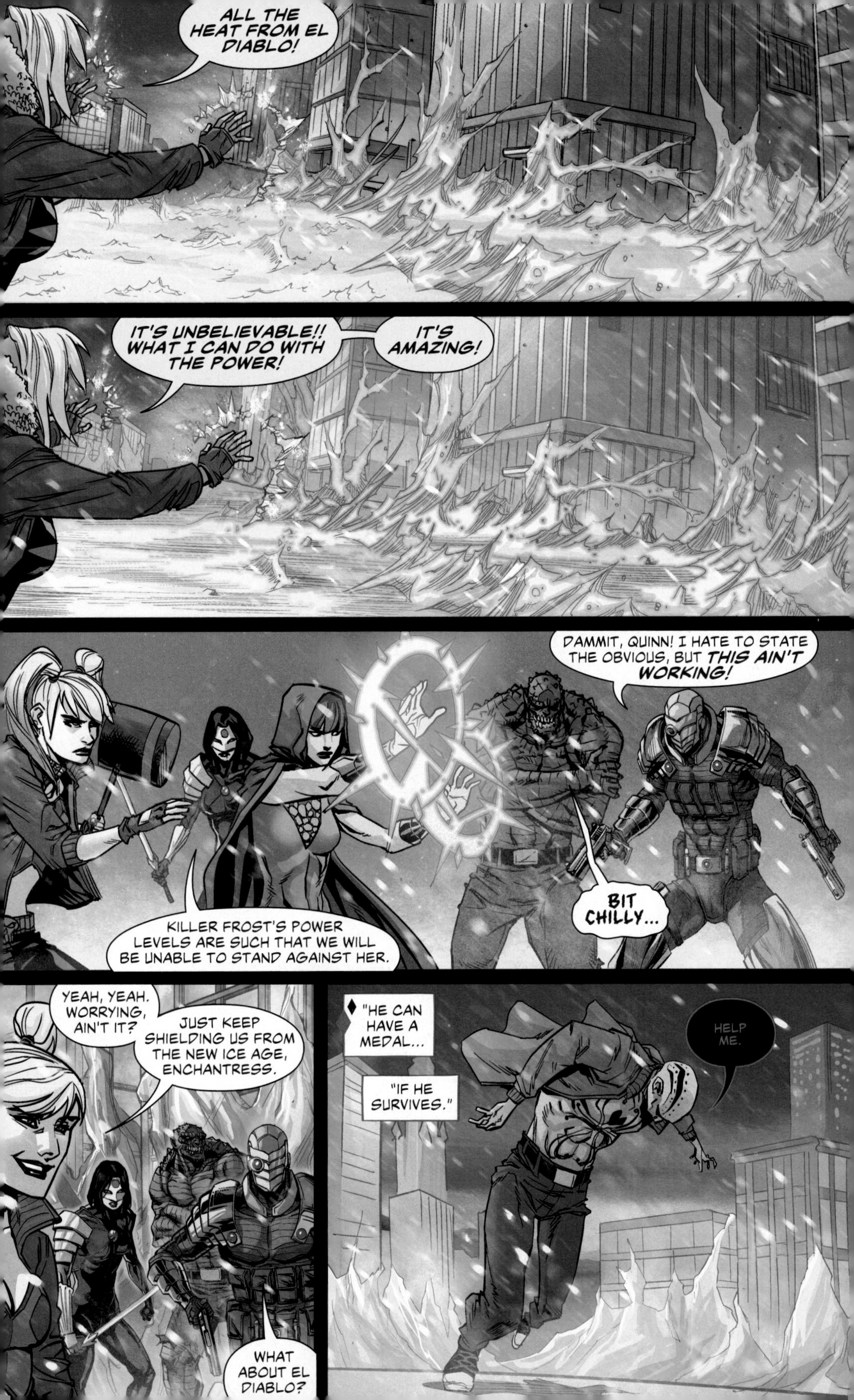
ALL THE HEAT FROM EL DIABLO!
IT'S UNBELIEVABLE!! WHAT I CAN DO WITH THE POWER!
IT'S AMAZING!
DAMMIT, QUINN! I HATE TO STATE THE OBVIOUS, BUT THIS AIN'T WORKING!
BIT CHILLY...
KILLER FROST'S POWER LEVELS ARE SUCH THAT WE WILL BE UNABLE TO STAND AGAINST HER.
YEAH, YEAH. WORRYING, AIN'T IT?
JUST KEEP SHIELDING US FROM THE NEW ICE AGE, ENCHANTRESS.
WHAT ABOUT EL DIABLO?
"HE CAN HAVE A MEDAL...
"IF HE SURVIVES."
HELP ME.

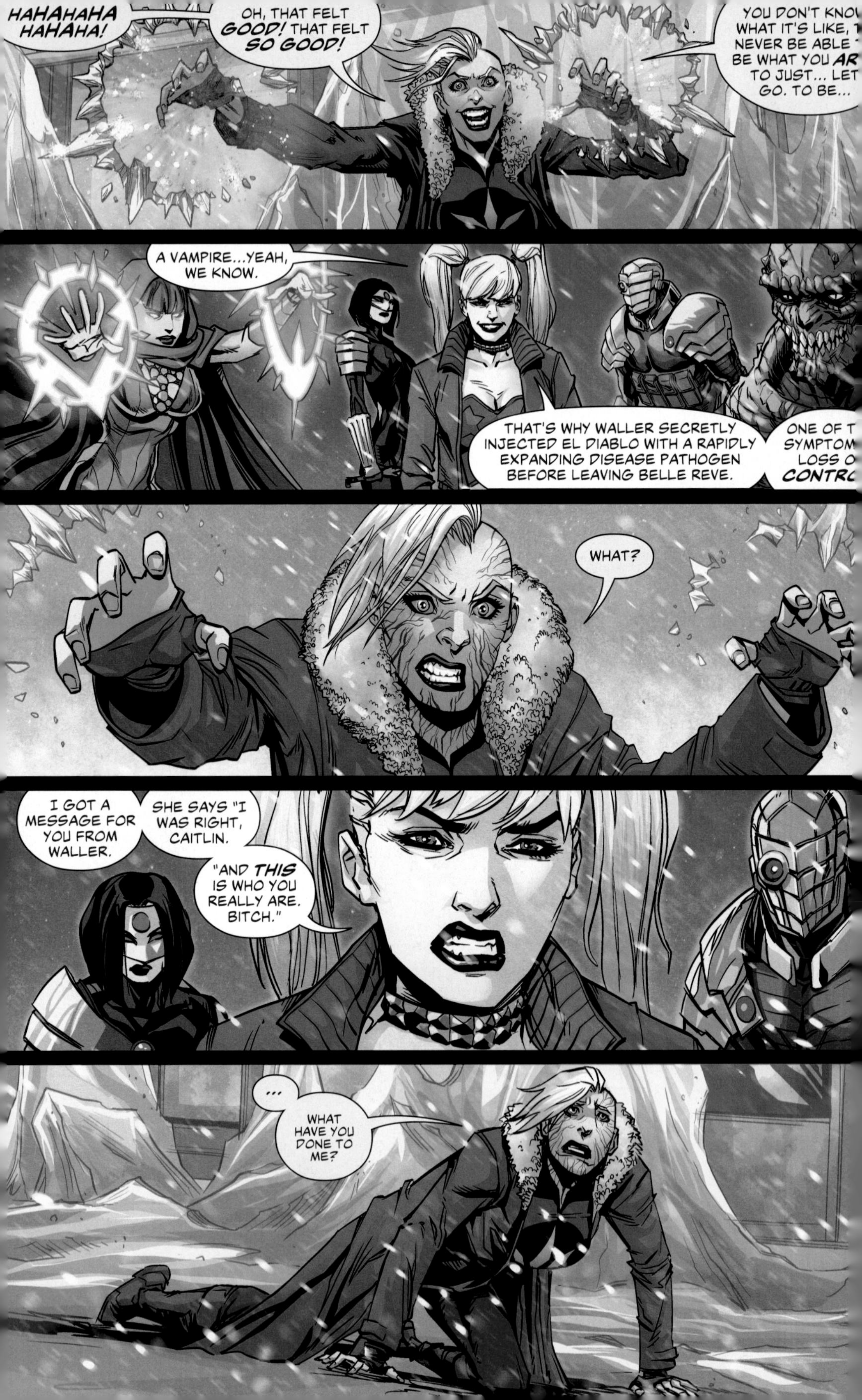
HAHAHAHA HAHAHA!
OH, THAT FELT GOOD! THAT FELT SO GOOD!
YOU DON'T KNOW WHAT IT'S LIKE, TO NEVER BE ABLE TO BE WHAT YOU ARE TO JUST... LET GO. TO BE...
A VAMPIRE...YEAH, WE KNOW.
THAT'S WHY WALLER SECRETLY INJECTED EL DIABLO WITH A RAPIDLY EXPANDING DISEASE PATHOGEN BEFORE LEAVING BELLE REVE.
ONE OF THE SYMPTOMS LOSS OF CONTROL
WHAT?
I GOT A MESSAGE FOR YOU FROM WALLER.
SHE SAYS "I WAS RIGHT, CAITLIN.
"AND THIS IS WHO YOU REALLY ARE. BITCH."
...
WHAT HAVE YOU DONE TO ME?

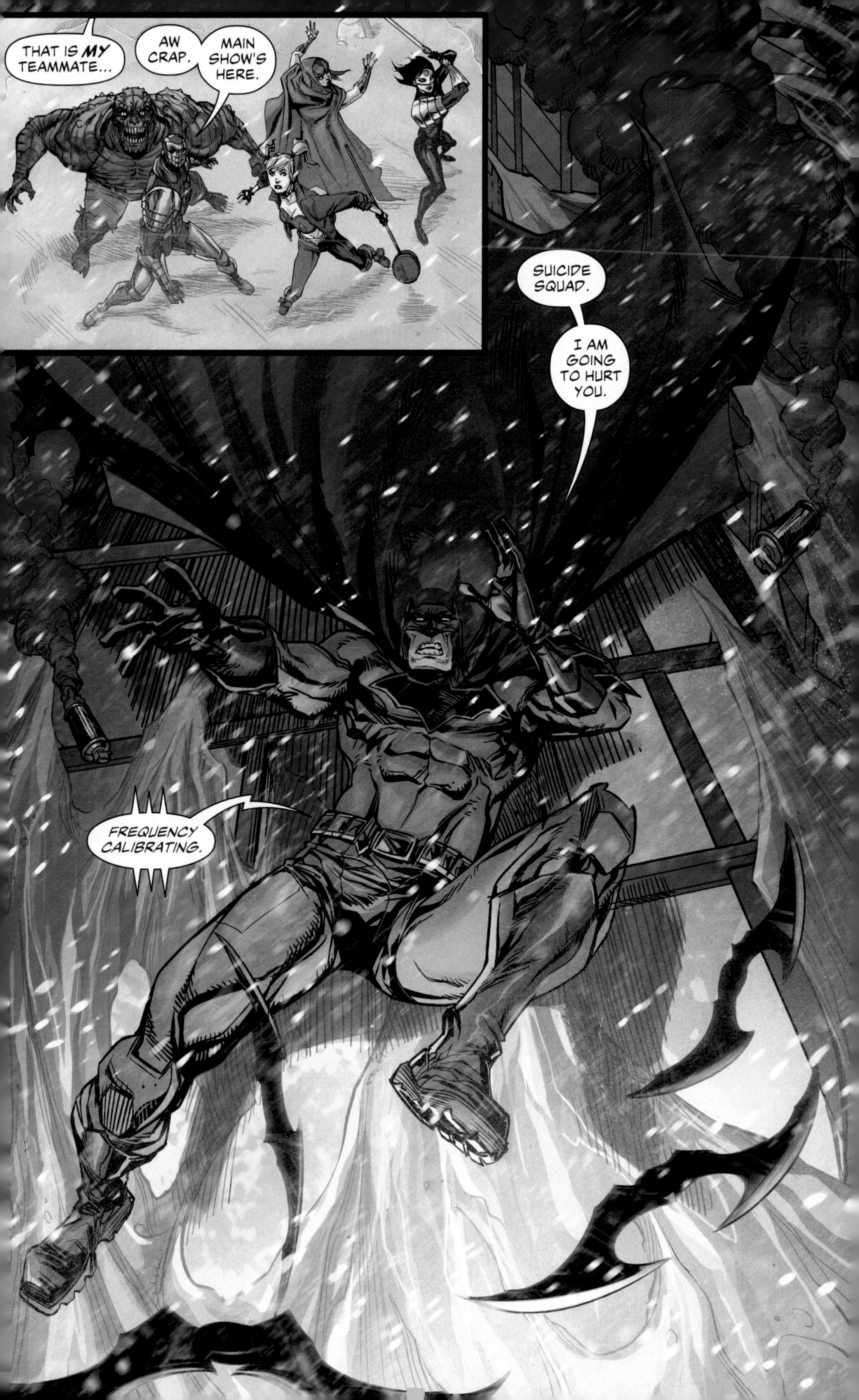
THAT IS ***MY*** TEAMMATE...
AW CRAP.
MAIN SHOW'S HERE.
SUICIDE SQUAD.
I AM GOING TO HURT YOU.
FREQUENCY CALIBRATING.

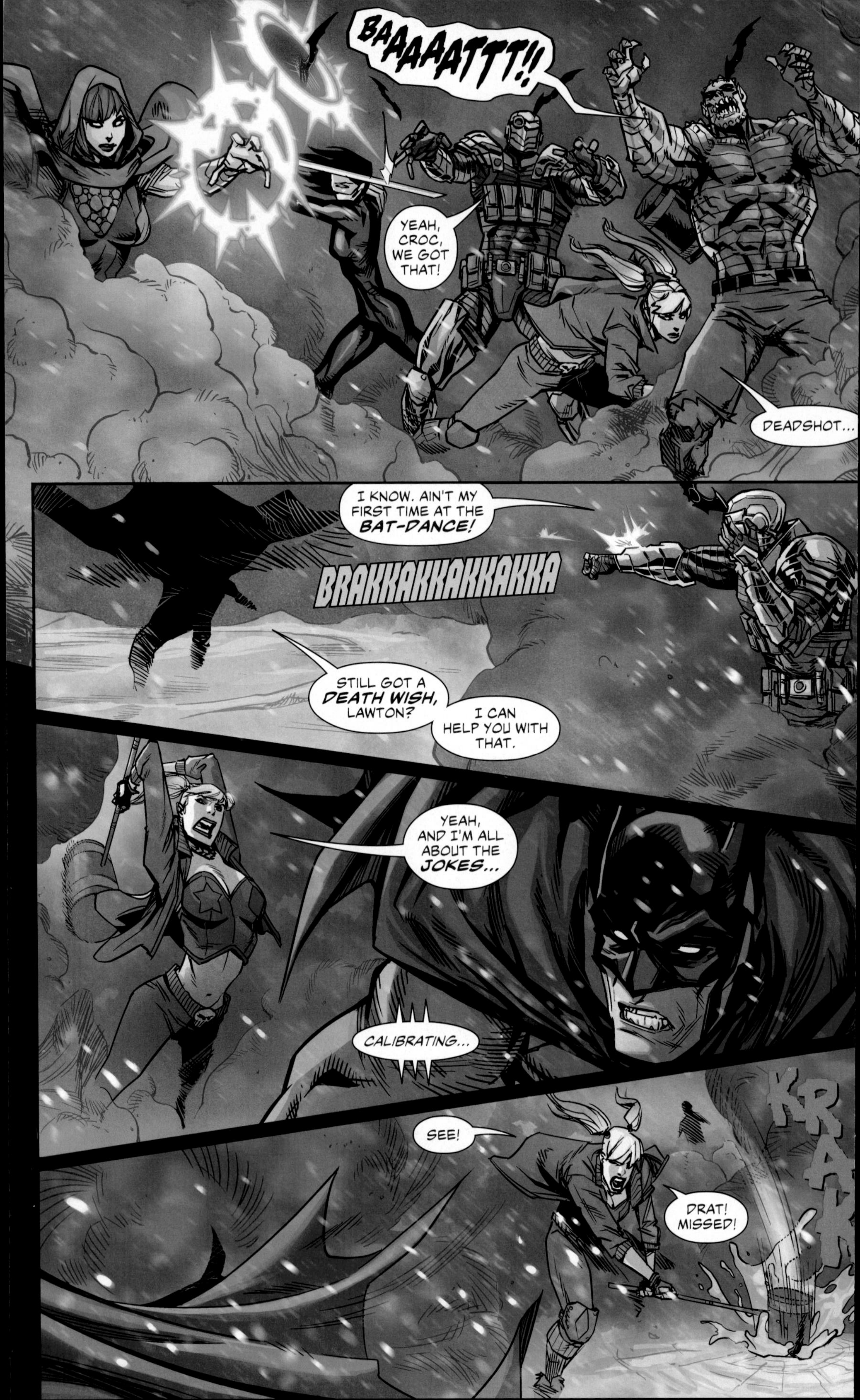
BAAAAATTT!!
YEAH, CROC, WE GOT THAT!
DEADSHOT...
I KNOW. AIN'T MY FIRST TIME AT THE BAT-DANCE!
BRAKKAKKAKKAKKA
STILL GOT A DEATH WISH, LAWTON?
I CAN HELP YOU WITH THAT.
YEAH, AND I'M ALL ABOUT THE JOKES...
CALIBRATING...
SEE!
DRAT! MISSED!

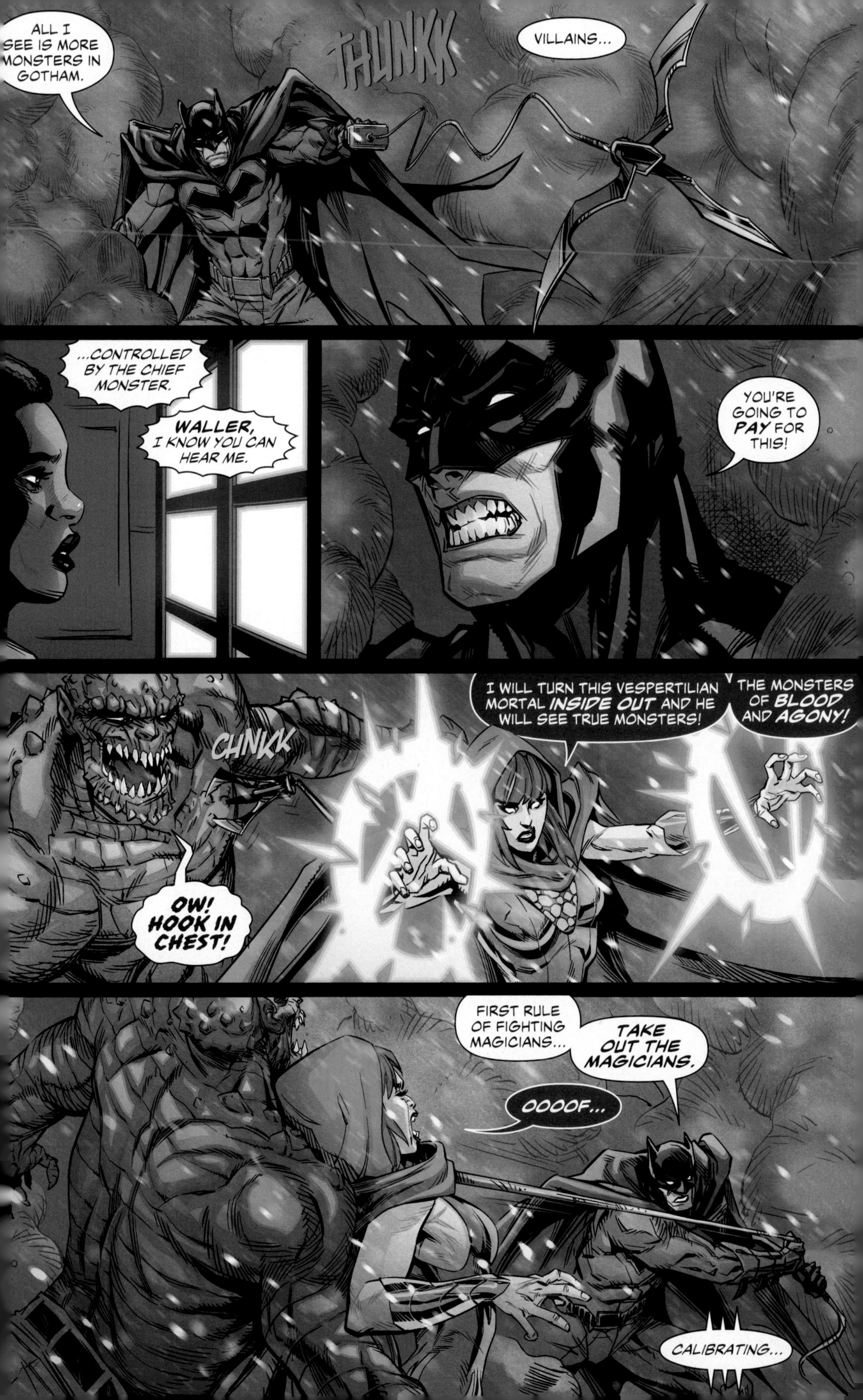

ALL I SEE IS MORE MONSTERS IN GOTHAM.
THUNKK
VILLAINS...
...CONTROLLED BY THE CHIEF MONSTER.
WALLER, I KNOW YOU CAN HEAR ME.
YOU'RE GOING TO PAY FOR THIS!
CHINKK
I WILL TURN THIS VESPERTILIAN MORTAL INSIDE OUT AND HE WILL SEE TRUE MONSTERS!
THE MONSTERS OF BLOOD AND AGONY!
OW! HOOK IN CHEST!
FIRST RULE OF FIGHTING MAGICIANS...
TAKE OUT THE MAGICIANS.
OOOOF...
CALIBRATING...

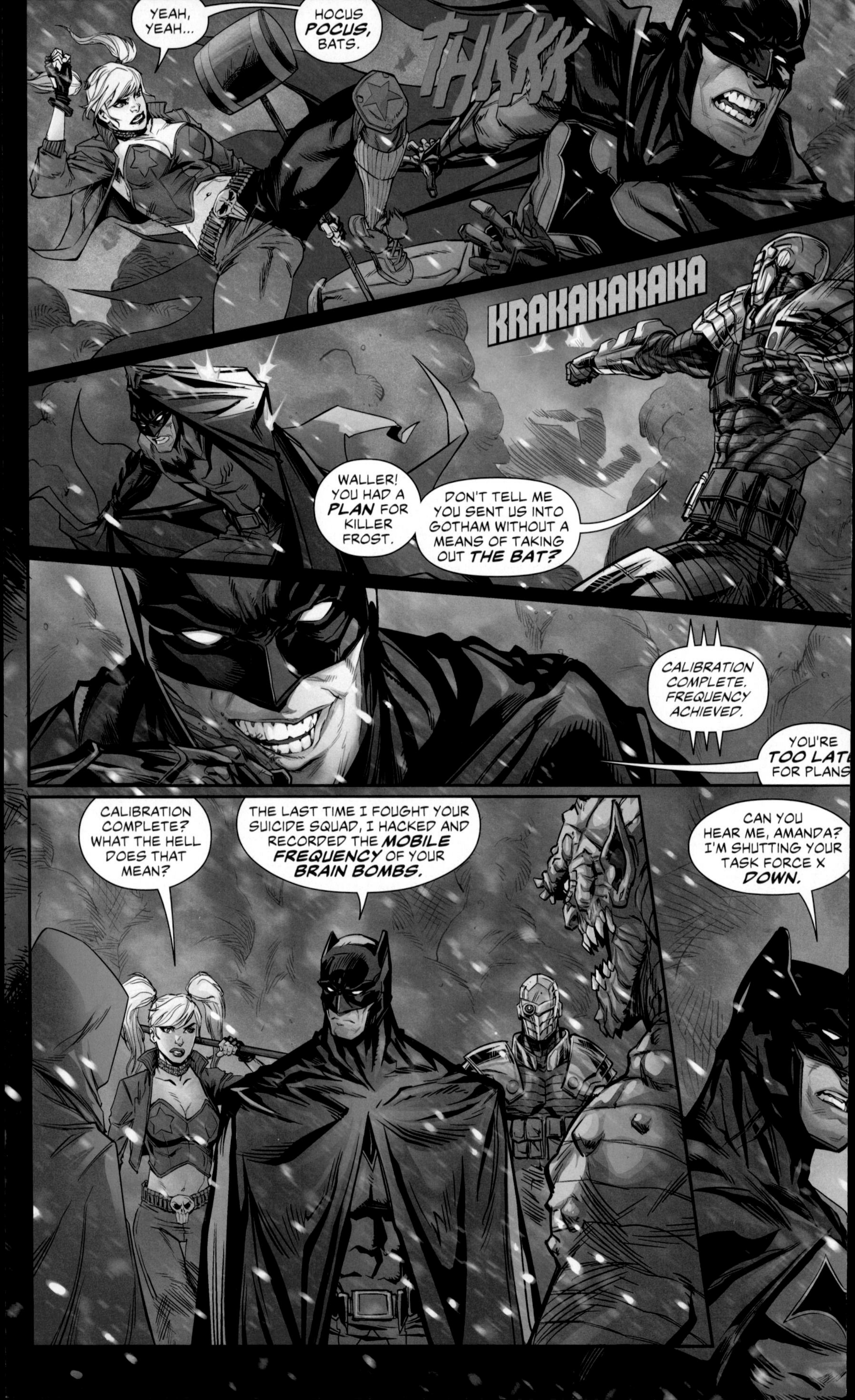
YEAH, YEAH...
HOCUS POCUS, BATS.
THKKK
KRAKAKAKAKA
WALLER! YOU HAD A PLAN FOR KILLER FROST.
DON'T TELL ME YOU SENT US INTO GOTHAM WITHOUT A MEANS OF TAKING OUT THE BAT?
CALIBRATION COMPLETE. FREQUENCY ACHIEVED.
YOU'RE TOO LATE FOR PLANS
CALIBRATION COMPLETE? WHAT THE HELL DOES THAT MEAN?
THE LAST TIME I FOUGHT YOUR SUICIDE SQUAD, I HACKED AND RECORDED THE MOBILE FREQUENCY OF YOUR BRAIN BOMBS.
CAN YOU HEAR ME, AMANDA? I'M SHUTTING YOUR TASK FORCE X DOWN.

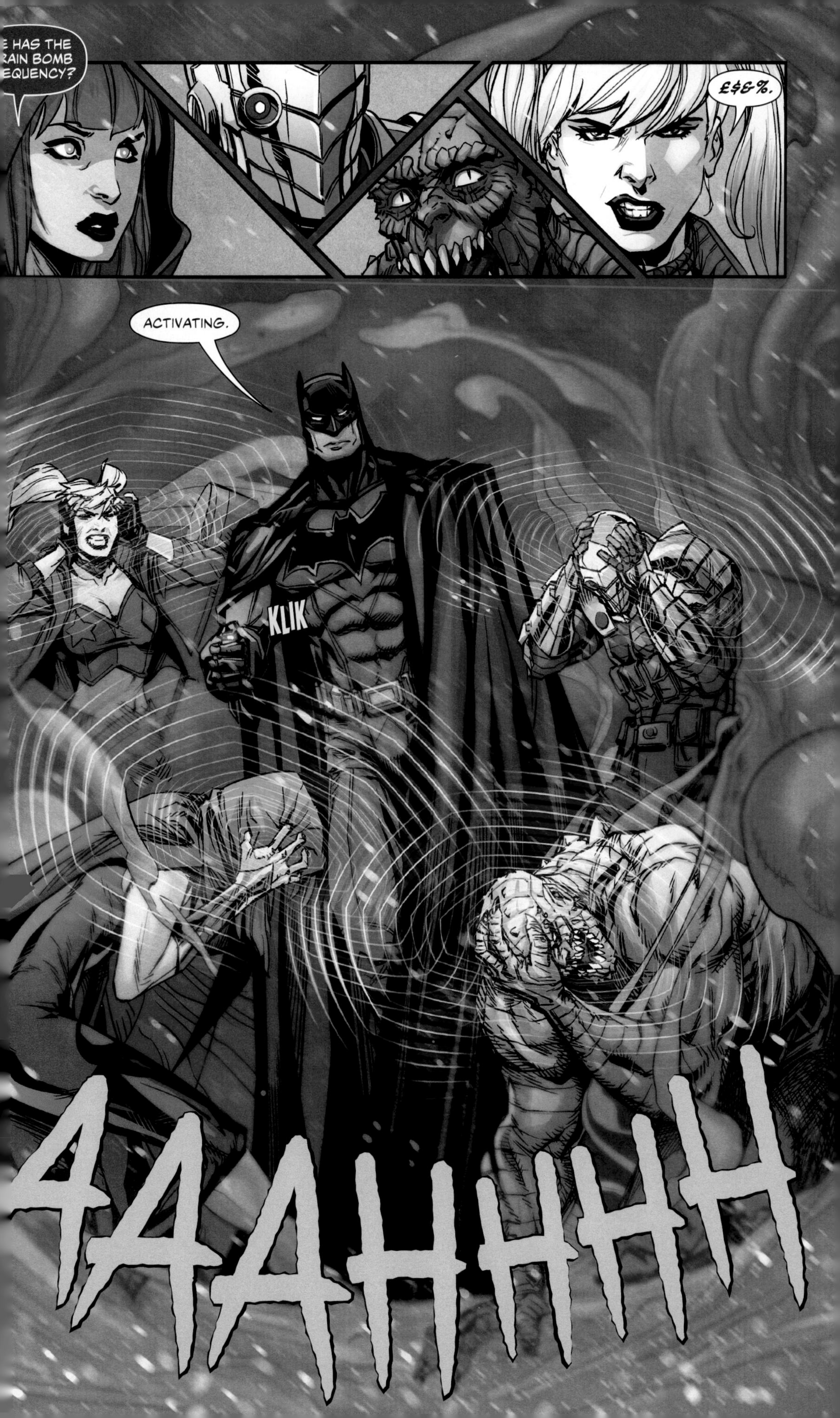
E HAS THE RAIN BOMB EQUENCY?
£$&%.
ACTIVATING.
KLIK
AAAHHH

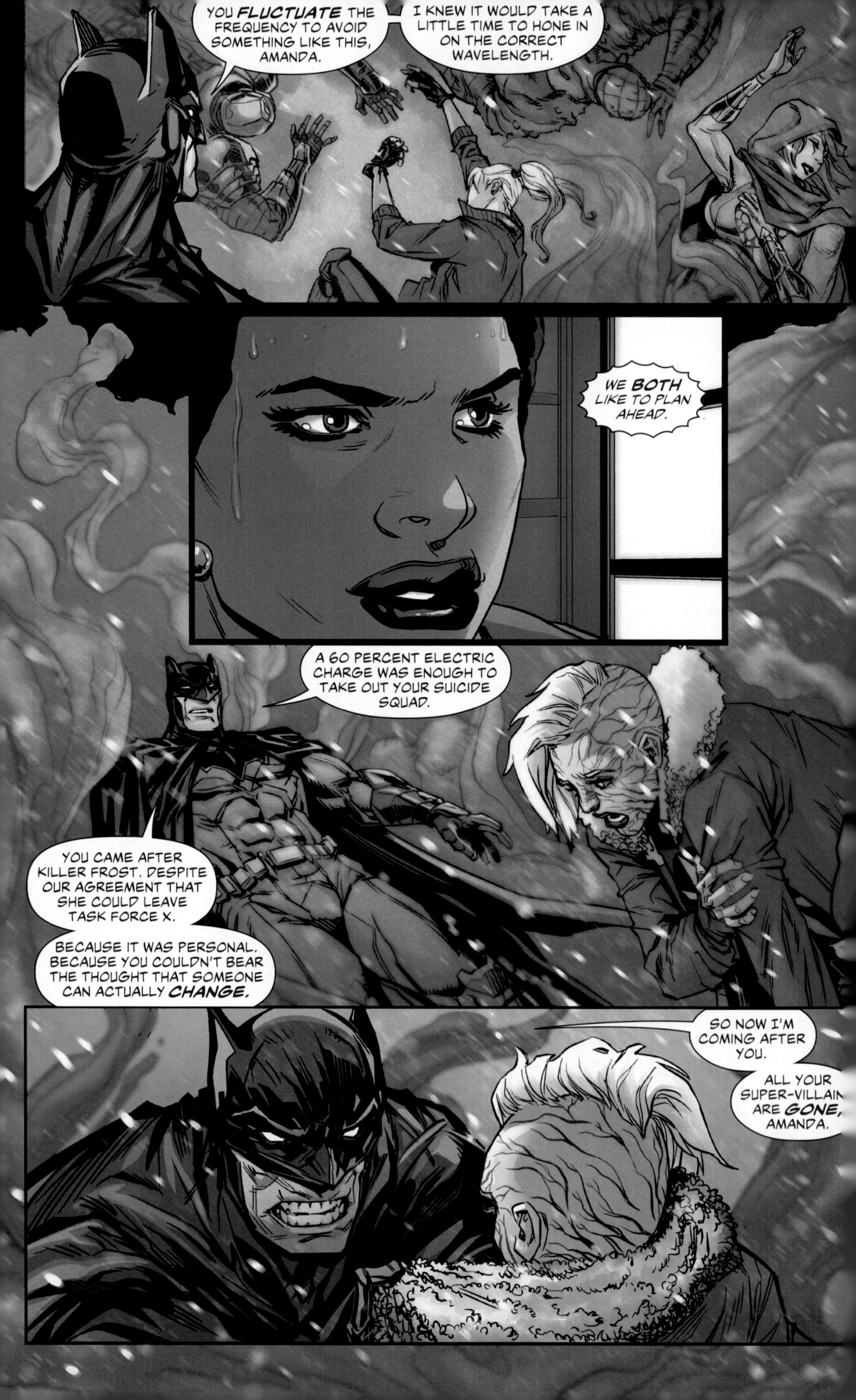
YOU FLUCTUATE THE FREQUENCY TO AVOID SOMETHING LIKE THIS, AMANDA.
I KNEW IT WOULD TAKE A LITTLE TIME TO HONE IN ON THE CORRECT WAVELENGTH.
WE BOTH LIKE TO PLAN AHEAD.
A 60 PERCENT ELECTRIC CHARGE WAS ENOUGH TO TAKE OUT YOUR SUICIDE SQUAD.
YOU CAME AFTER KILLER FROST. DESPITE OUR AGREEMENT THAT SHE COULD LEAVE TASK FORCE X.
BECAUSE IT WAS PERSONAL. BECAUSE YOU COULDN'T BEAR THE THOUGHT THAT SOMEONE CAN ACTUALLY CHANGE.
SO NOW I'M COMING AFTER YOU.
ALL YOUR SUPER-VILLAIN ARE GONE, AMANDA.

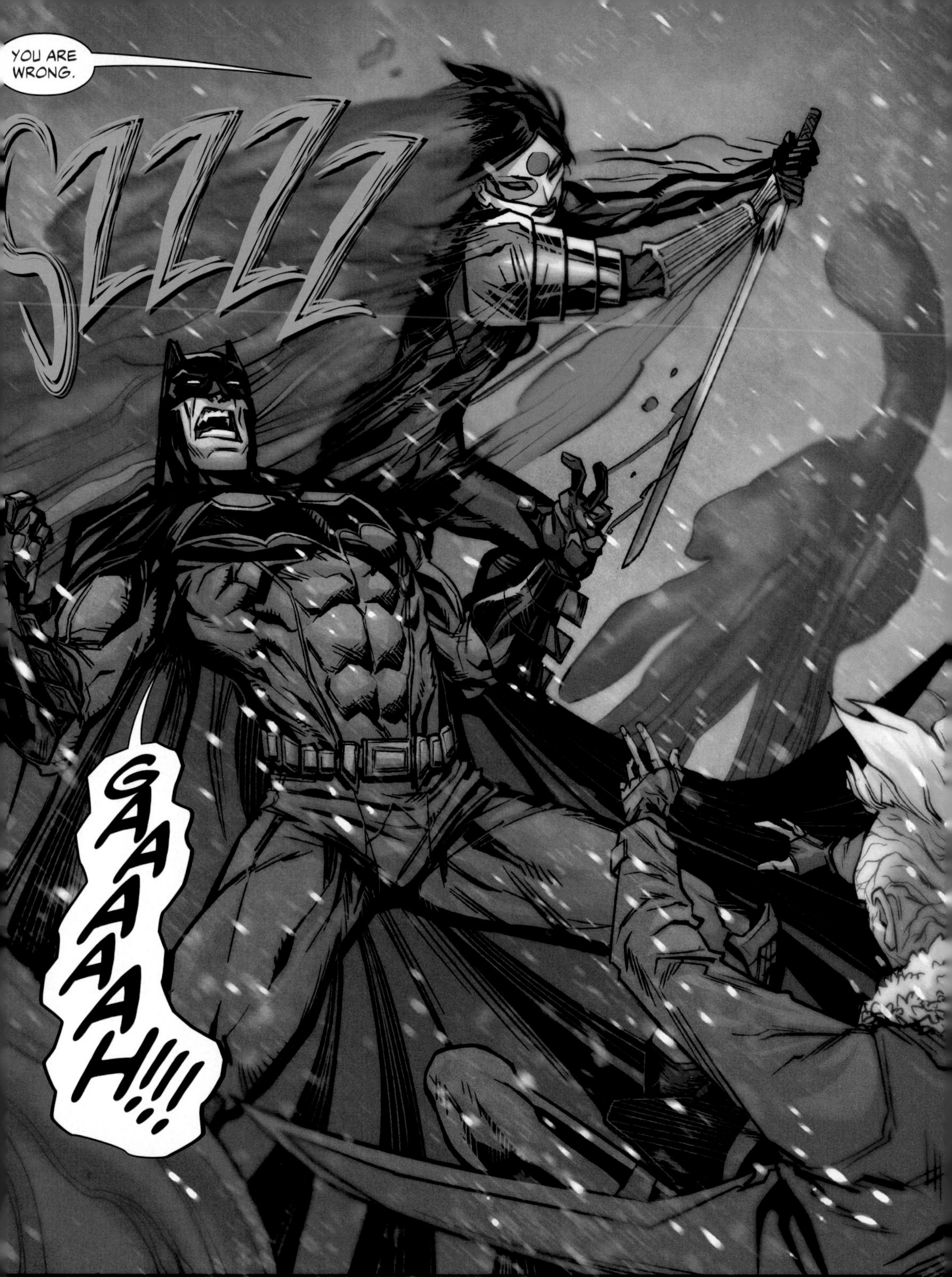
YOU ARE WRONG.
SZZZZ
GAAAAH!!!

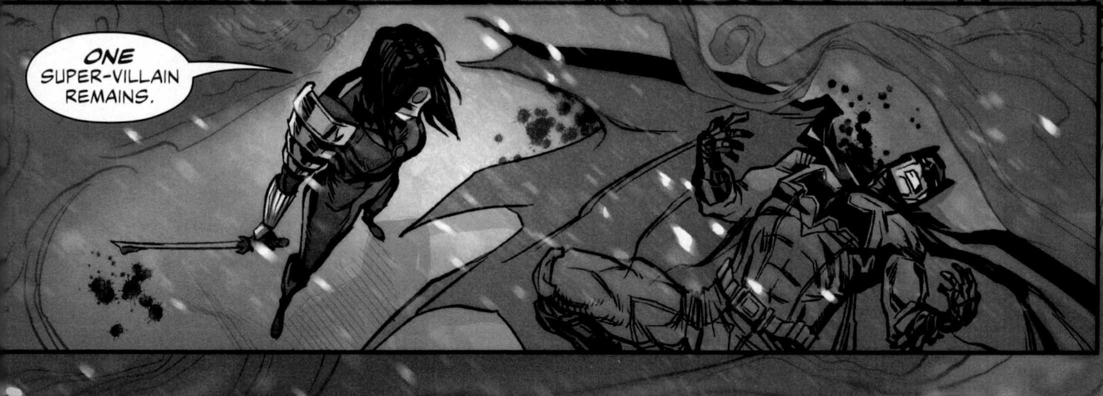
ONE SUPER-VILLAIN REMAINS.

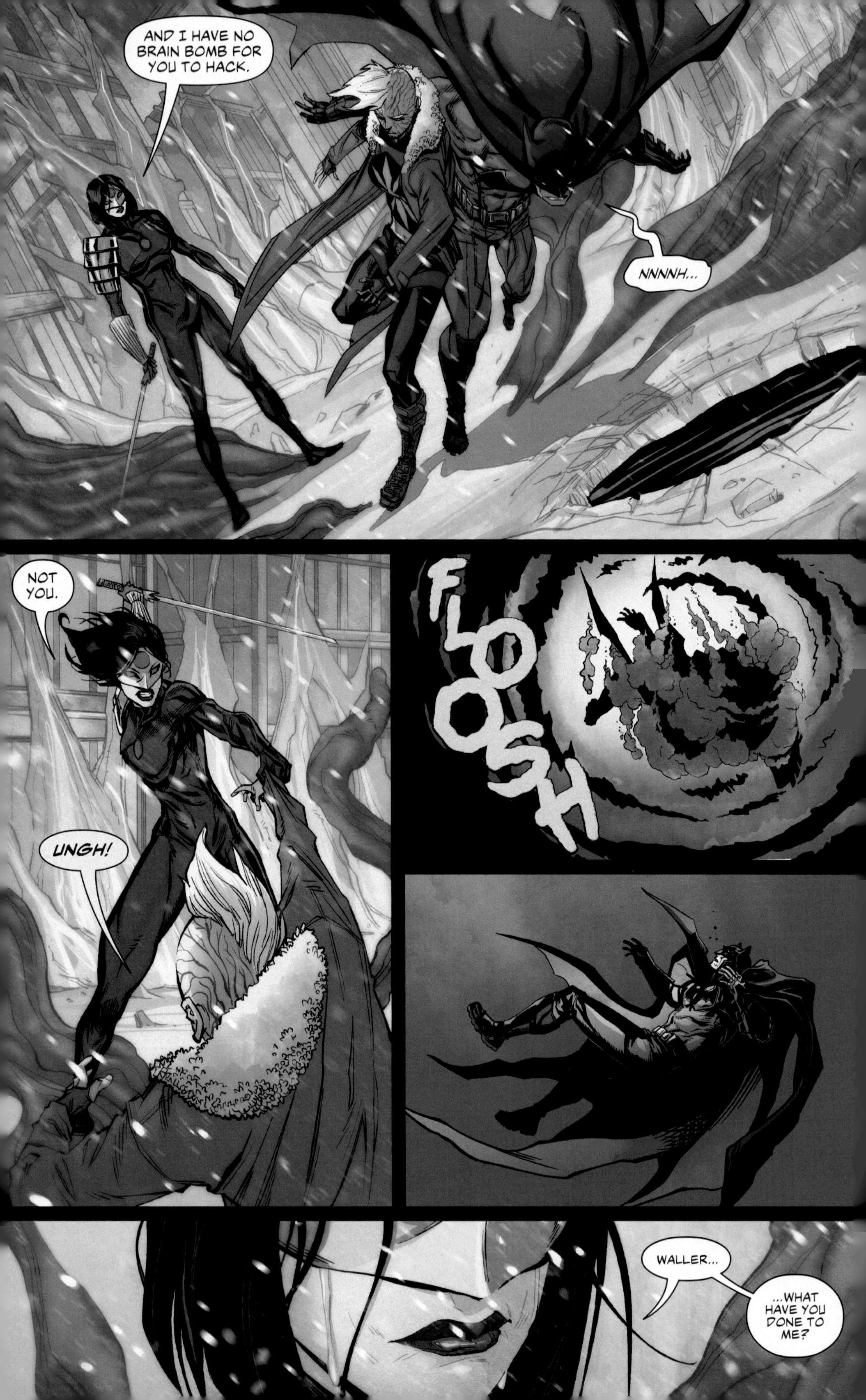
AND I HAVE NO BRAIN BOMB FOR YOU TO HACK.
NNNNH...
NOT YOU.
UNGH!
FLOOSH
WALLER...
...WHAT HAVE YOU DONE TO ME?

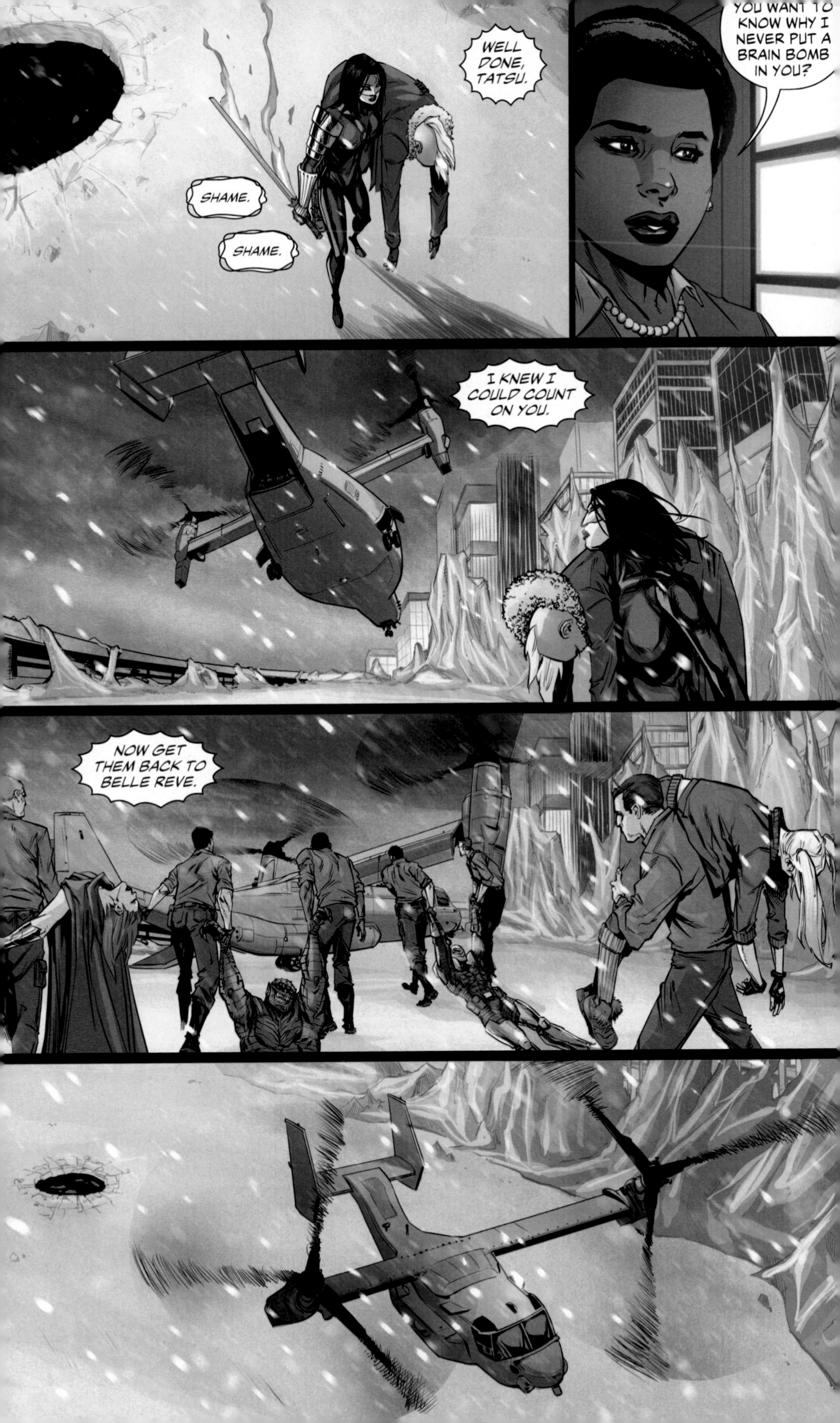

WELL DONE, TATSU.
SHAME.
SHAME.
YOU WANT TO KNOW WHY I NEVER PUT A BRAIN BOMB IN YOU?
I KNEW I COULD COUNT ON YOU.
NOW GET THEM BACK TO BELLE REVE.

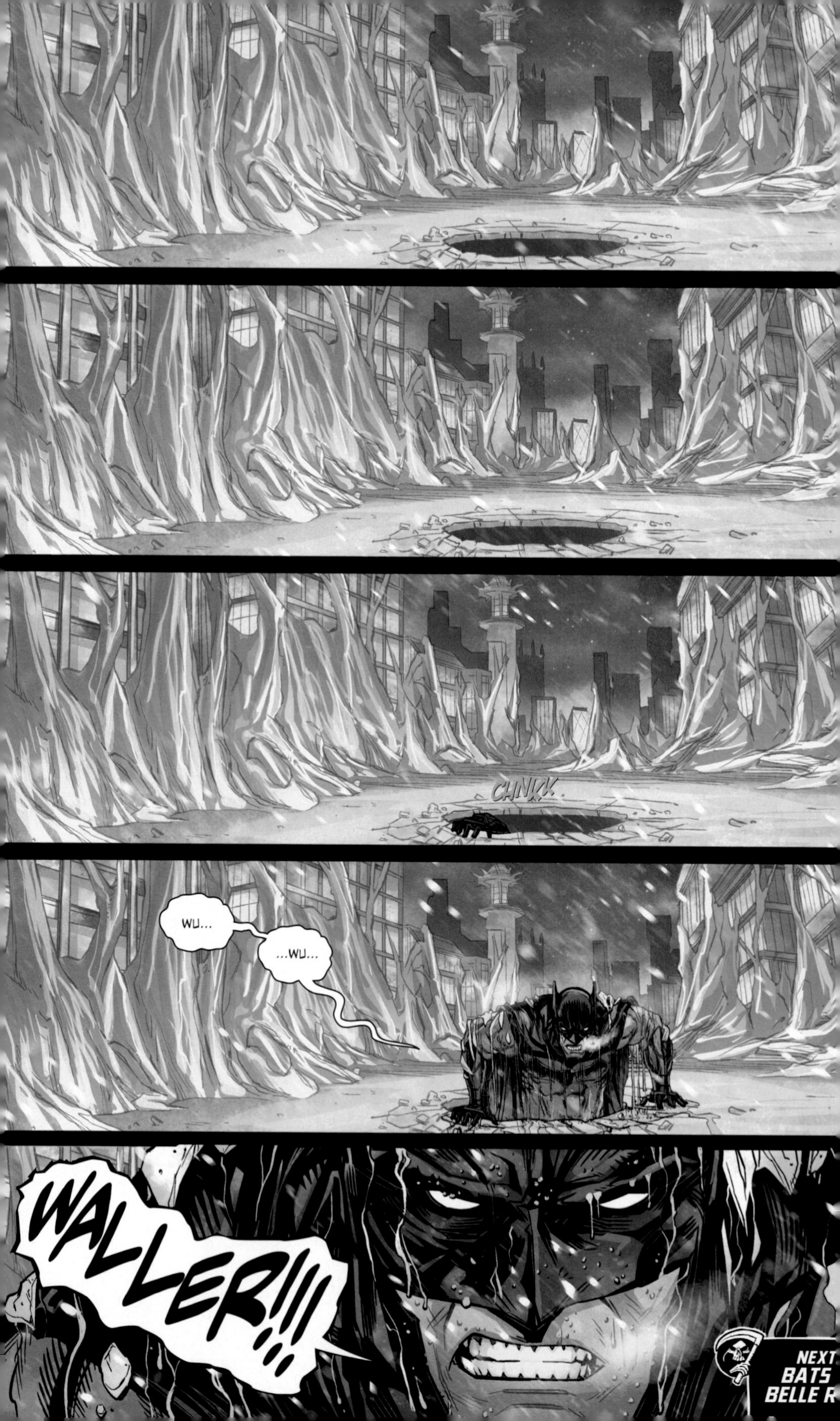
CHNKK
WU...
...WU...
WALLER!!!
NEXT
BATS
BELLE R

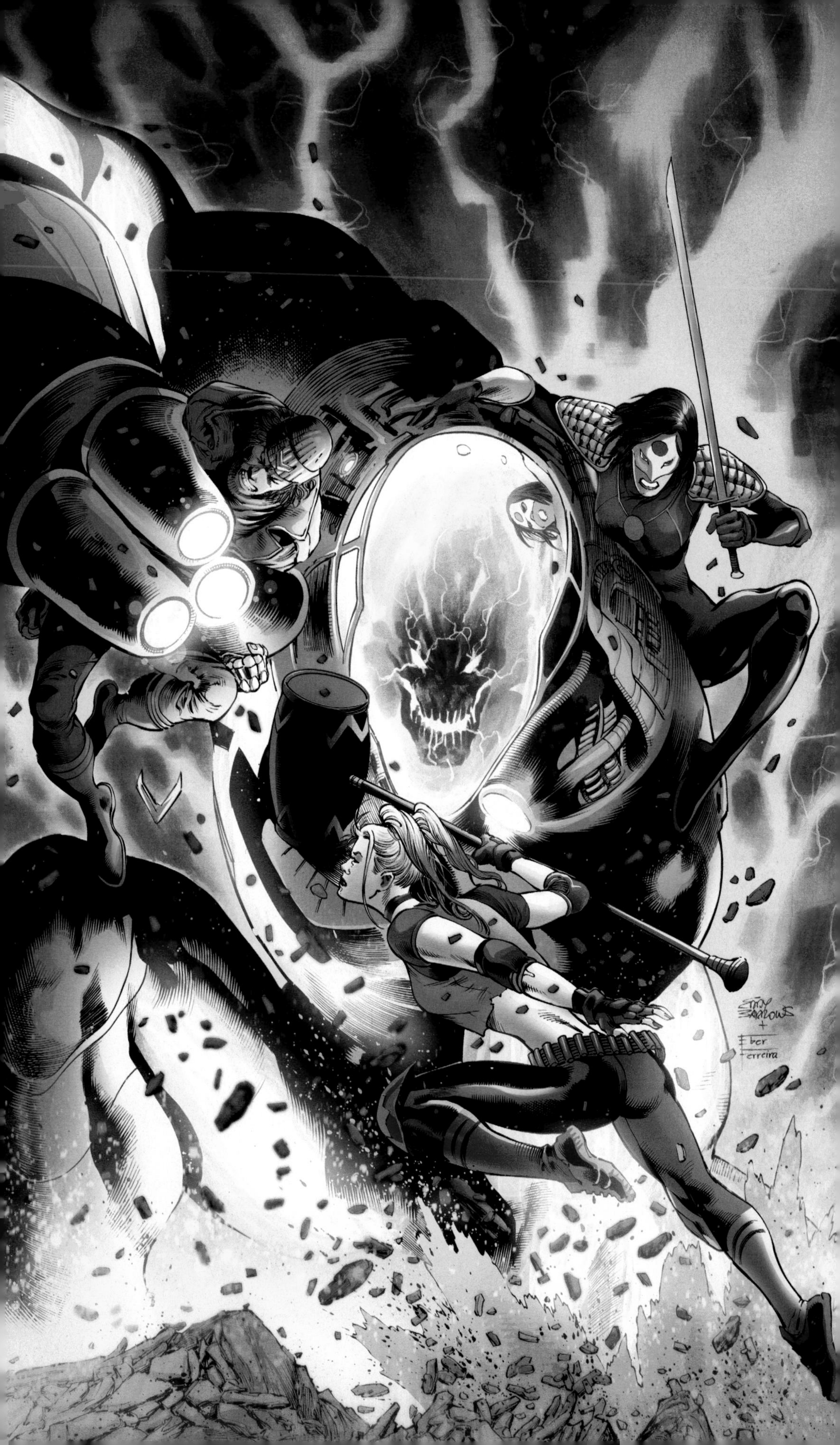

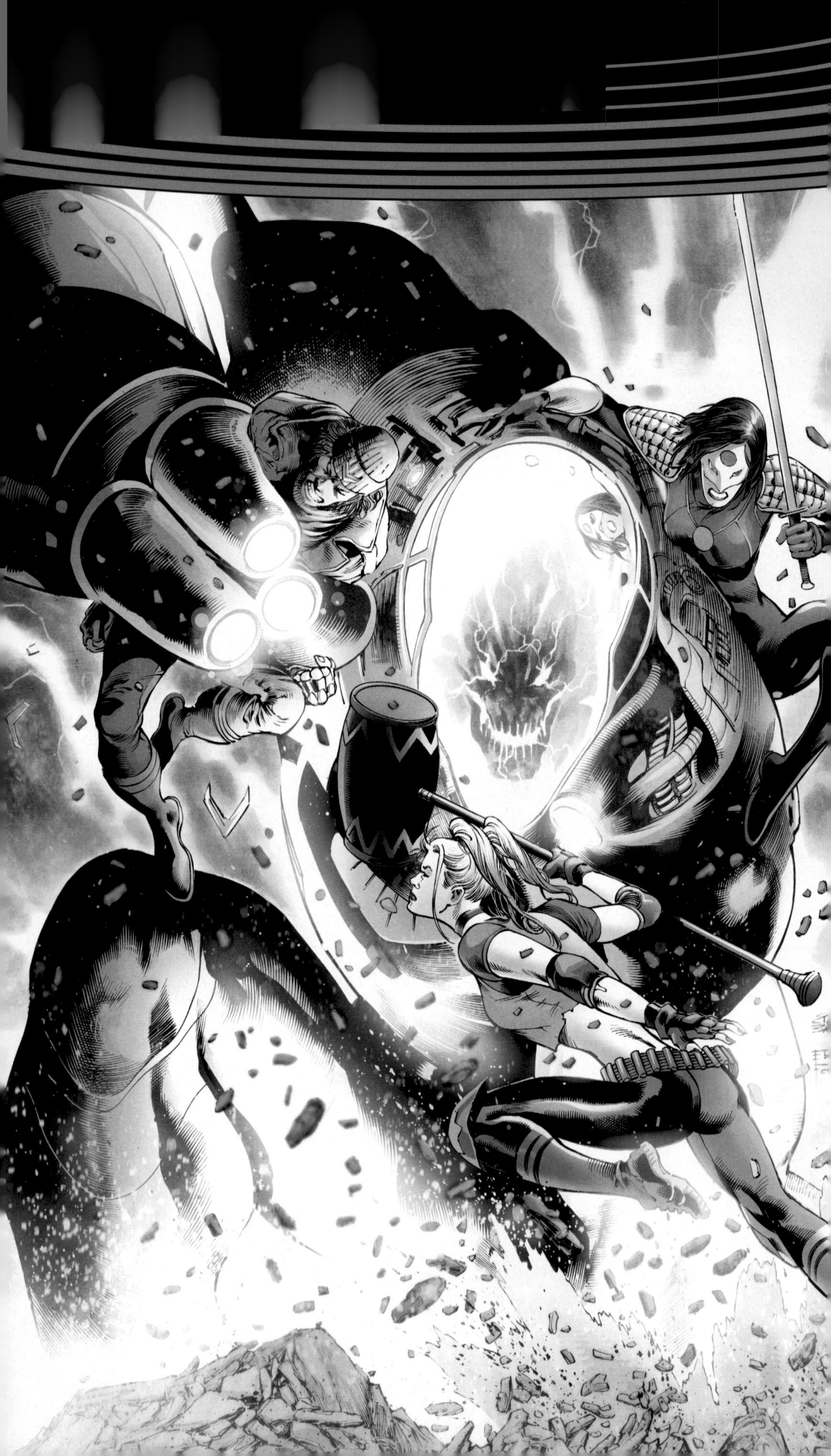

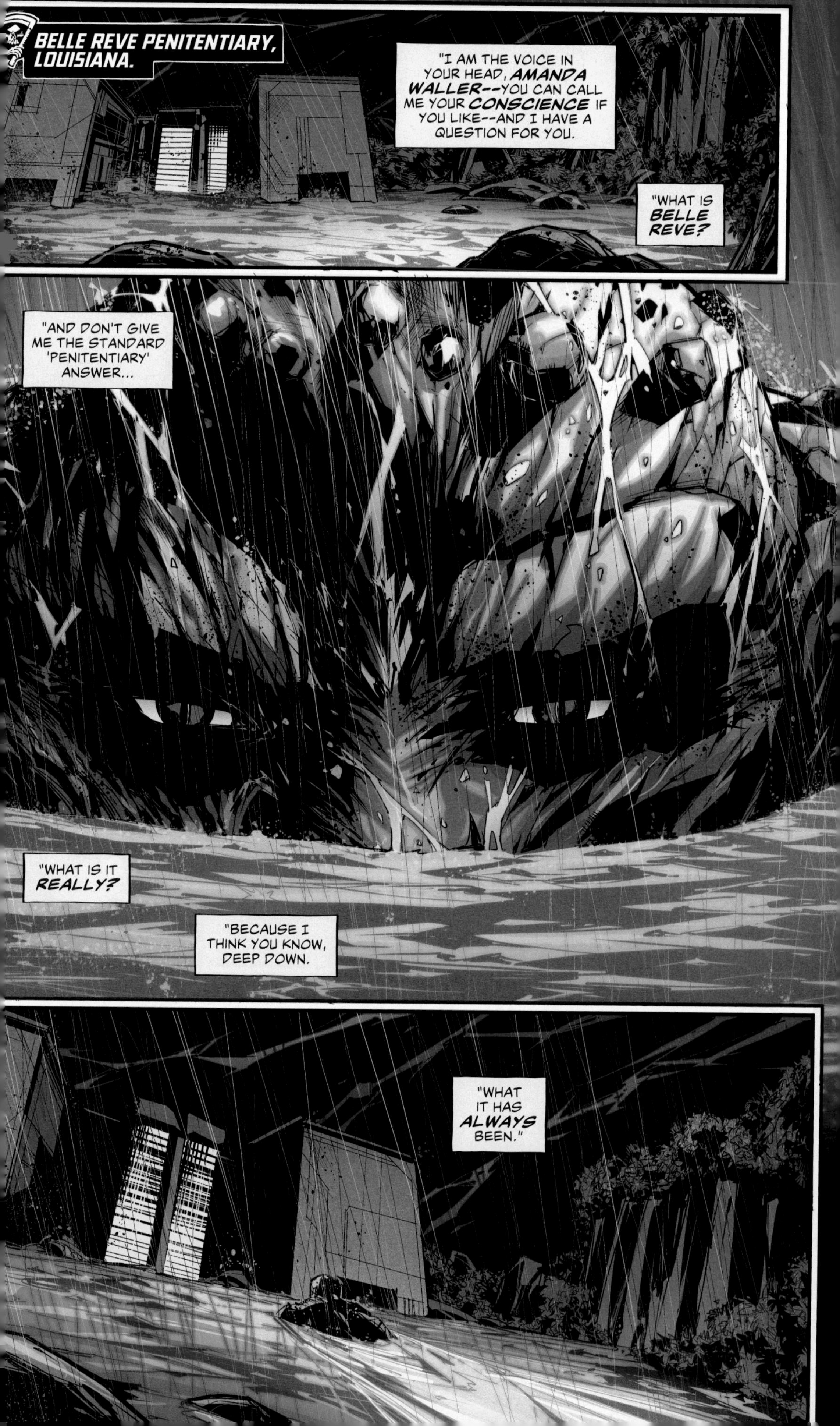
BELLE REVE PENITENTIARY, LOUISIANA.
"I AM THE VOICE IN YOUR HEAD, AMANDA WALLER--YOU CAN CALL ME YOUR CONSCIENCE IF YOU LIKE--AND I HAVE A QUESTION FOR YOU.
"WHAT IS BELLE REVE?
"AND DON'T GIVE ME THE STANDARD 'PENITENTIARY' ANSWER...
"WHAT IS IT REALLY?
"BECAUSE I THINK YOU KNOW, DEEP DOWN.
"WHAT IT HAS ALWAYS BEEN."

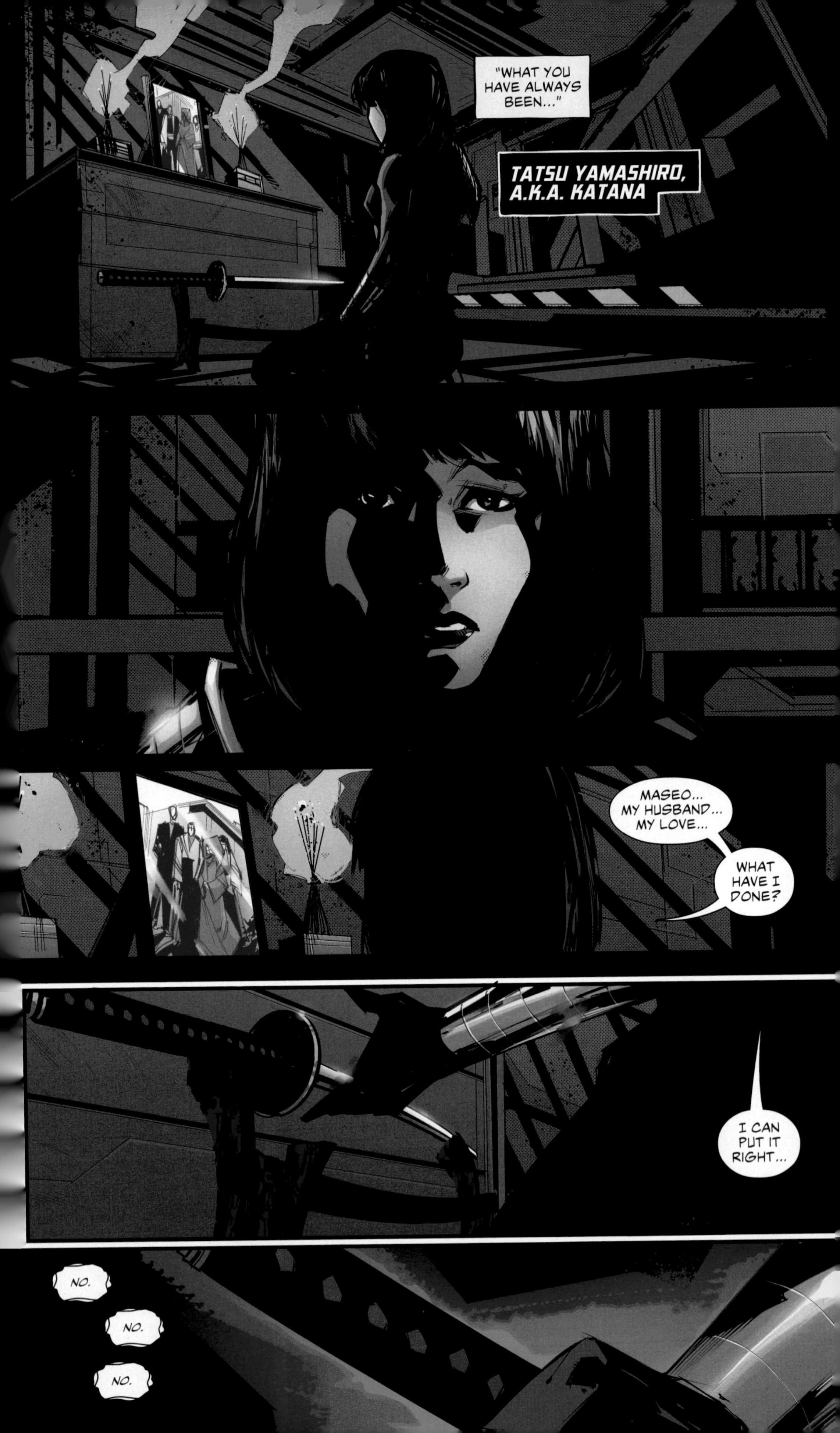
"WHAT YOU HAVE ALWAYS BEEN..."
TATSU YAMASHIRO, A.K.A. KATANA
MASEO... MY HUSBAND... MY LOVE...
WHAT HAVE I DONE?
I CAN PUT IT RIGHT...
NO.
NO.
NO.

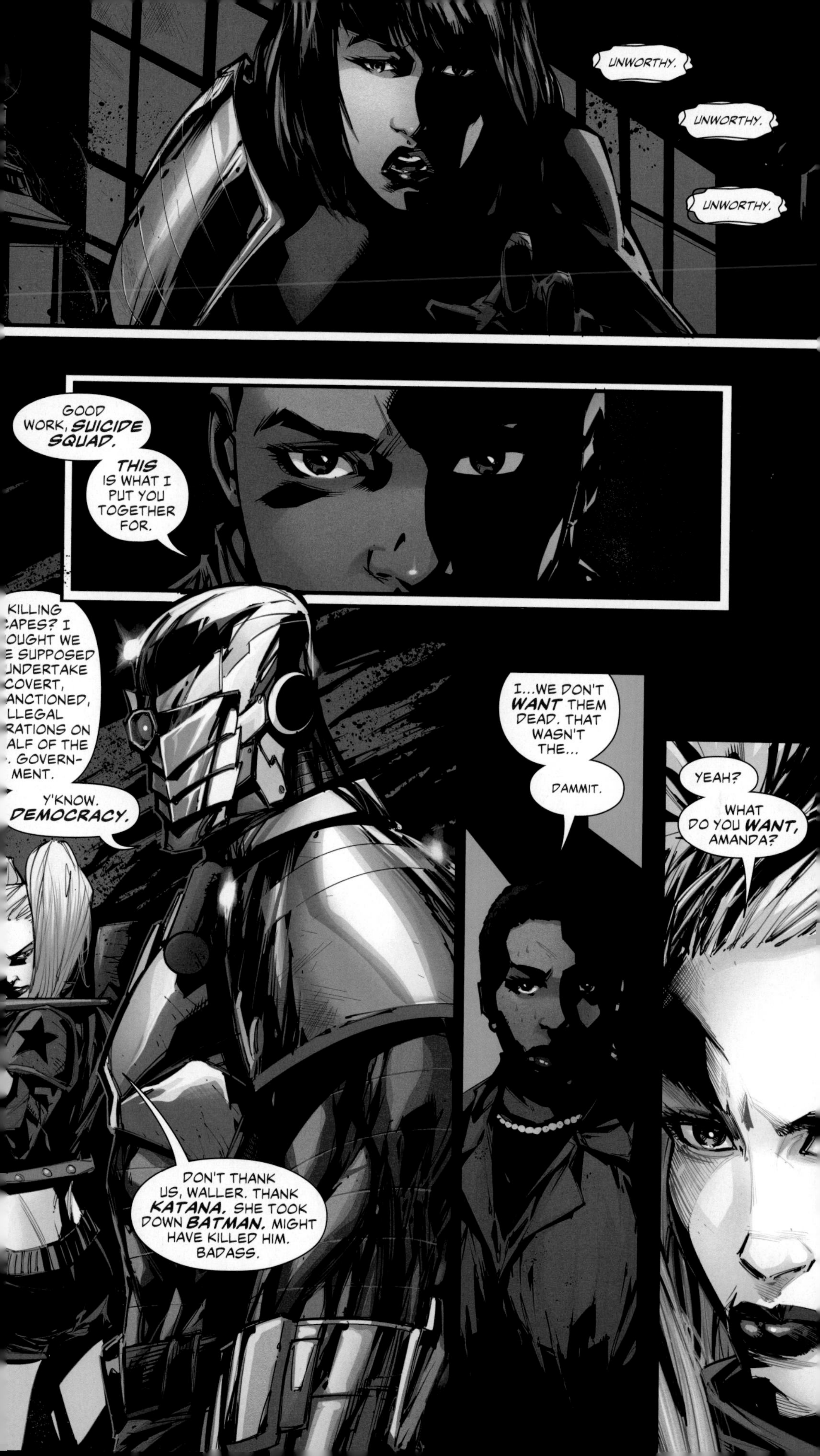

UNWORTHY.
UNWORTHY.
UNWORTHY.
GOOD WORK, SUICIDE SQUAD.
THIS IS WHAT I PUT YOU TOGETHER FOR.
KILLING CAPES? I OUGHT WE E SUPPOSED UNDERTAKE COVERT, ANCTIONED, LLEGAL RATIONS ON ALF OF THE . GOVERN-MENT.
Y'KNOW. DEMOCRACY.
DON'T THANK US, WALLER. THANK KATANA. SHE TOOK DOWN BATMAN. MIGHT HAVE KILLED HIM. BADASS.
I...WE DON'T WANT THEM DEAD. THAT WASN'T THE...
DAMMIT.
YEAH?
WHAT DO YOU WANT, AMANDA?

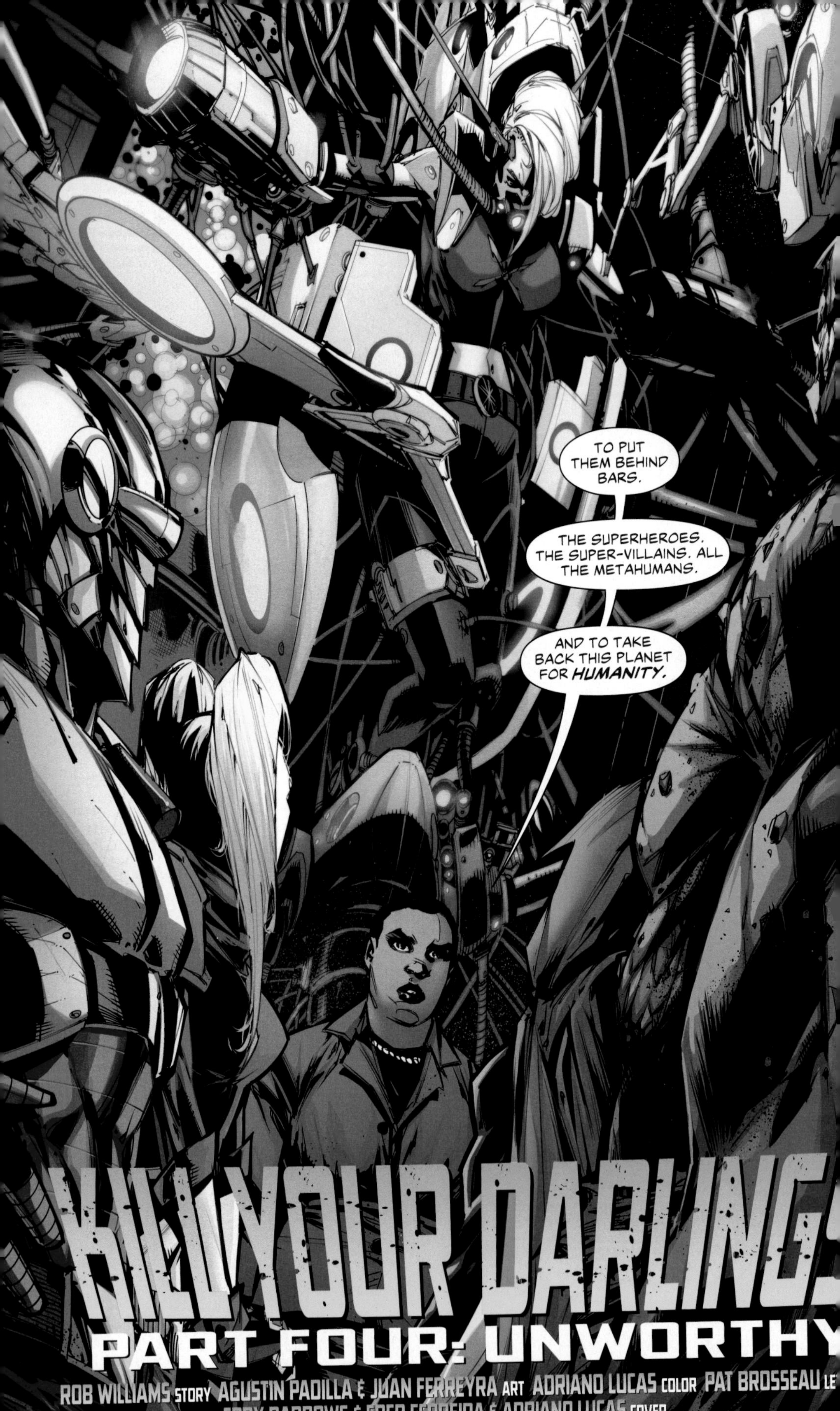
TO PUT THEM BEHIND BARS.
THE SUPERHEROES. THE SUPER-VILLAINS. ALL THE METAHUMANS.
AND TO TAKE BACK THIS PLANET FOR *HUMANITY.*
KILL YOUR DARLINGS
PART FOUR: UNWORTHY
ROB WILLIAMS STORY AGUSTIN PADILLA & JUAN FERREYRA ART ADRIANO LUCAS COLOR PAT BROSSEAU LE
EDDY BARROWS & EBER FERREIRA & ADRIANO LUCAS COVER
BRIAN CUNNINGHAM GROUP EDITOR HARVEY RICHARDS ASSOCIATE EDITOR ANDY KHOURI EDITOR

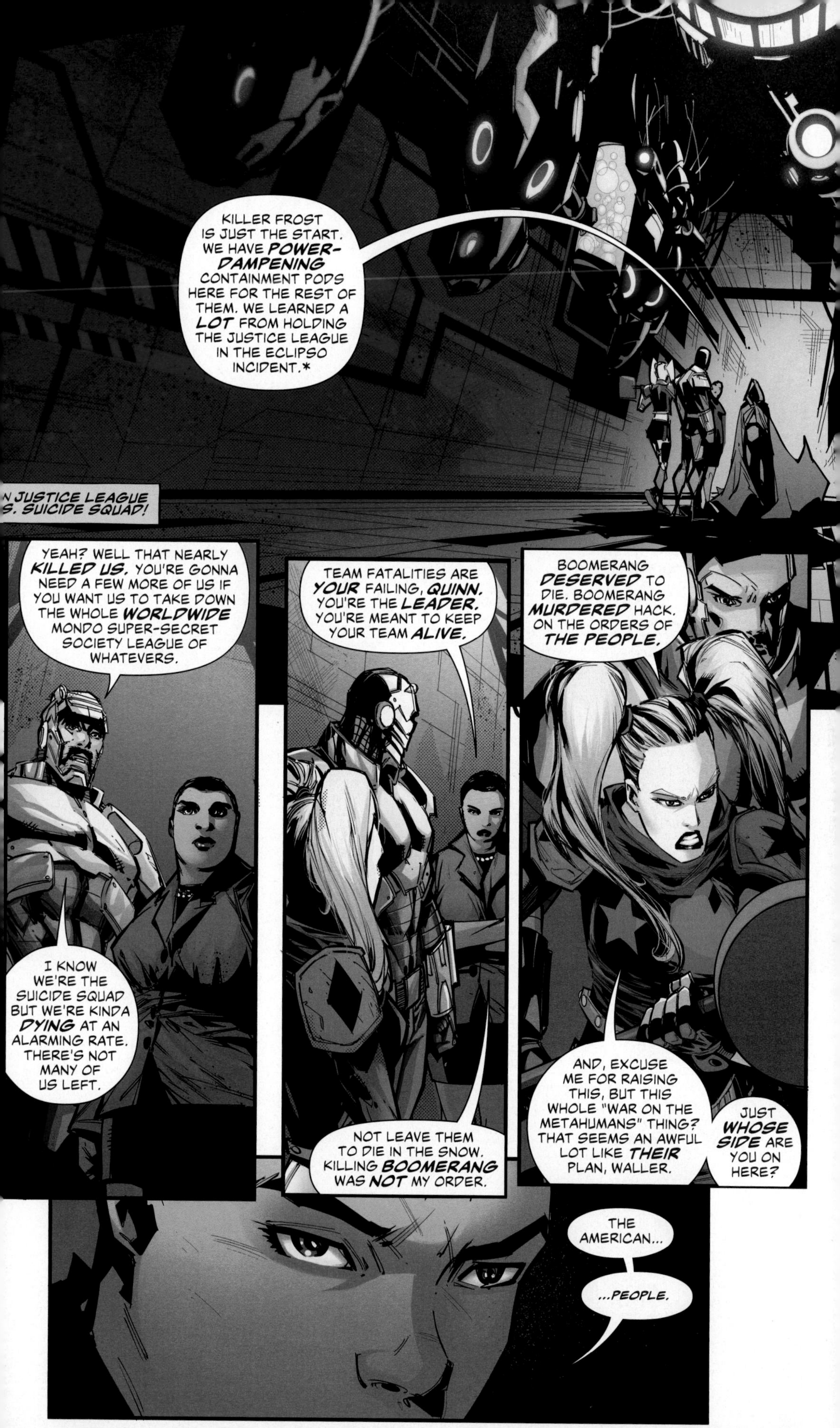
KILLER FROST IS JUST THE START. WE HAVE POWER-DAMPENING CONTAINMENT PODS HERE FOR THE REST OF THEM. WE LEARNED A LOT FROM HOLDING THE JUSTICE LEAGUE IN THE ECLIPSO INCIDENT.*
N JUSTICE LEAGUE
S. SUICIDE SQUAD!
YEAH? WELL THAT NEARLY KILLED US. YOU'RE GONNA NEED A FEW MORE OF US IF YOU WANT US TO TAKE DOWN THE WHOLE WORLDWIDE MONDO SUPER-SECRET SOCIETY LEAGUE OF WHATEVERS.
I KNOW WE'RE THE SUICIDE SQUAD BUT WE'RE KINDA DYING AT AN ALARMING RATE. THERE'S NOT MANY OF US LEFT.
TEAM FATALITIES ARE YOUR FAILING, QUINN. YOU'RE THE LEADER. YOU'RE MEANT TO KEEP YOUR TEAM ALIVE.
NOT LEAVE THEM TO DIE IN THE SNOW. KILLING BOOMERANG WAS NOT MY ORDER.
BOOMERANG DESERVED TO DIE. BOOMERANG MURDERED HACK. ON THE ORDERS OF THE PEOPLE.
AND, EXCUSE ME FOR RAISING THIS, BUT THIS WHOLE "WAR ON THE METAHUMANS" THING? THAT SEEMS AN AWFUL LOT LIKE THEIR PLAN, WALLER.
JUST WHOSE SIDE ARE YOU ON HERE?
THE AMERICAN...
...PEOPLE.

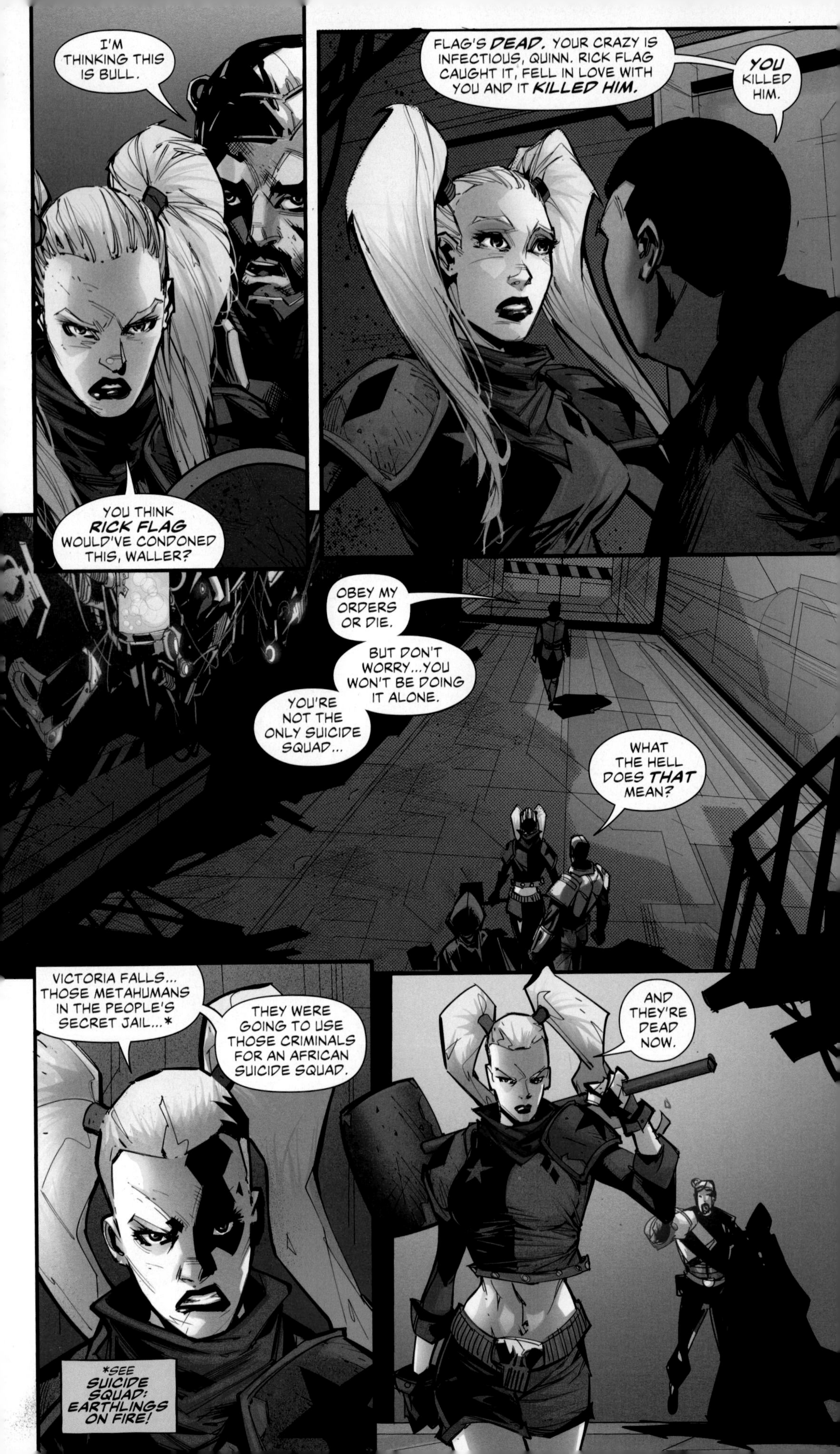
I'M THINKING THIS IS BULL.
YOU THINK RICK FLAG WOULD'VE CONDONED THIS, WALLER?
FLAG'S DEAD. YOUR CRAZY IS INFECTIOUS, QUINN. RICK FLAG CAUGHT IT, FELL IN LOVE WITH YOU AND IT KILLED HIM.
YOU KILLED HIM.
OBEY MY ORDERS OR DIE.
BUT DON'T WORRY...YOU WON'T BE DOING IT ALONE.
YOU'RE NOT THE ONLY SUICIDE SQUAD...
WHAT THE HELL DOES THAT MEAN?
VICTORIA FALLS... THOSE METAHUMANS IN THE PEOPLE'S SECRET JAIL...*
THEY WERE GOING TO USE THOSE CRIMINALS FOR AN AFRICAN SUICIDE SQUAD.
AND THEY'RE DEAD NOW.
*SEE SUICIDE SQUAD: EARTHLINGS ON FIRE!

THANK YOU FOR AGREEING TO THIS HOLOGRAPHIC CONFERENCE CALL, AMANDA.

I SPEAK FOR **THE PEOPLE** WHEN I SAY THAT WE ARE READY.

OUR SUICIDE SQUADS POSITIONED AROUND THE GLOBE ARE PREPARED TO STRIKE. WE ONLY WAIT FOR YOUR SIGNAL.

DIREKTOR KARLA...

I UNDERSTAND YOUR RETICENCE BUT YOU HAVE PROVEN, WITH THE KILLER FROST TRIAL, THAT THIS CAN BE DONE **WITHOUT** FATALITIES.

BATMAN MAY HAVE BEEN **KILLED**...

UNFORTUNATE. BUT ANY WAR INVOLVES SACRIFICES.

WHAT MAKES THAT WORTHWHILE IS A **JUST CAUSE.** WE WILL SAVE MILLIONS OF LIVES THIS DAY.

THIS ... ABOUT ...URING THE ...TURE OF ...E HUMAN RACE.

AND TO PROCEED WE NEED YOUR 'JOSEPH' PROTOCOLS, AMANDA. WE NEED TO KNOW THE **WEAKNESSES** OF THE SUPERHEROES, THEIR **SECRET** IDENTITIES...

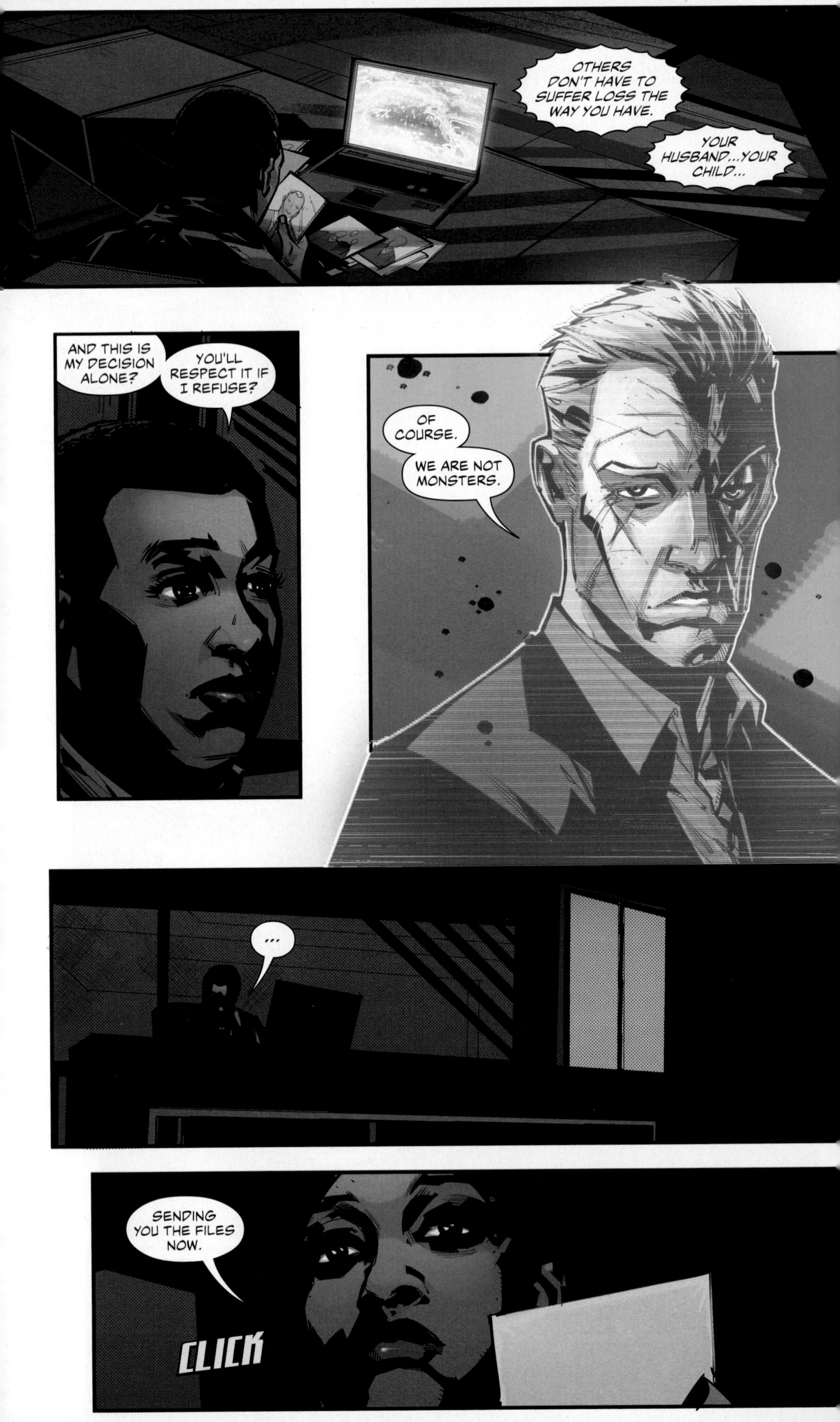
OTHERS DON'T HAVE TO SUFFER LOSS THE WAY YOU HAVE.
YOUR HUSBAND...YOUR CHILD...
AND THIS IS MY DECISION ALONE?
YOU'LL RESPECT IT IF I REFUSE?
OF COURSE.
WE ARE NOT MONSTERS.
...
SENDING YOU THE FILES NOW.
CLICK

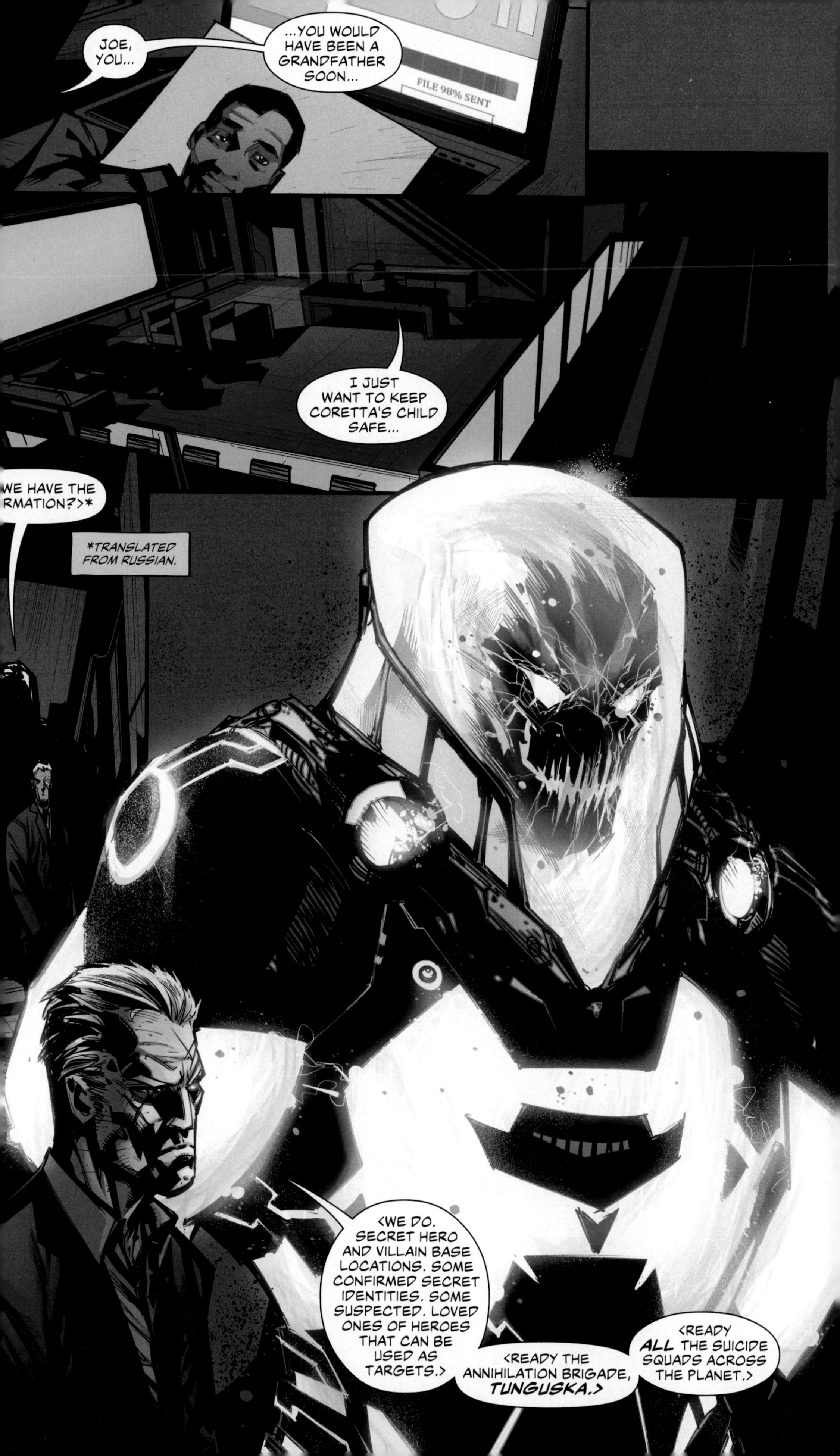

JOE, YOU...
...YOU WOULD HAVE BEEN A GRANDFATHER SOON...
FILE 98% SENT
I JUST WANT TO KEEP CORETTA'S CHILD SAFE...
WE HAVE THE RMATION?>*
*TRANSLATED FROM RUSSIAN.
<WE DO. SECRET HERO AND VILLAIN BASE LOCATIONS. SOME CONFIRMED SECRET IDENTITIES. SOME SUSPECTED. LOVED ONES OF HEROES THAT CAN BE USED AS TARGETS.>
<READY THE ANNIHILATION BRIGADE, TUNGUSKA.>
<READY ALL THE SUICIDE SQUADS ACROSS THE PLANET.>

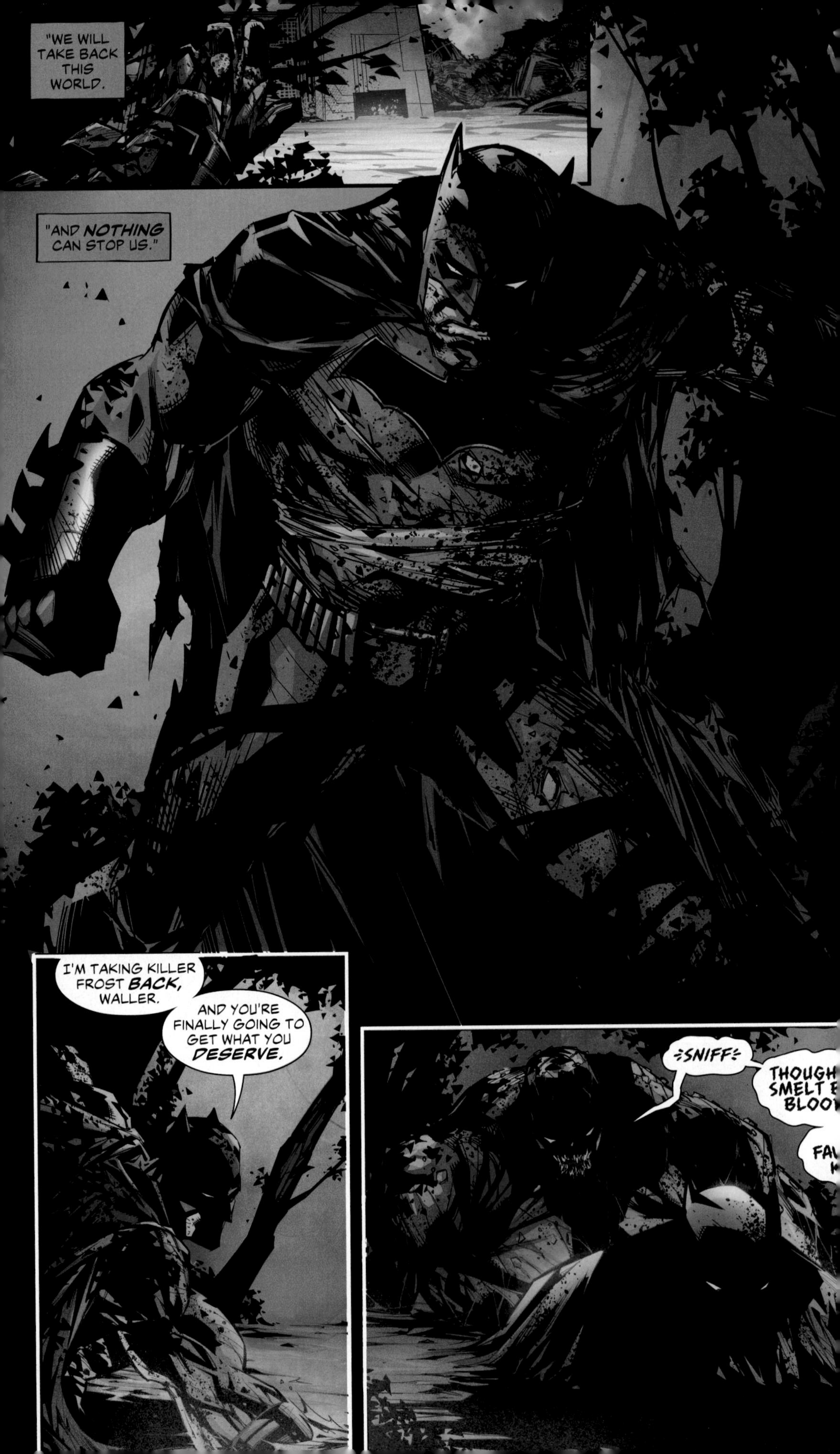
"WE WILL TAKE BACK THIS WORLD.
"AND NOTHING CAN STOP US."
I'M TAKING KILLER FROST BACK, WALLER.
AND YOU'RE FINALLY GOING TO GET WHAT YOU DESERVE.
~SNIFF~

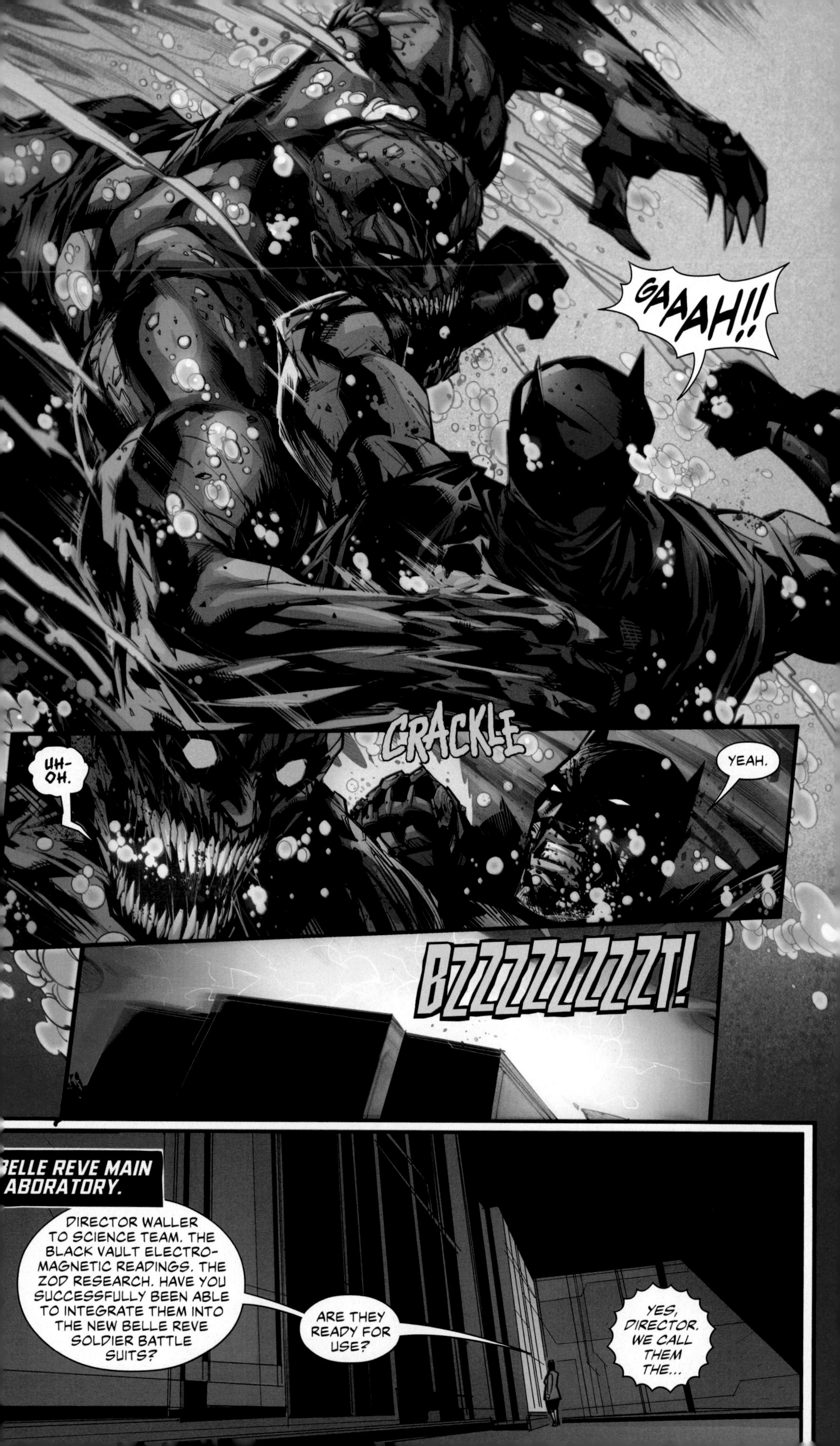
GAAAH!!
CRACKLE
UH-OH.
YEAH.
BZZZZZZZZZT!
BELLE REVE MAIN LABORATORY.
DIRECTOR WALLER TO SCIENCE TEAM. THE BLACK VAULT ELECTRO-MAGNETIC READINGS. THE ZOD RESEARCH. HAVE YOU SUCCESSFULLY BEEN ABLE TO INTEGRATE THEM INTO THE NEW BELLE REVE SOLDIER BATTLE SUITS?
ARE THEY READY FOR USE?
YES, DIRECTOR. WE CALL THEM THE...

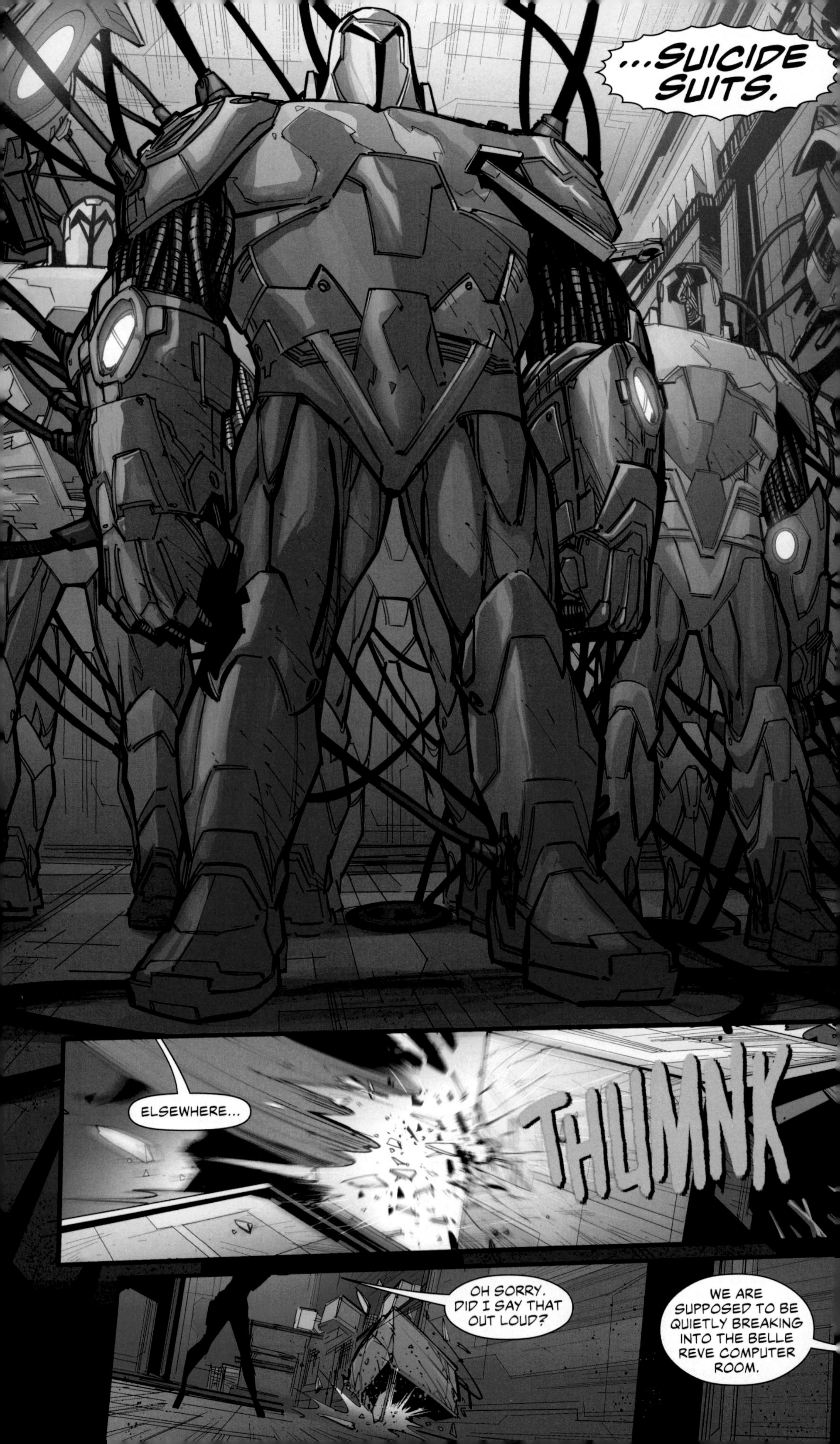
...SUICIDE SUITS.
ELSEWHERE...
THUMNK
OH SORRY. DID I SAY THAT OUT LOUD?
WE ARE SUPPOSED TO BE QUIETLY BREAKING INTO THE BELLE REVE COMPUTER ROOM.

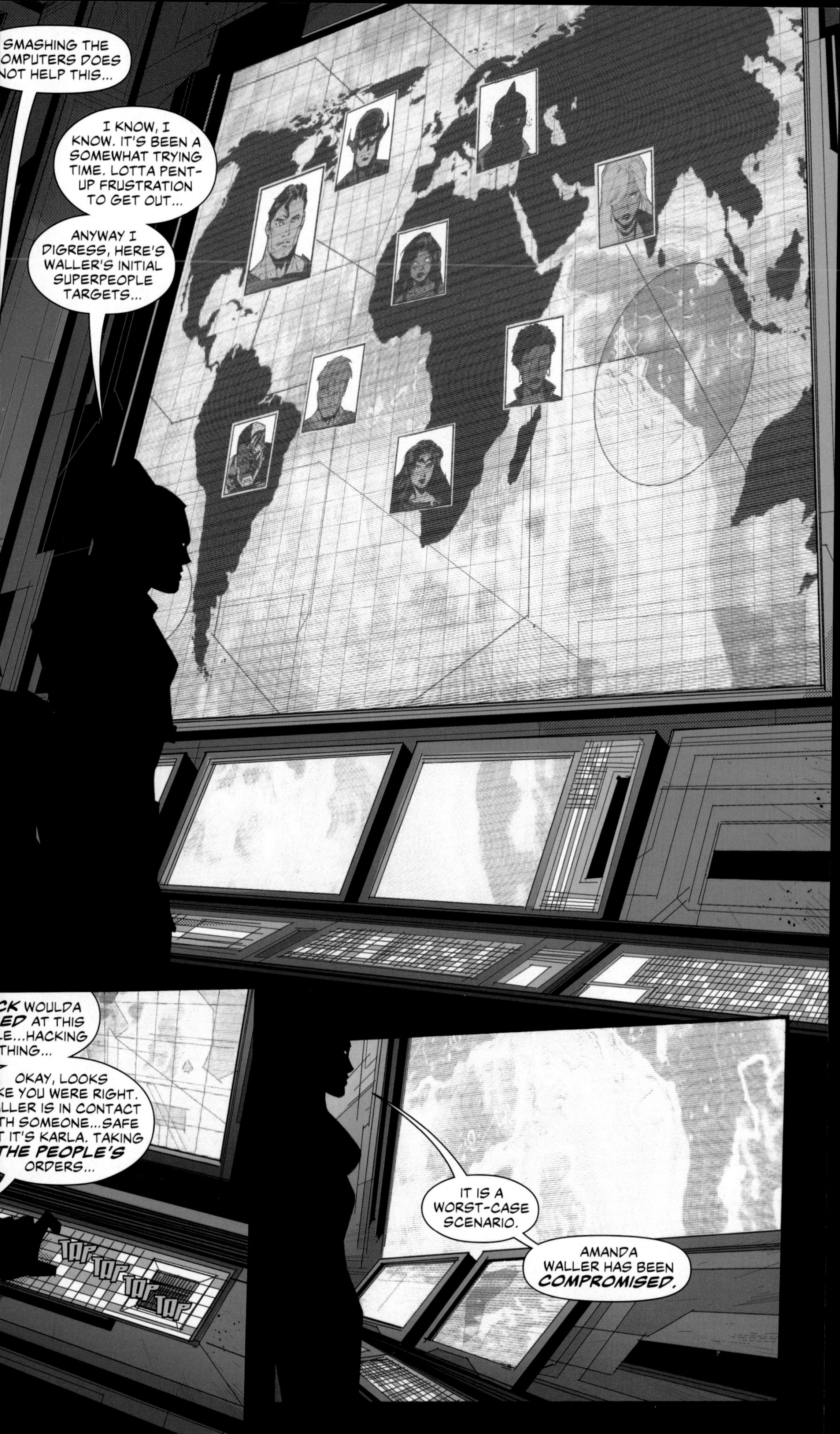
SMASHING THE
OMPUTERS DOES
NOT HELP THIS...
I KNOW, I KNOW. IT'S BEEN A SOMEWHAT TRYING TIME. LOTTA PENT-UP FRUSTRATION TO GET OUT...
ANYWAY I DIGRESS, HERE'S WALLER'S INITIAL SUPERPEOPLE TARGETS...
CK WOULDA ED AT THIS E...HACKING THING...
OKAY, LOOKS E YOU WERE RIGHT. ALLER IS IN CONTACT TH SOMEONE...SAFE T IT'S KARLA. TAKING THE PEOPLE'S ORDERS...
TAP TAP TAP TAP
IT IS A WORST-CASE SCENARIO.
AMANDA WALLER HAS BEEN COMPROMISED.

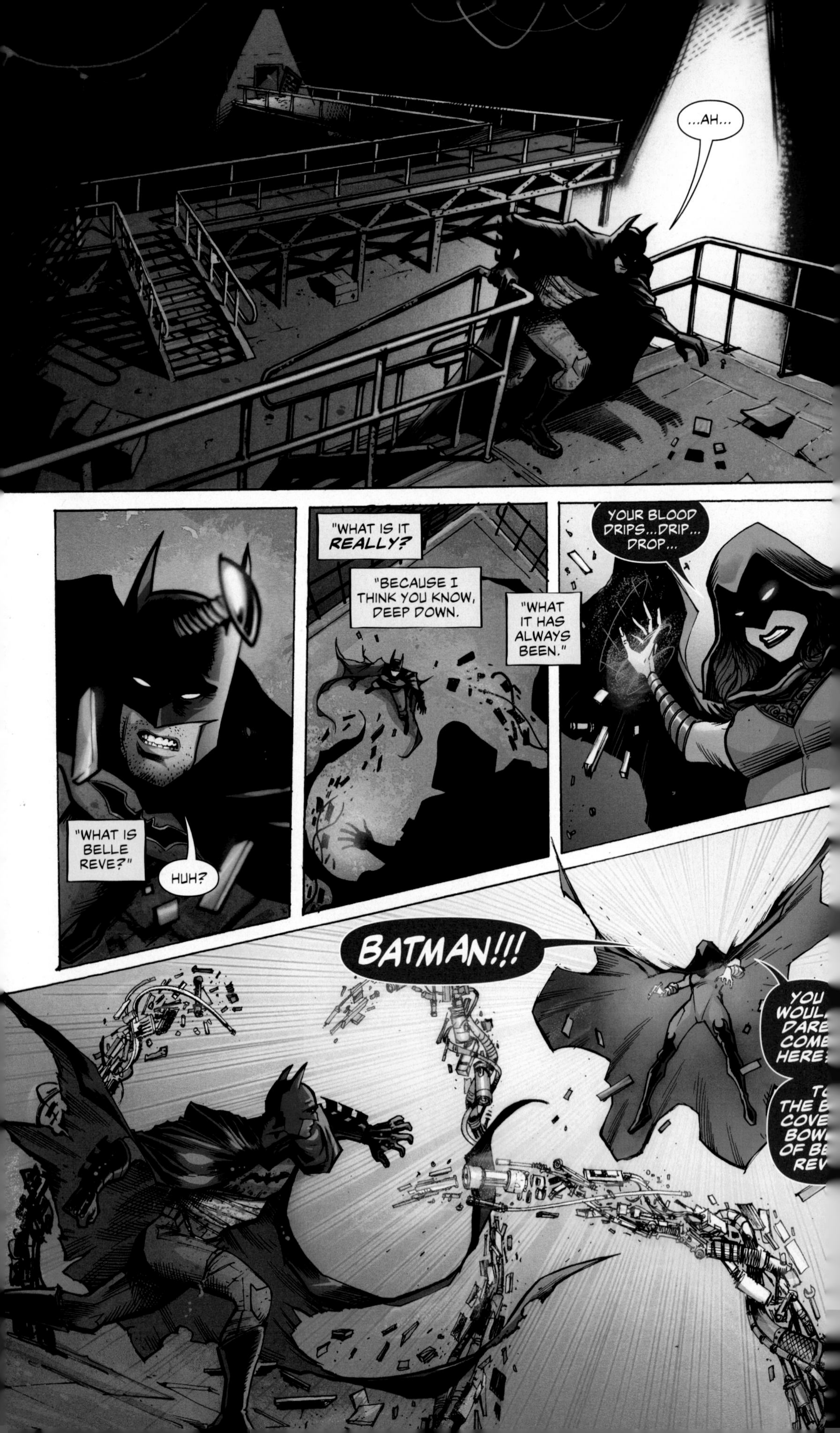

...AH...
"WHAT IS BELLE REVE?"
HUH?
"WHAT IS IT REALLY?
"BECAUSE I THINK YOU KNOW, DEEP DOWN.
"WHAT IT HAS ALWAYS BEEN."
YOUR BLOOD DRIPS...DRIP... DROP...
BATMAN!!!
YOU

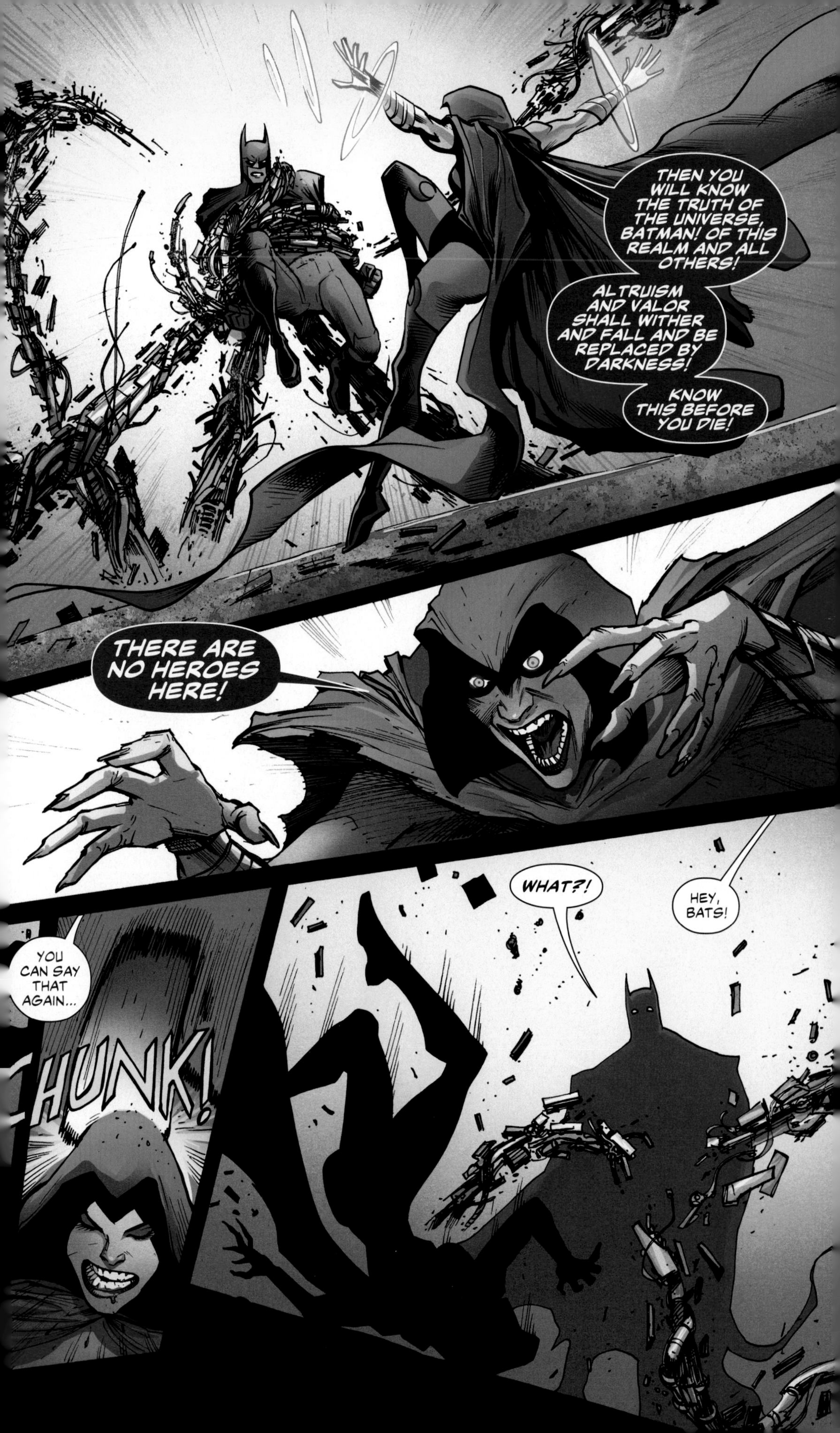
THEN YOU WILL KNOW THE TRUTH OF THE UNIVERSE, BATMAN! OF THIS REALM AND ALL OTHERS!
ALTRUISM AND VALOR SHALL WITHER AND FALL AND BE REPLACED BY DARKNESS!
KNOW THIS BEFORE YOU DIE!
THERE ARE NO HEROES HERE!
YOU CAN SAY THAT AGAIN...
CHUNK!
WHAT?!
HEY, BATS!

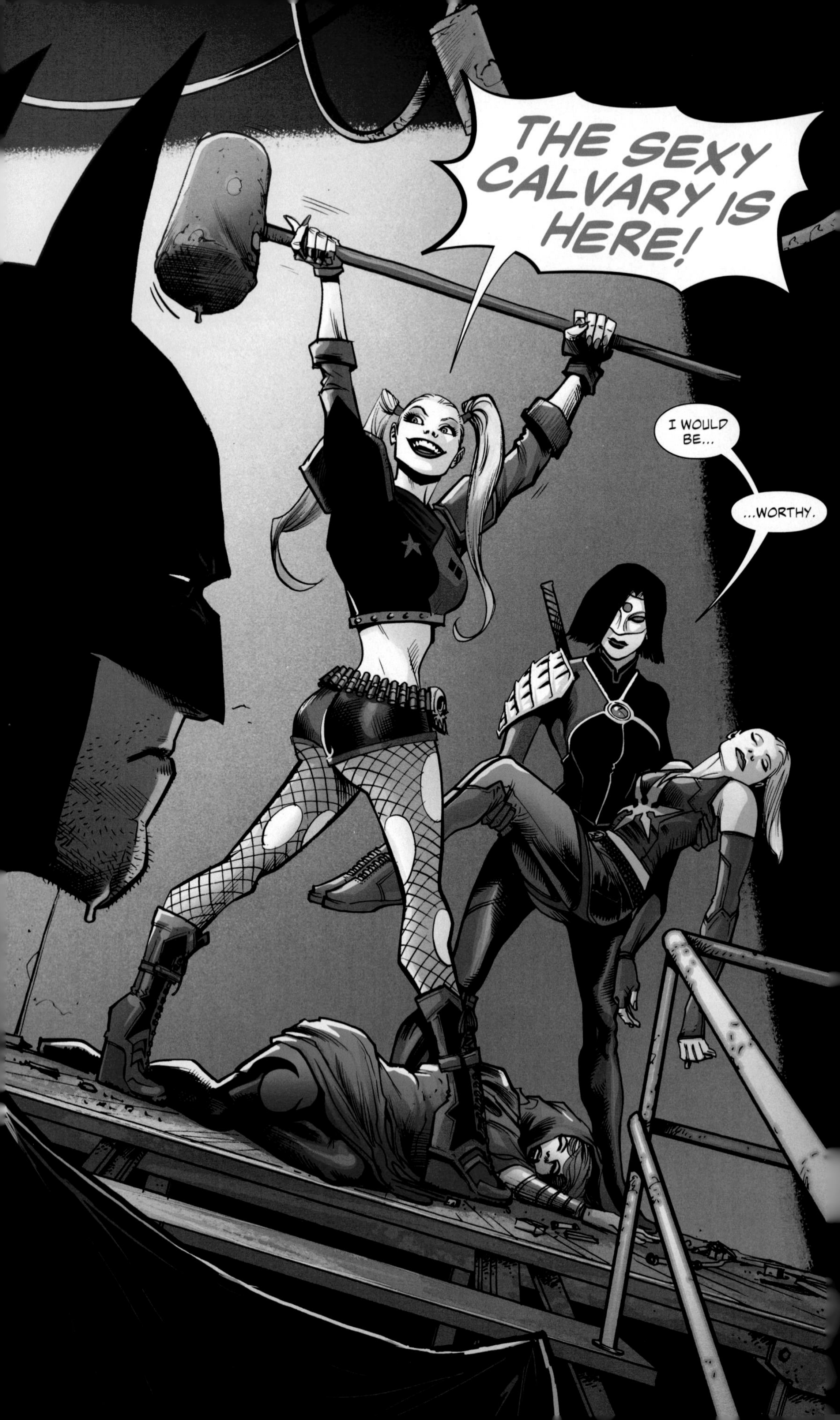
THE SEXY CALVARY IS HERE!
I WOULD BE...
...WORTHY.

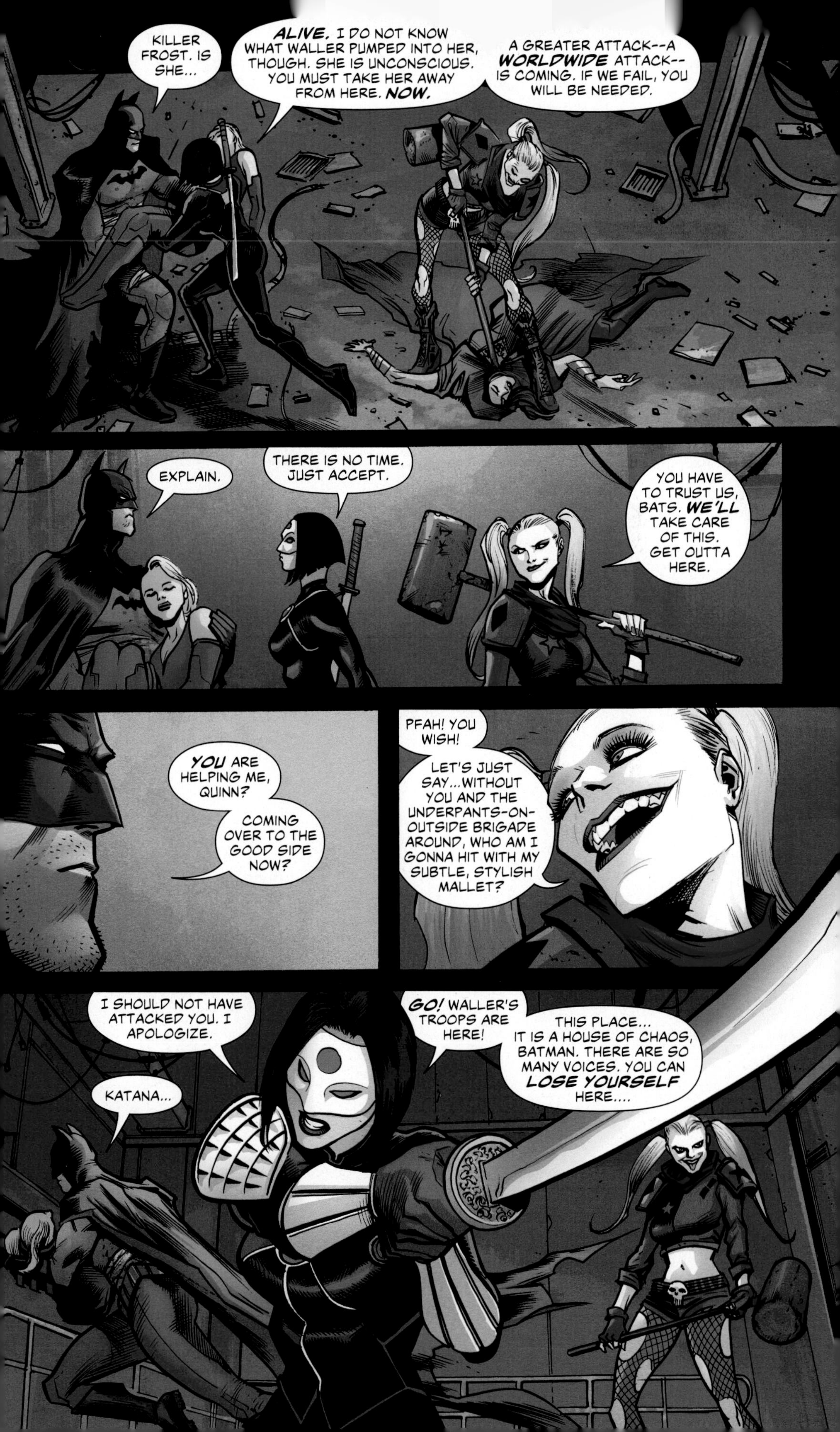
KILLER FROST. IS SHE...
ALIVE. I DO NOT KNOW WHAT WALLER PUMPED INTO HER, THOUGH. SHE IS UNCONSCIOUS. YOU MUST TAKE HER AWAY FROM HERE. NOW.
A GREATER ATTACK--A WORLDWIDE ATTACK--IS COMING. IF WE FAIL, YOU WILL BE NEEDED.
EXPLAIN.
THERE IS NO TIME. JUST ACCEPT.
YOU HAVE TO TRUST US, BATS. WE'LL TAKE CARE OF THIS. GET OUTTA HERE.
YOU ARE HELPING ME, QUINN?
COMING OVER TO THE GOOD SIDE NOW?
PFAH! YOU WISH!
LET'S JUST SAY...WITHOUT YOU AND THE UNDERPANTS-ON-OUTSIDE BRIGADE AROUND, WHO AM I GONNA HIT WITH MY SUBTLE, STYLISH MALLET?
I SHOULD NOT HAVE ATTACKED YOU. I APOLOGIZE.
KATANA...
GO! WALLER'S TROOPS ARE HERE!
THIS PLACE... IT IS A HOUSE OF CHAOS, BATMAN. THERE ARE SO MANY VOICES. YOU CAN LOSE YOURSELF HERE....

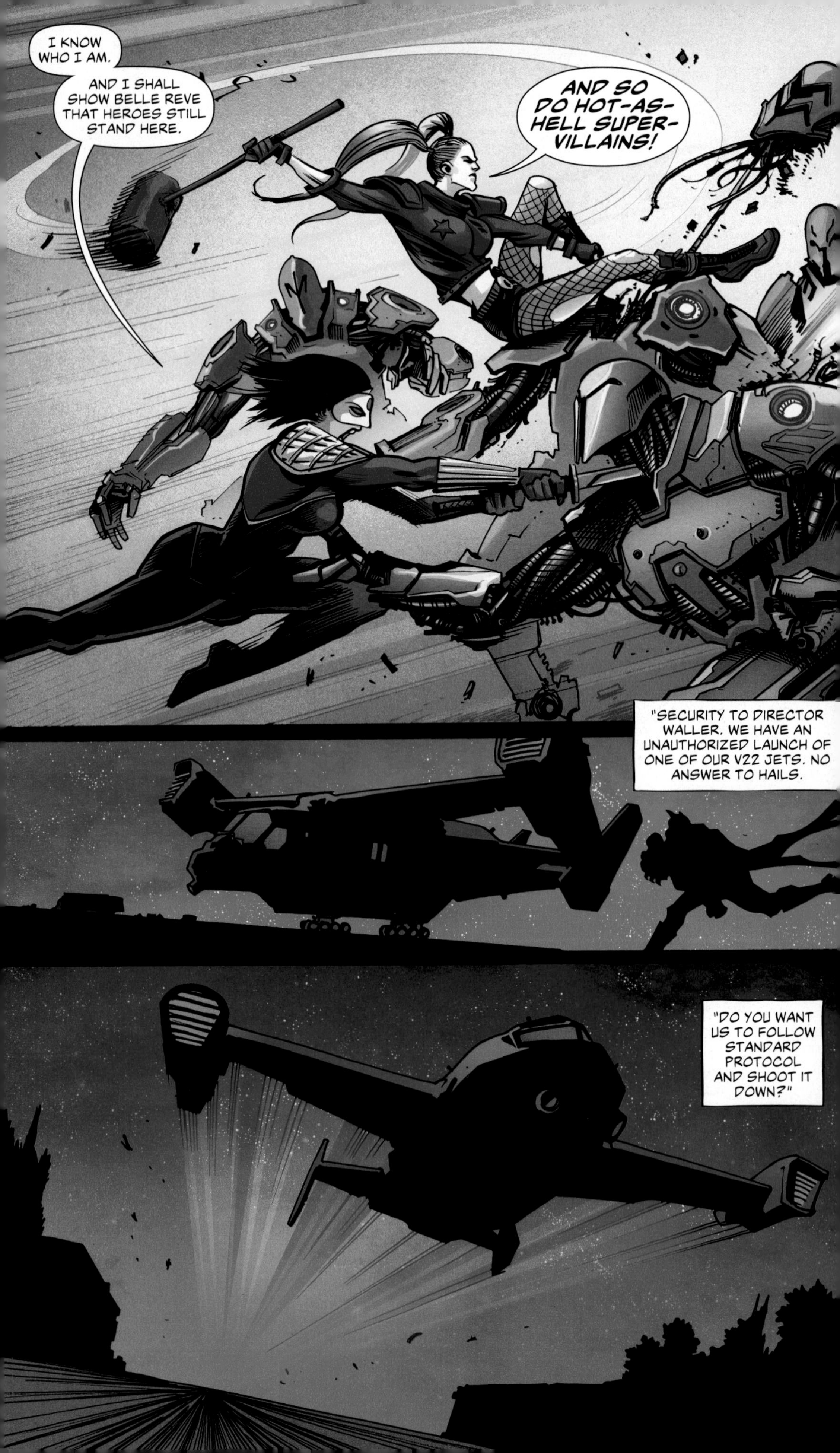
I KNOW WHO I AM.
AND I SHALL SHOW BELLE REVE THAT HEROES STILL STAND HERE.
AND SO DO HOT-AS-HELL SUPER-VILLAINS!
"SECURITY TO DIRECTOR WALLER. WE HAVE AN UNAUTHORIZED LAUNCH OF ONE OF OUR V22 JETS. NO ANSWER TO HAILS.
"DO YOU WANT US TO FOLLOW STANDARD PROTOCOL AND SHOOT IT DOWN?"

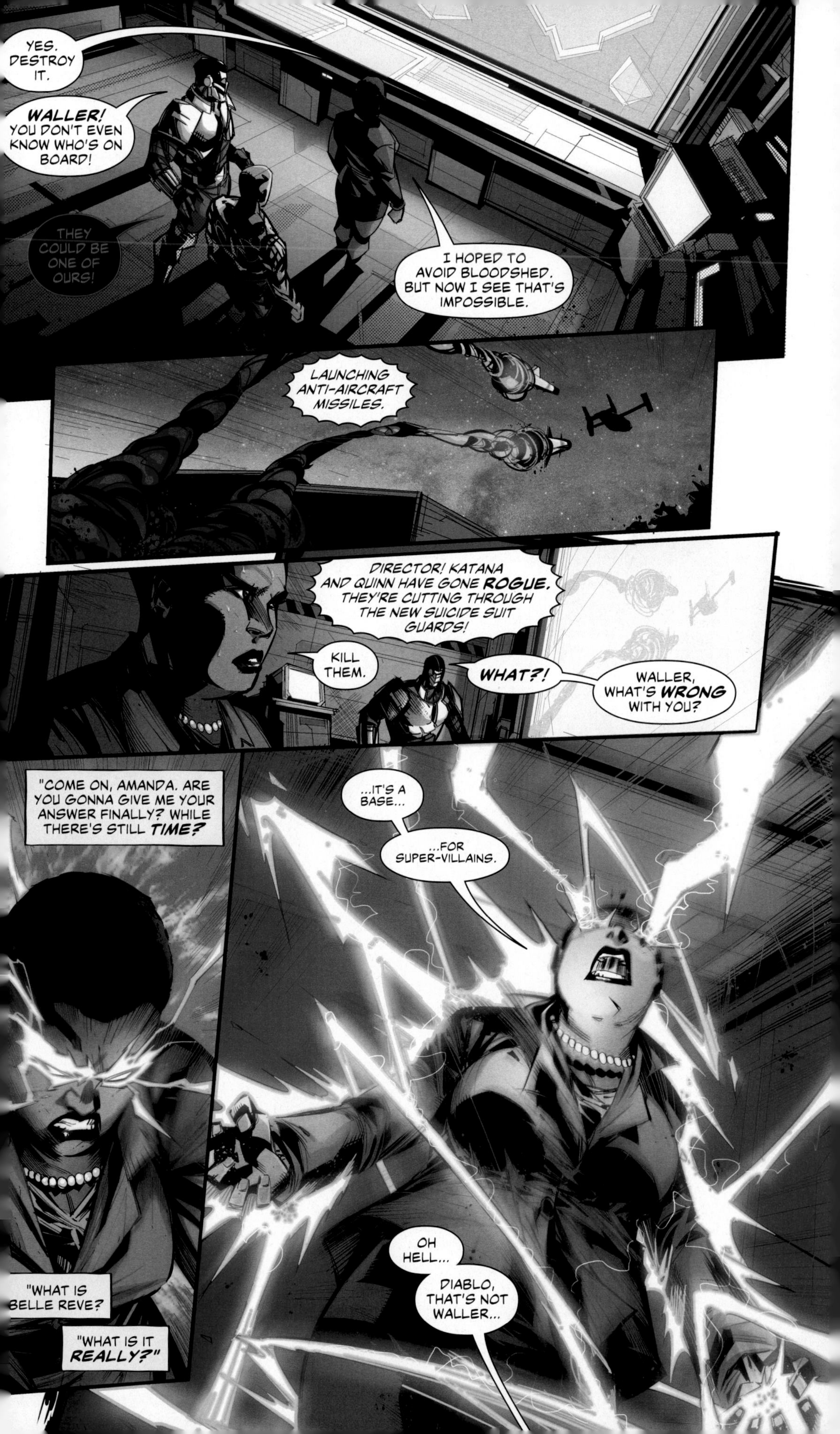
YES. DESTROY IT.
WALLER! YOU DON'T EVEN KNOW WHO'S ON BOARD!
THEY COULD BE ONE OF OURS!
I HOPED TO AVOID BLOODSHED. BUT NOW I SEE THAT'S IMPOSSIBLE.
LAUNCHING ANTI-AIRCRAFT MISSILES.
DIRECTOR! KATANA AND QUINN HAVE GONE ROGUE. THEY'RE CUTTING THROUGH THE NEW SUICIDE SUIT GUARDS!
KILL THEM.
WHAT?!
WALLER, WHAT'S WRONG WITH YOU?
"COME ON, AMANDA. ARE YOU GONNA GIVE ME YOUR ANSWER FINALLY? WHILE THERE'S STILL TIME?
...IT'S A BASE...
...FOR SUPER-VILLAINS.
"WHAT IS BELLE REVE?
"WHAT IS IT REALLY?"
OH HELL...
DIABLO, THAT'S NOT WALLER...

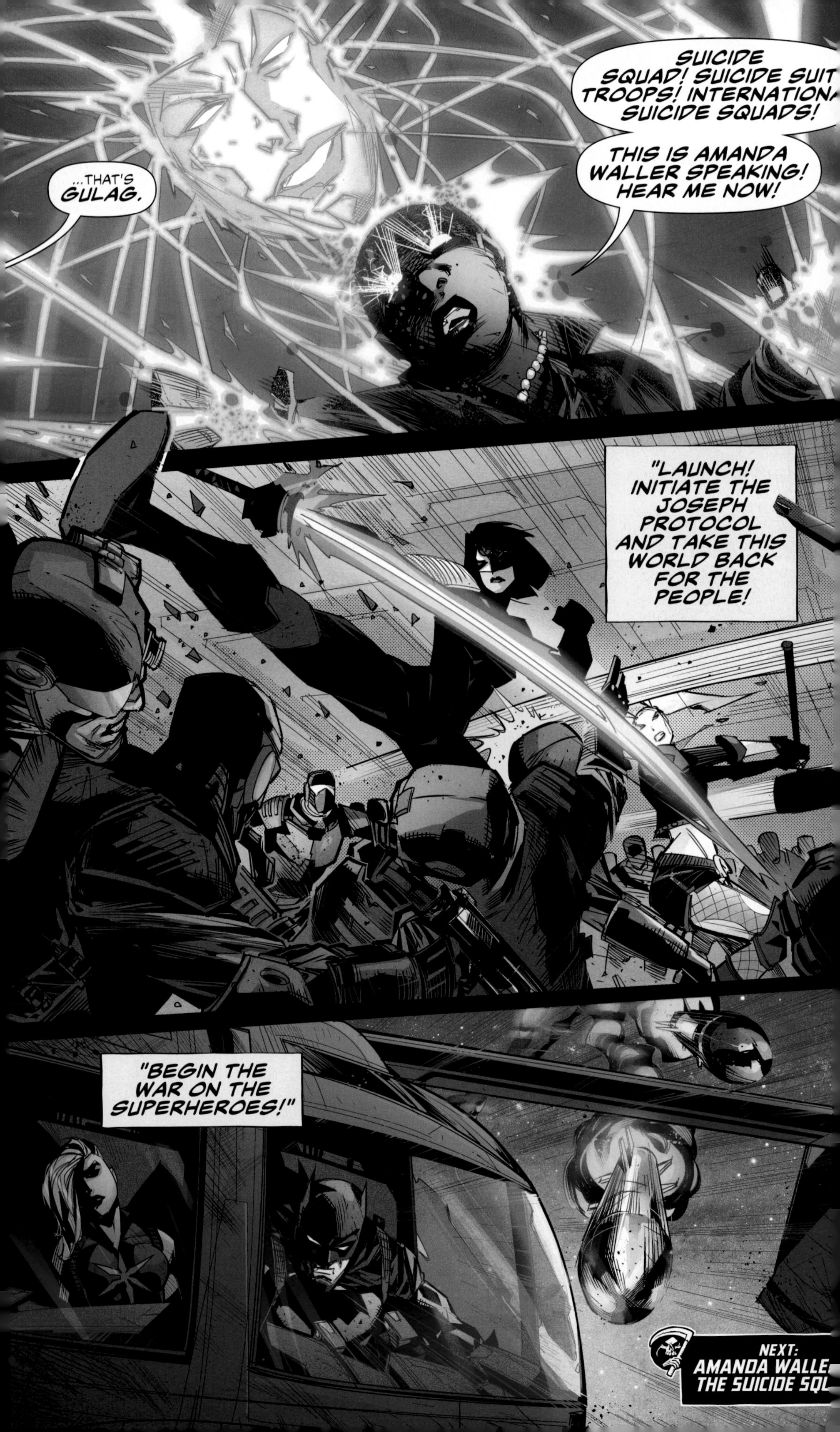
...THAT'S GULAG.
SUICIDE SQUAD! SUICIDE SUIT TROOPS! INTERNATIONA SUICIDE SQUADS!
THIS IS AMANDA WALLER SPEAKING! HEAR ME NOW!
"LAUNCH! INITIATE THE JOSEPH PROTOCOL AND TAKE THIS WORLD BACK FOR THE PEOPLE!
"BEGIN THE WAR ON THE SUPERHEROES!"
NEXT:
AMANDA WALLE
THE SUICIDE SQU

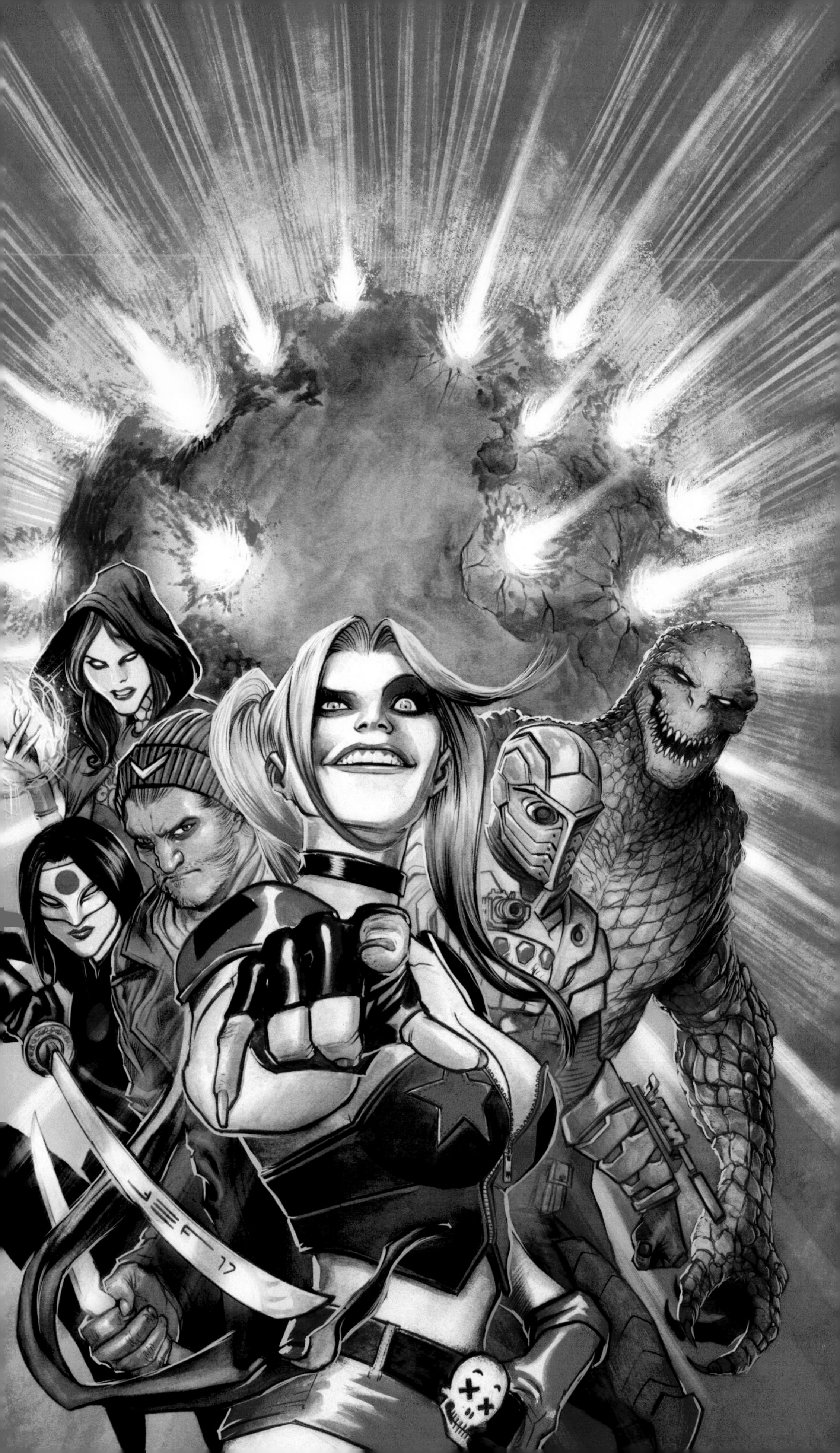

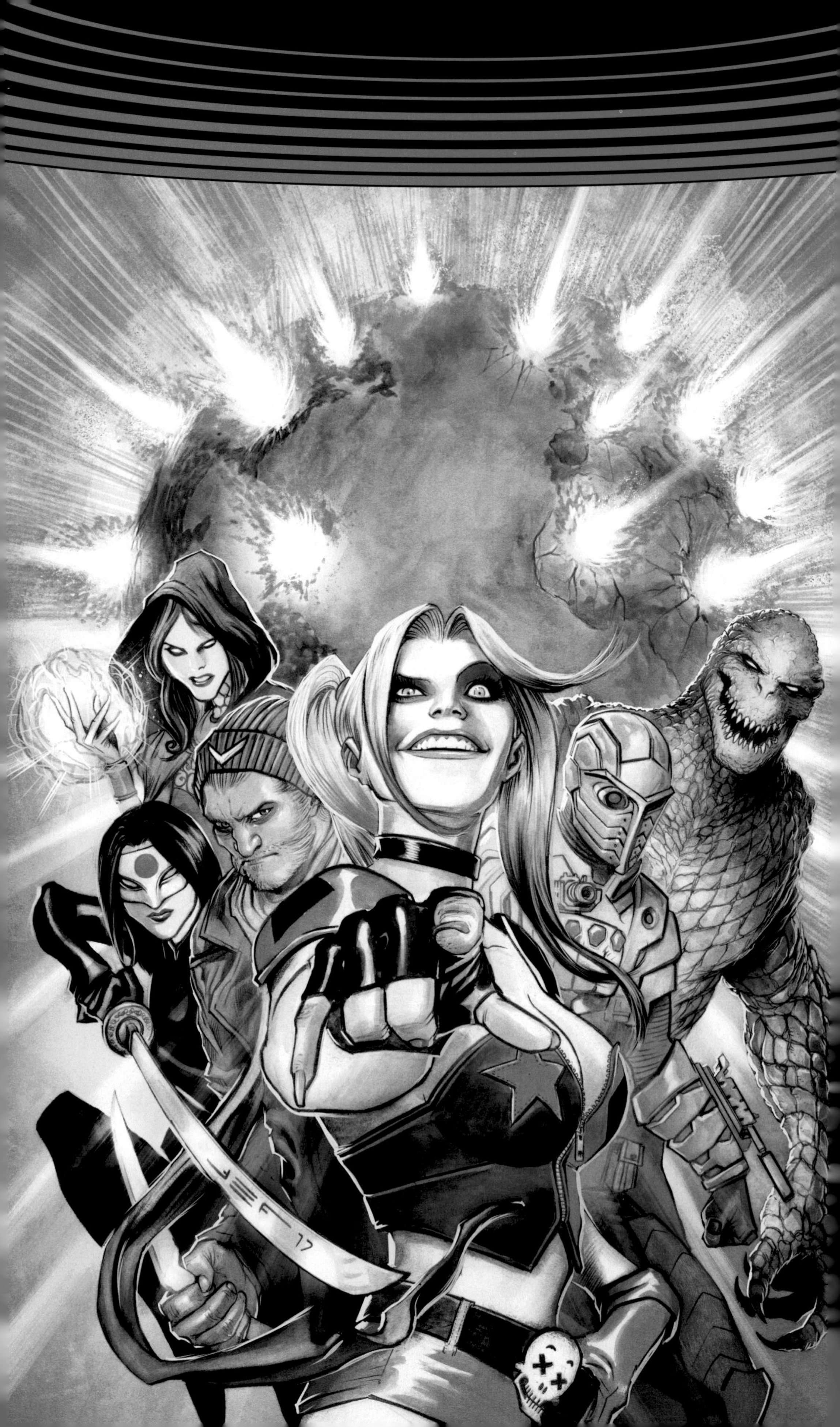

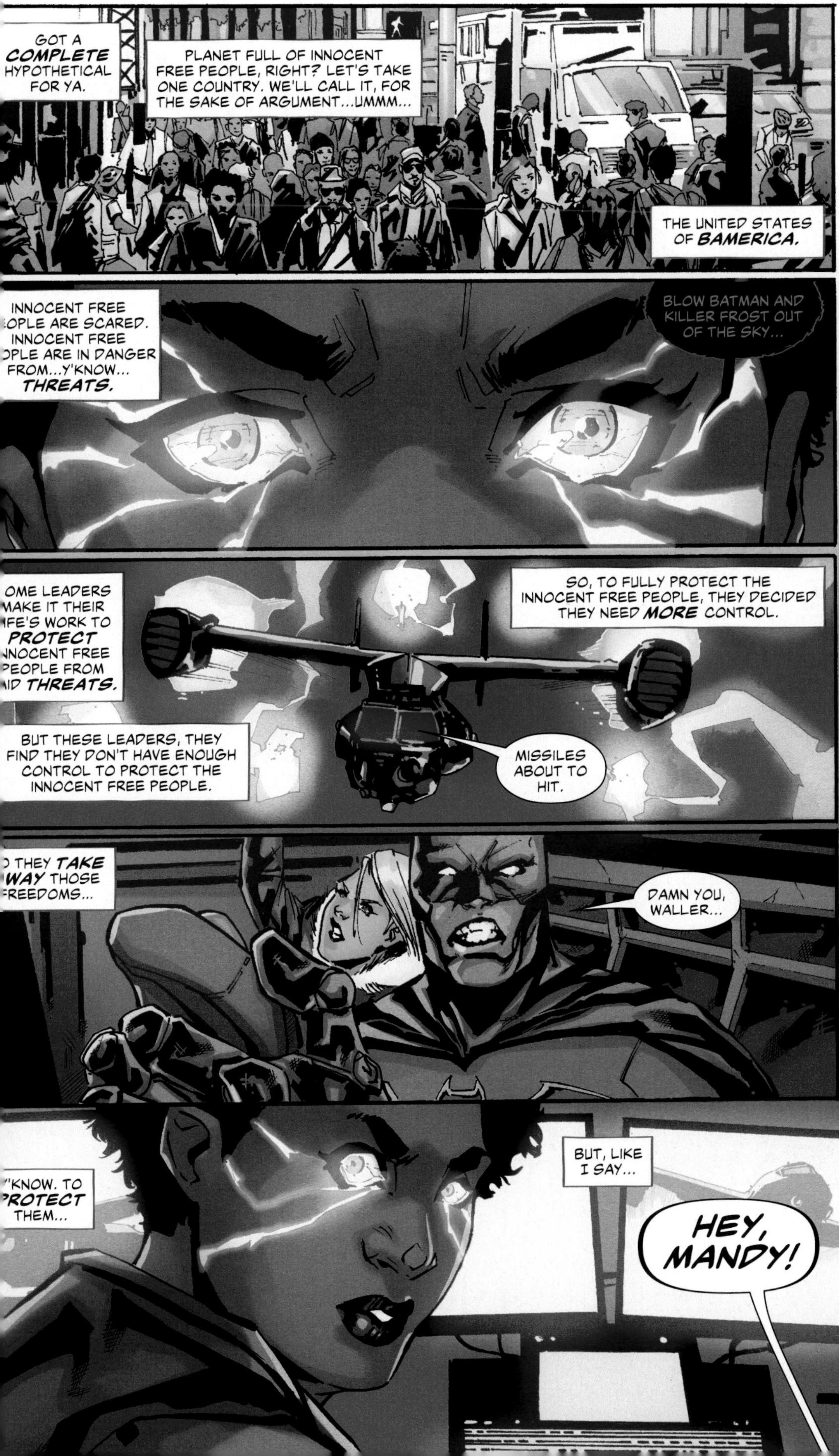
GOT A COMPLETE HYPOTHETICAL FOR YA.
PLANET FULL OF INNOCENT FREE PEOPLE, RIGHT? LET'S TAKE ONE COUNTRY. WE'LL CALL IT, FOR THE SAKE OF ARGUMENT...UMMM...
THE UNITED STATES OF BAMERICA.
INNOCENT FREE EOPLE ARE SCARED. INNOCENT FREE OPLE ARE IN DANGER FROM...Y'KNOW... THREATS.
BLOW BATMAN AND KILLER FROST OUT OF THE SKY...
OME LEADERS MAKE IT THEIR IFE'S WORK TO PROTECT NNOCENT FREE PEOPLE FROM ID THREATS.
SO, TO FULLY PROTECT THE INNOCENT FREE PEOPLE, THEY DECIDED THEY NEED MORE CONTROL.
BUT THESE LEADERS, THEY FIND THEY DON'T HAVE ENOUGH CONTROL TO PROTECT THE INNOCENT FREE PEOPLE.
MISSILES ABOUT TO HIT.
O THEY TAKE WAY THOSE FREEDOMS...
DAMN YOU, WALLER...
'KNOW. TO PROTECT THEM...
BUT, LIKE I SAY...
HEY, MANDY!

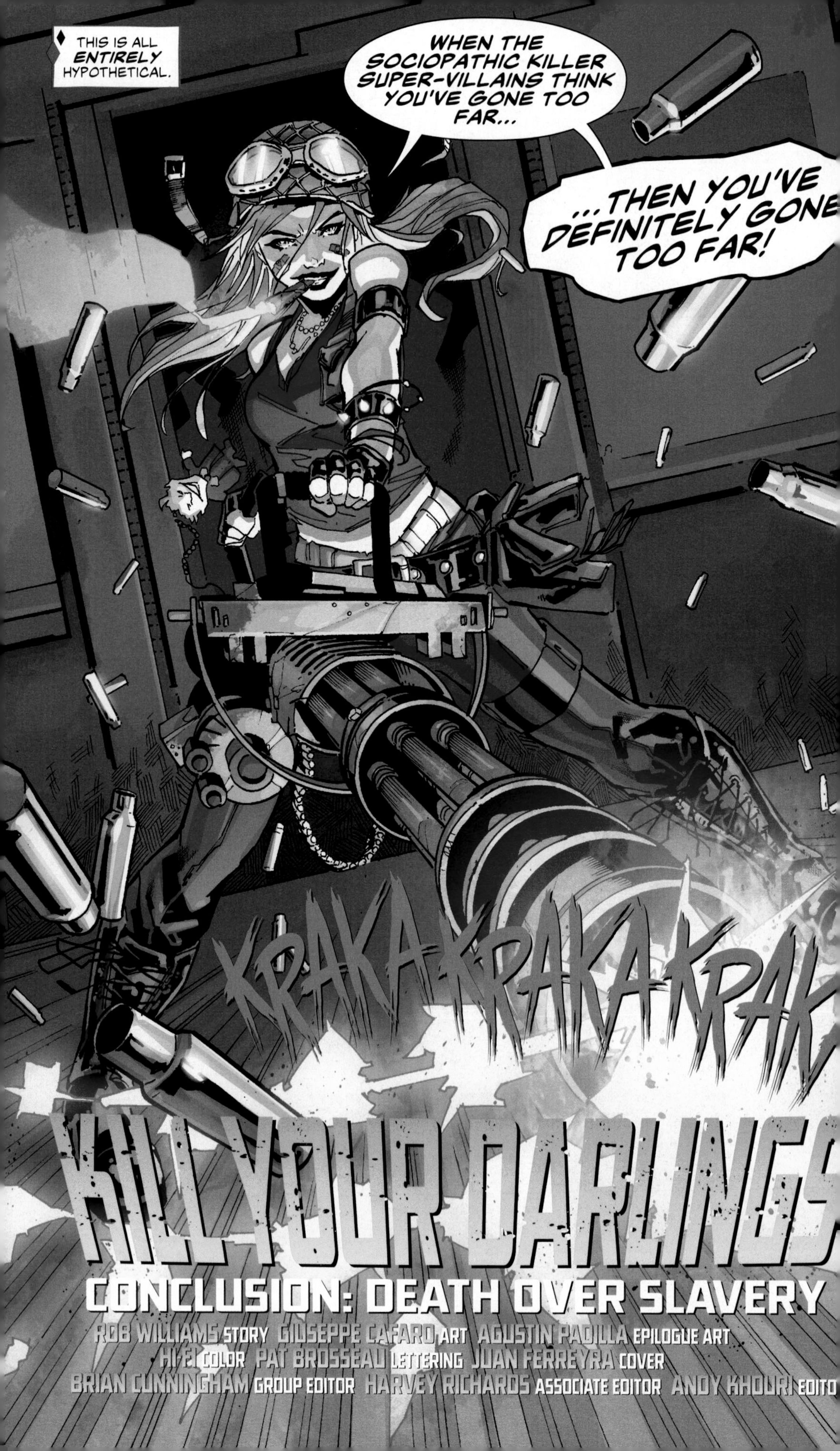

THIS IS ALL ENTIRELY HYPOTHETICAL.
WHEN THE SOCIOPATHIC KILLER SUPER-VILLAINS THINK YOU'VE GONE TOO FAR...
...THEN YOU'VE DEFINITELY GONE TOO FAR!
KRAKAKRAKAKRAK
KILL YOUR DARLINGS
CONCLUSION: DEATH OVER SLAVERY
ROB WILLIAMS STORY GIUSEPPE CAFARO ART AGUSTIN PADILLA EPILOGUE ART
HI-FI COLOR PAT BROSSEAU LETTERING JUAN FERREYRA COVER
BRIAN CUNNINGHAM GROUP EDITOR HARVEY RICHARDS ASSOCIATE EDITOR ANDY KHOURI EDITO

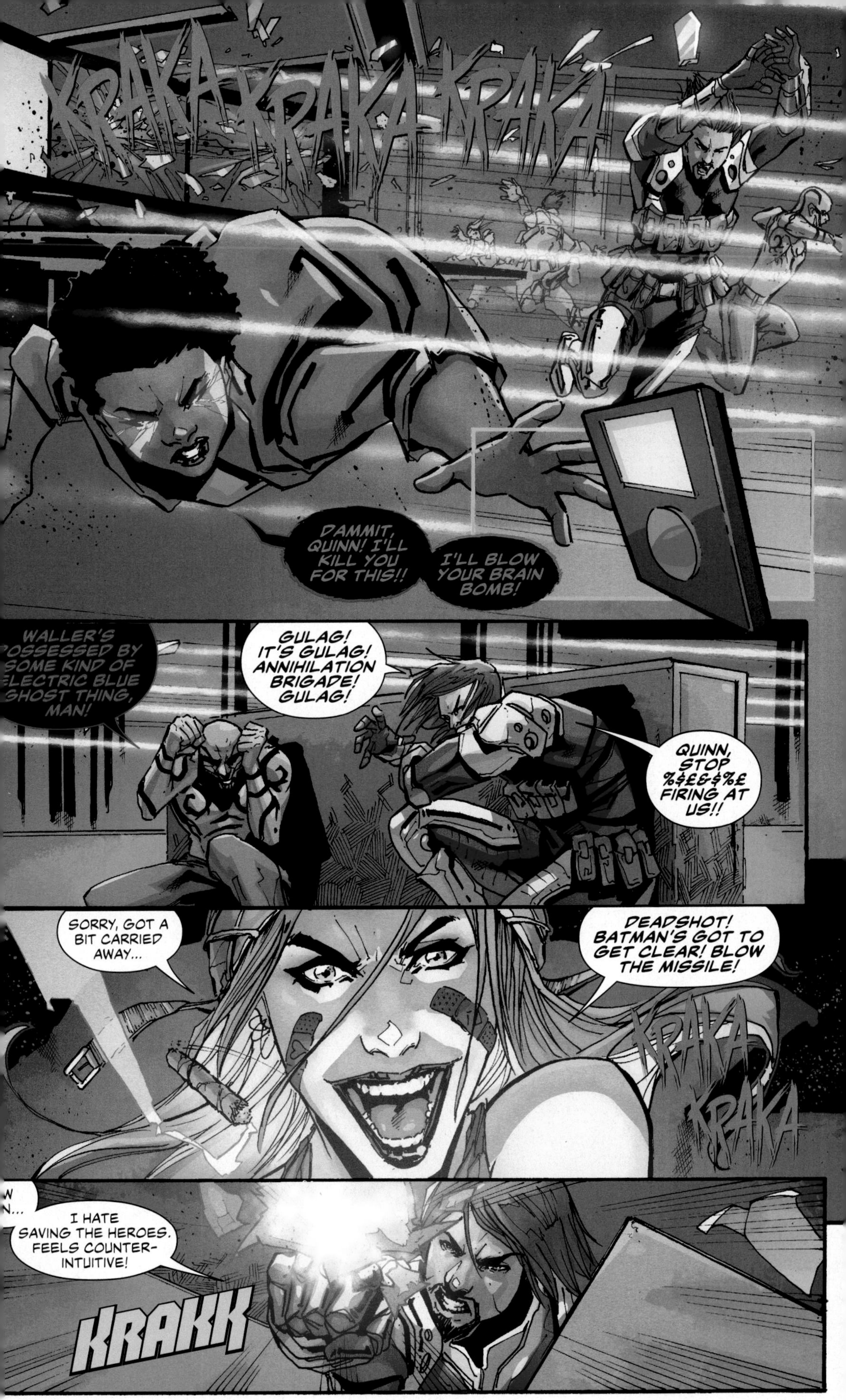
KRAKA KRAKA KRAKA
DAMMIT, QUINN! I'LL KILL YOU FOR THIS!!
I'LL BLOW YOUR BRAIN BOMB!
WALLER'S OSSESSED BY SOME KIND OF LECTRIC BLUE GHOST THING, MAN!
GULAG! IT'S GULAG! ANNIHILATION BRIGADE! GULAG!
QUINN, STOP %$£&$%£ FIRING AT US!!
SORRY, GOT A BIT CARRIED AWAY...
DEADSHOT! BATMAN'S GOT TO GET CLEAR! BLOW THE MISSILE!
KRAKA KRAKA
I HATE SAVING THE HEROES. FEELS COUNTER-INTUITIVE!
KRAKK

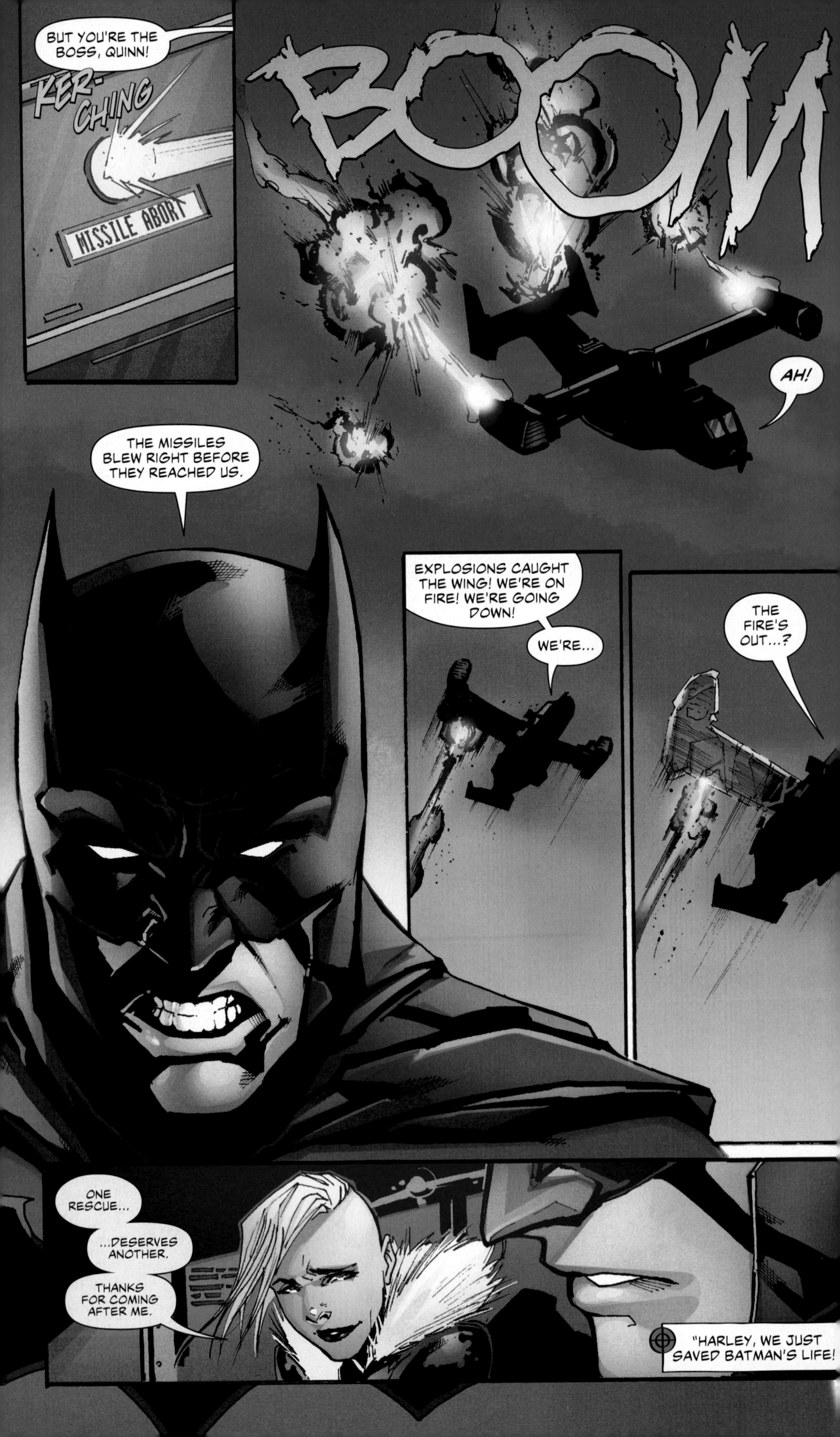

BUT YOU'RE THE BOSS, QUINN!
KER-CHING
MISSILE ABORT
BOOM
AH!
THE MISSILES BLEW RIGHT BEFORE THEY REACHED US.
EXPLOSIONS CAUGHT THE WING! WE'RE ON FIRE! WE'RE GOING DOWN!
WE'RE...
THE FIRE'S OUT...?
ONE RESCUE...
...DESERVES ANOTHER.
THANKS FOR COMING AFTER ME.
"HARLEY, WE JUST SAVED BATMAN'S LIFE!

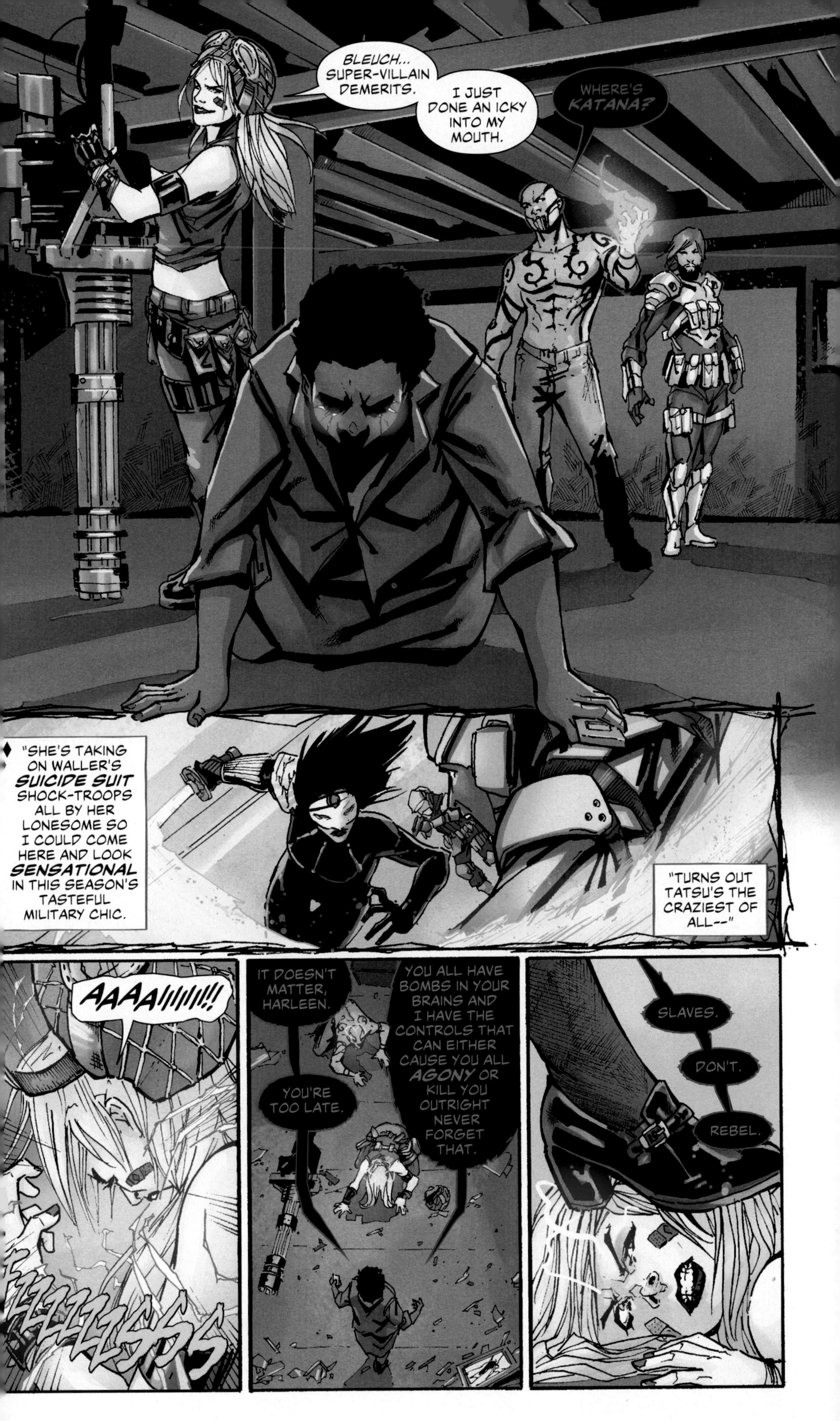

BLEUCH... SUPER-VILLAIN DEMERITS.
I JUST DONE AN ICKY INTO MY MOUTH.
WHERE'S KATANA?
"SHE'S TAKING ON WALLER'S SUICIDE SUIT SHOCK-TROOPS ALL BY HER LONESOME SO I COULD COME HERE AND LOOK SENSATIONAL IN THIS SEASON'S TASTEFUL MILITARY CHIC.
"TURNS OUT TATSU'S THE CRAZIEST OF ALL--"
AAAAIIIIII!!
FZZZZZZSSSS
IT DOESN'T MATTER, HARLEEN.
YOU'RE TOO LATE.
YOU ALL HAVE BOMBS IN YOUR BRAINS AND I HAVE THE CONTROLS THAT CAN EITHER CAUSE YOU ALL AGONY OR KILL YOU OUTRIGHT NEVER FORGET THAT.
SLAVES.
DON'T.
REBEL.

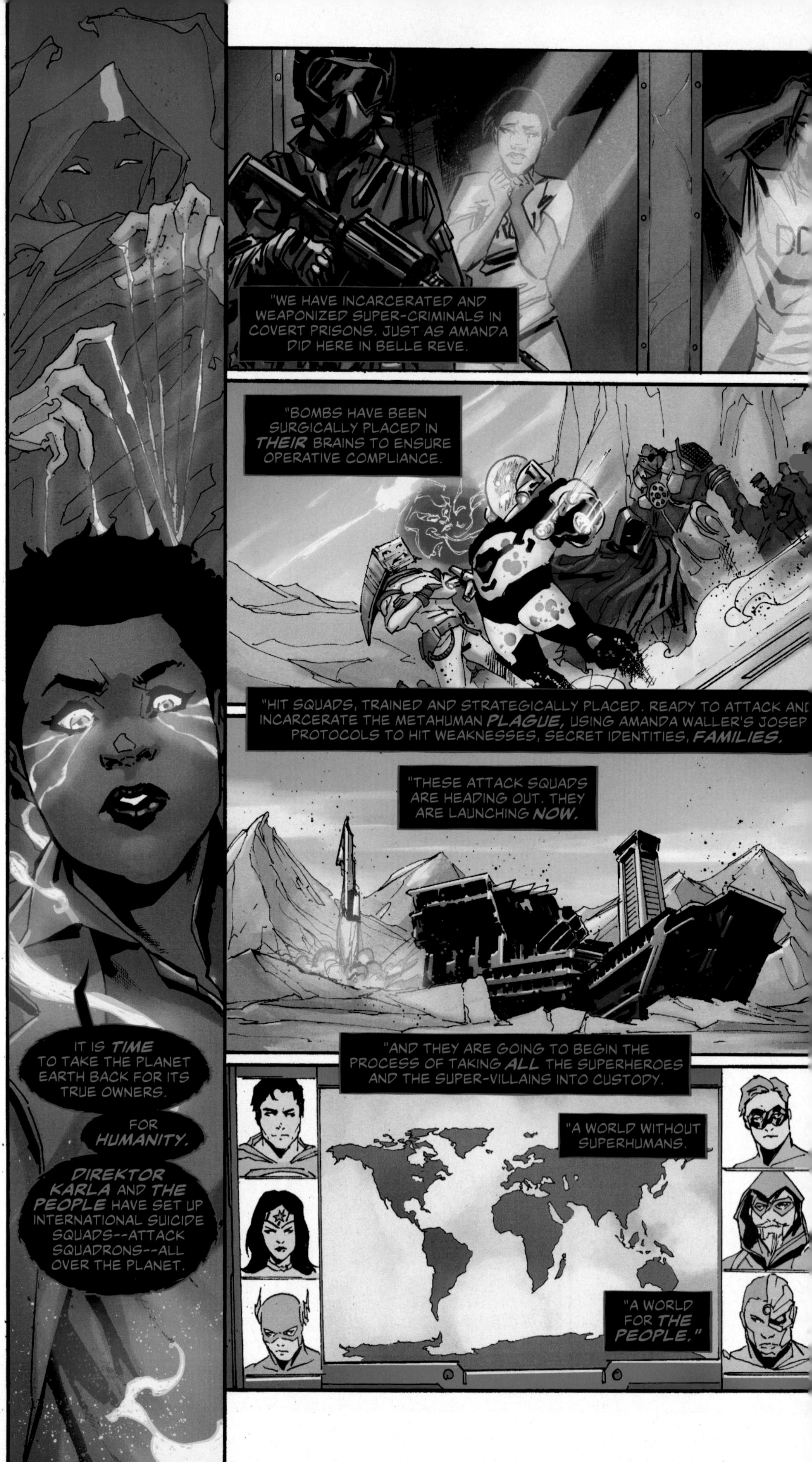
"WE HAVE INCARCERATED AND WEAPONIZED SUPER-CRIMINALS IN COVERT PRISONS. JUST AS AMANDA DID HERE IN BELLE REVE.
"BOMBS HAVE BEEN SURGICALLY PLACED IN THEIR BRAINS TO ENSURE OPERATIVE COMPLIANCE.
"HIT SQUADS, TRAINED AND STRATEGICALLY PLACED. READY TO ATTACK AND INCARCERATE THE METAHUMAN PLAGUE, USING AMANDA WALLER'S JOSEP PROTOCOLS TO HIT WEAKNESSES, SECRET IDENTITIES, FAMILIES.
"THESE ATTACK SQUADS ARE HEADING OUT. THEY ARE LAUNCHING NOW.
"AND THEY ARE GOING TO BEGIN THE PROCESS OF TAKING ALL THE SUPERHEROES AND THE SUPER-VILLAINS INTO CUSTODY.
"A WORLD WITHOUT SUPERHUMANS.
"A WORLD FOR THE PEOPLE."
IT IS TIME TO TAKE THE PLANET EARTH BACK FOR ITS TRUE OWNERS.
FOR HUMANITY.
DIREKTOR KARLA AND THE PEOPLE HAVE SET UP INTERNATIONAL SUICIDE SQUADS--ATTACK SQUADRONS--ALL OVER THE PLANET.

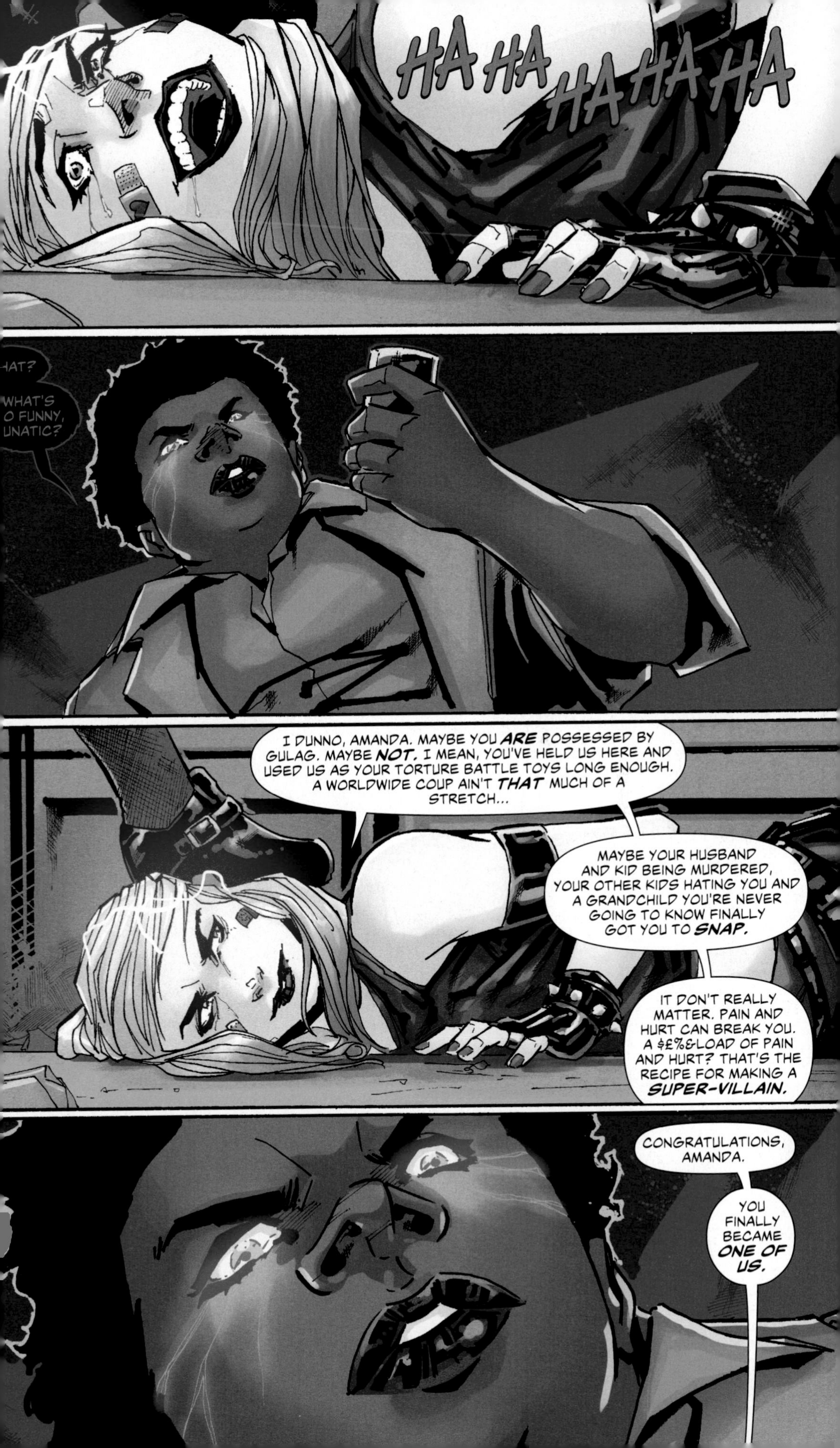

HA HA HA HA HA HA
HAT? WHAT'S O FUNNY, UNATIC?
I DUNNO, AMANDA. MAYBE YOU ARE POSSESSED BY GULAG. MAYBE NOT. I MEAN, YOU'VE HELD US HERE AND USED US AS YOUR TORTURE BATTLE TOYS LONG ENOUGH. A WORLDWIDE COUP AIN'T THAT MUCH OF A STRETCH...
MAYBE YOUR HUSBAND AND KID BEING MURDERED, YOUR OTHER KIDS HATING YOU AND A GRANDCHILD YOU'RE NEVER GOING TO KNOW FINALLY GOT YOU TO SNAP.
IT DON'T REALLY MATTER. PAIN AND HURT CAN BREAK YOU. A $£%&LOAD OF PAIN AND HURT? THAT'S THE RECIPE FOR MAKING A SUPER-VILLAIN.
CONGRATULATIONS, AMANDA.
YOU FINALLY BECAME ONE OF US.

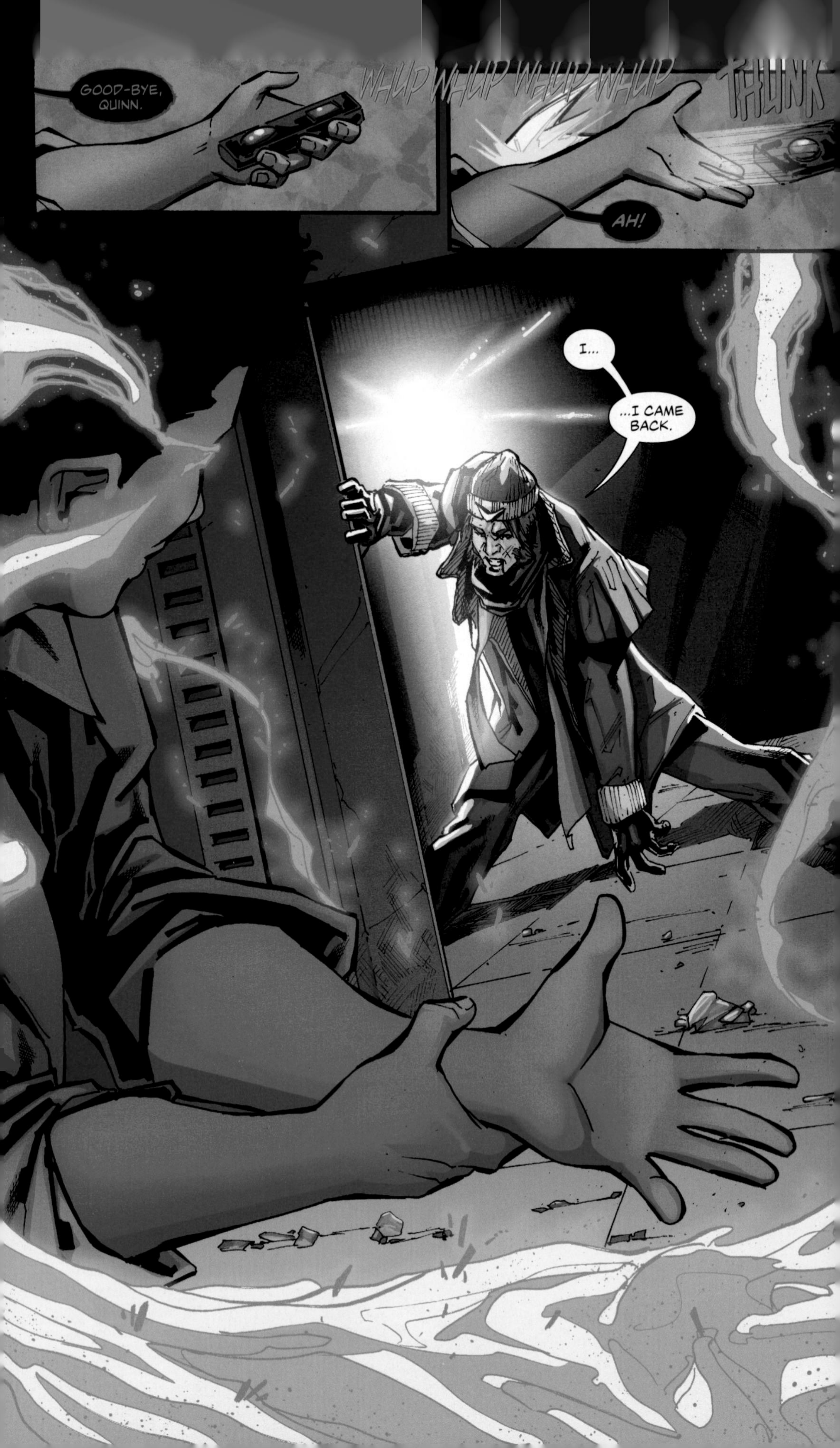
GOOD-BYE, QUINN.
WHUP WHUP WHUP WHUP
THUNK
AH!
I...
...I CAME BACK.

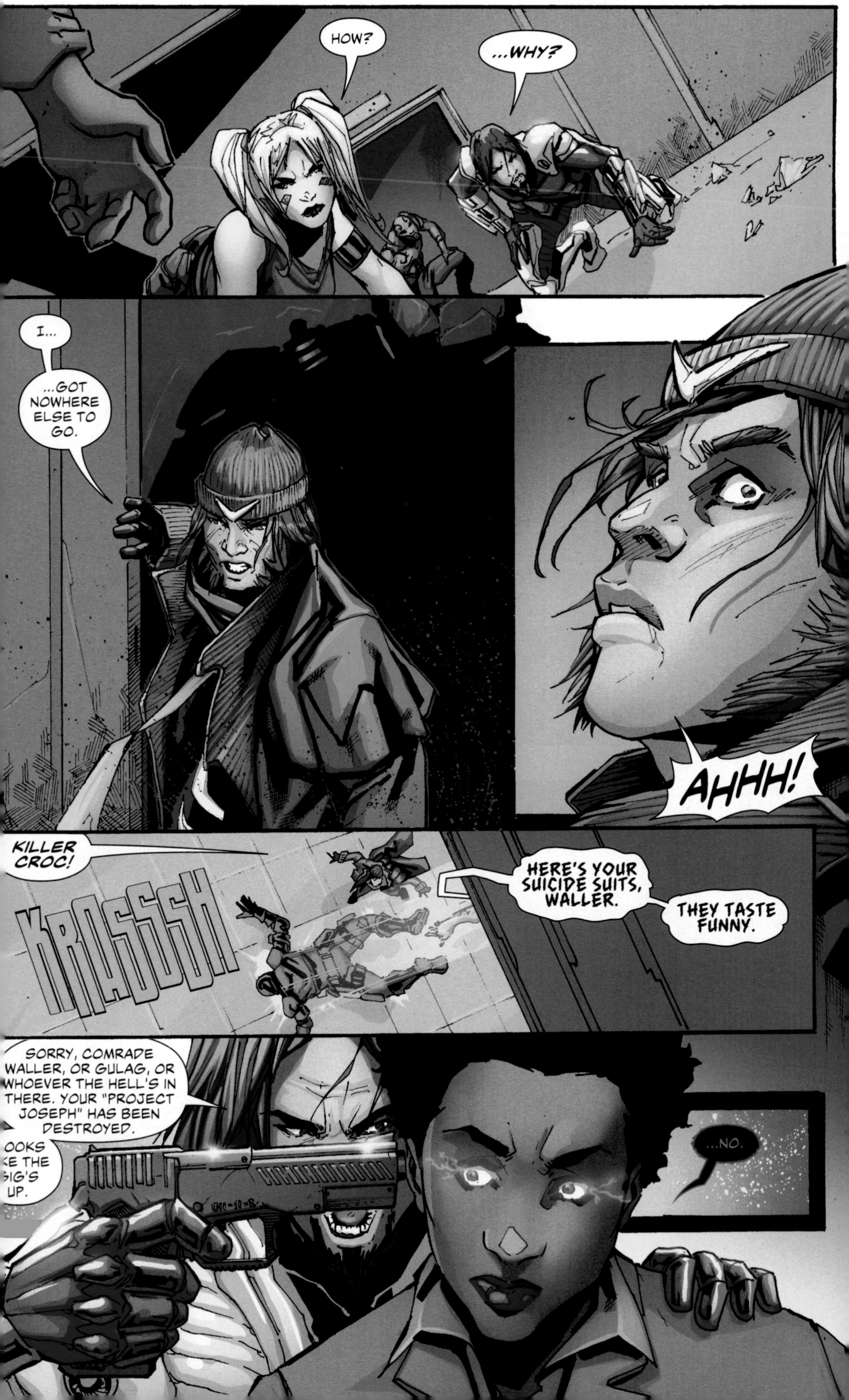
HOW?
...WHY?
I...
...GOT NOWHERE ELSE TO GO.
AHHH!
KILLER CROC!
KROSSSH
HERE'S YOUR SUICIDE SUITS, WALLER.
THEY TASTE FUNNY.
SORRY, COMRADE WALLER, OR GULAG, OR WHOEVER THE HELL'S IN THERE. YOUR "PROJECT JOSEPH" HAS BEEN DESTROYED.
OOKS KE THE GIG'S UP.
...NO.

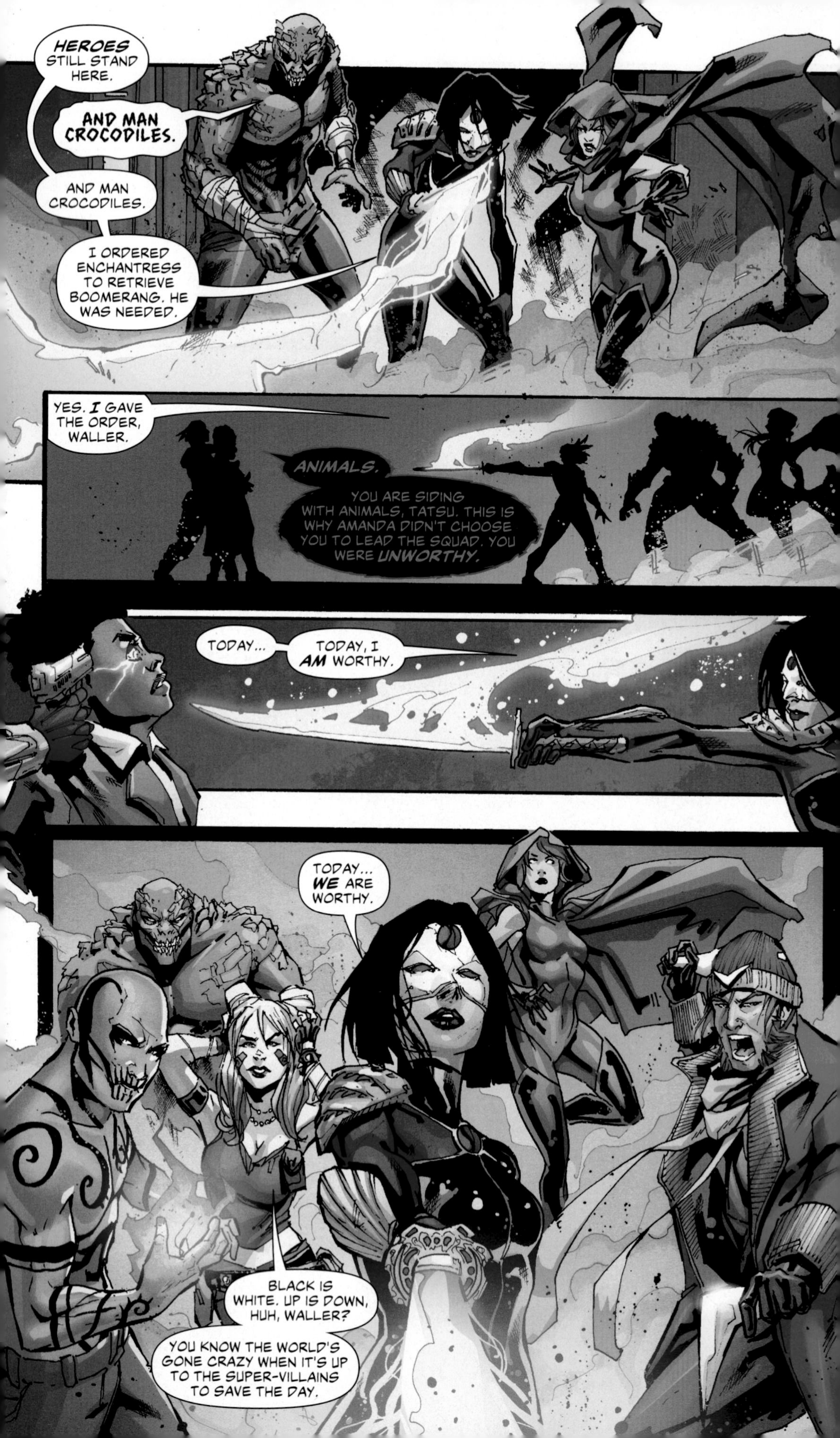
HEROES STILL STAND HERE.
AND MAN CROCODILES.
AND MAN CROCODILES.
I ORDERED ENCHANTRESS TO RETRIEVE BOOMERANG. HE WAS NEEDED.
YES. I GAVE THE ORDER, WALLER.
ANIMALS.
YOU ARE SIDING WITH ANIMALS, TATSU. THIS IS WHY AMANDA DIDN'T CHOOSE YOU TO LEAD THE SQUAD. YOU WERE UNWORTHY.
TODAY...
TODAY, I AM WORTHY.
TODAY... WE ARE WORTHY.
BLACK IS WHITE. UP IS DOWN, HUH, WALLER?
YOU KNOW THE WORLD'S GONE CRAZY WHEN IT'S UP TO THE SUPER-VILLAINS TO SAVE THE DAY.

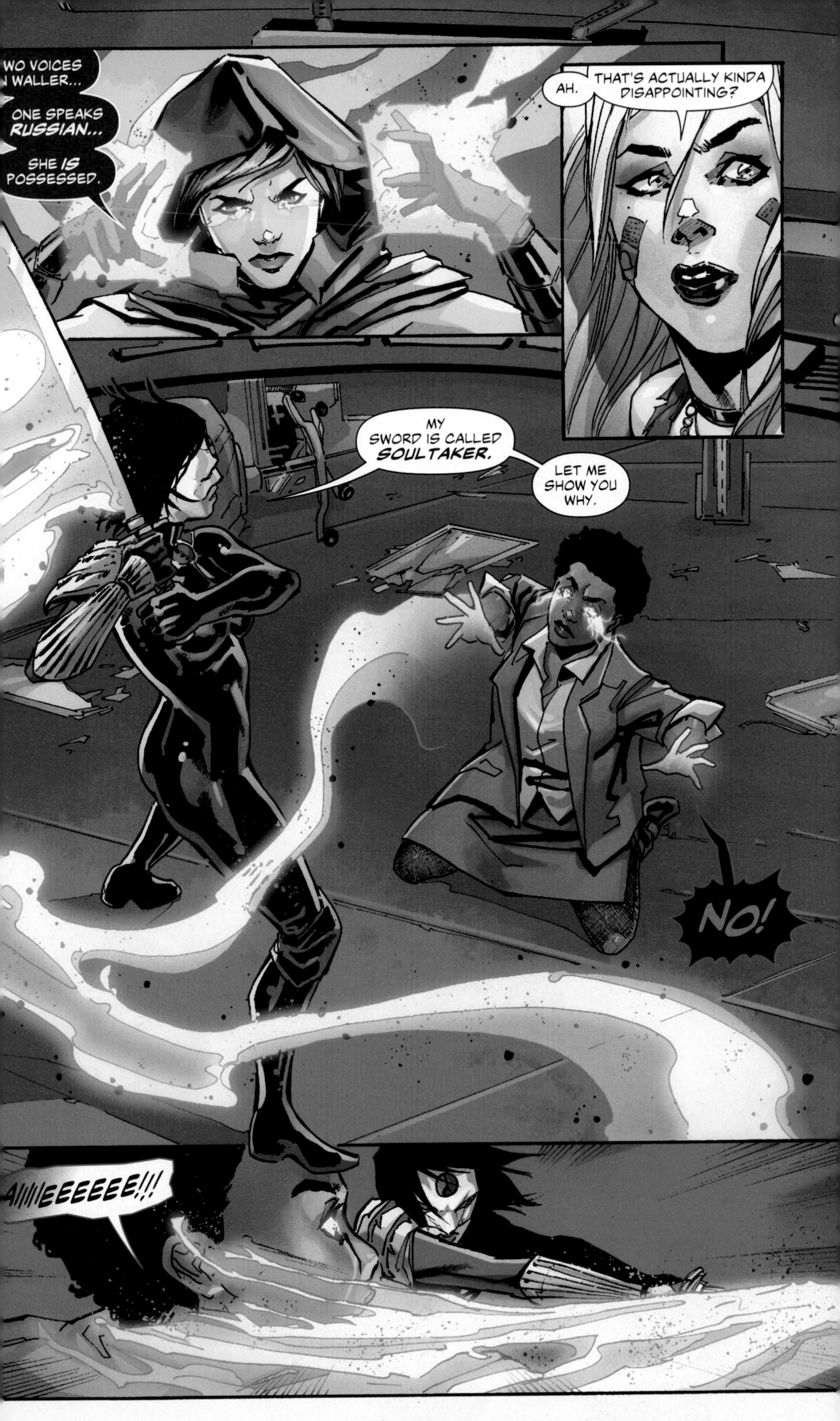

WO VOICES
N WALLER...
ONE SPEAKS
RUSSIAN...
SHE IS
POSSESSED.
AH.
THAT'S ACTUALLY KINDA
DISAPPOINTING?
MY
SWORD IS CALLED
SOULTAKER.
LET ME
SHOW YOU
WHY.
NO!
AIIIIEEEEEEE!!!

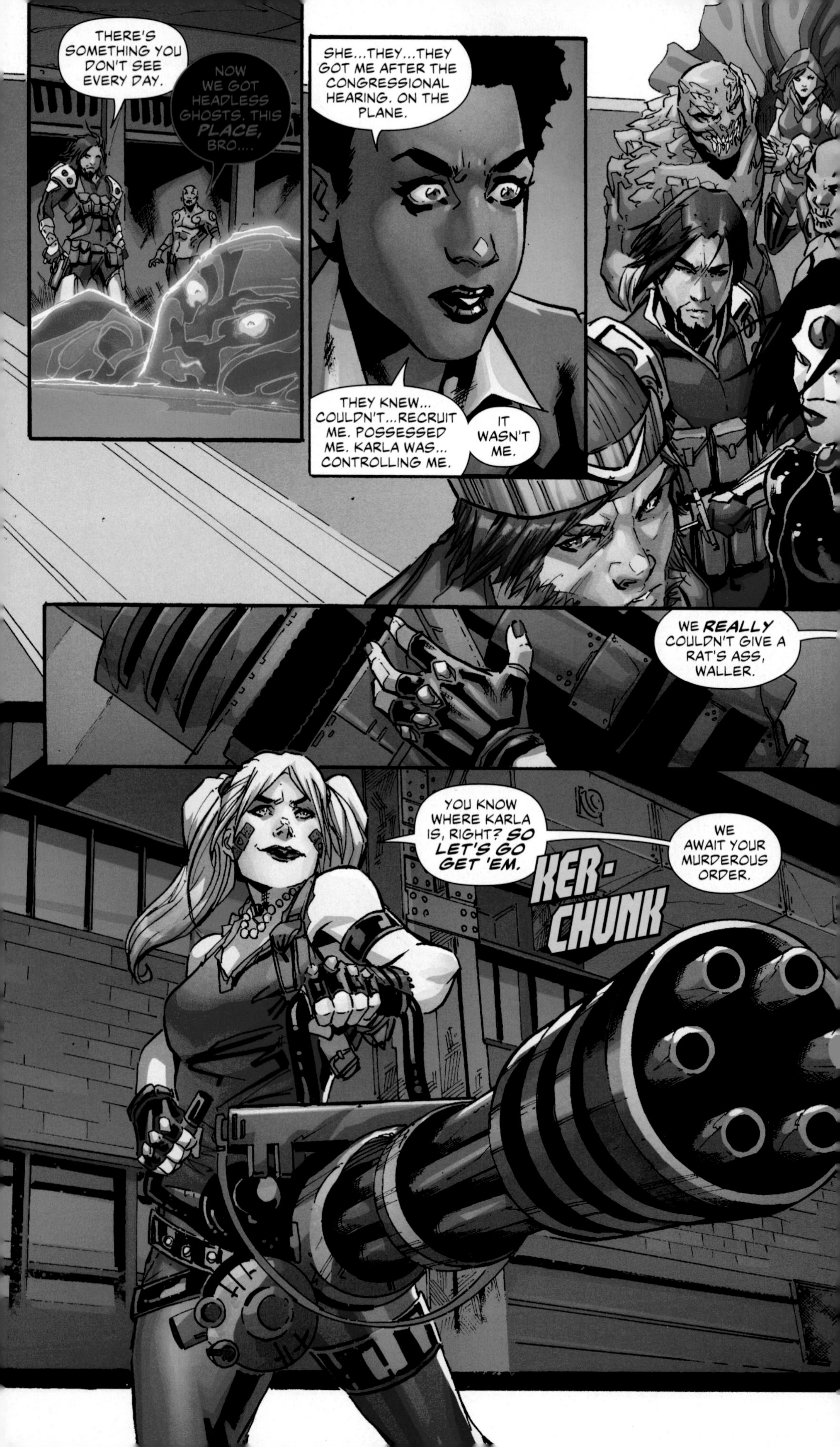
THERE'S SOMETHING YOU DON'T SEE EVERY DAY.
NOW WE GOT HEADLESS GHOSTS. THIS PLACE, BRO....
SHE...THEY...THEY GOT ME AFTER THE CONGRESSIONAL HEARING. ON THE PLANE.
THEY KNEW... COULDN'T...RECRUIT ME. POSSESSED ME. KARLA WAS... CONTROLLING ME.
IT WASN'T ME.
WE REALLY COULDN'T GIVE A RAT'S ASS, WALLER.
YOU KNOW WHERE KARLA IS, RIGHT? SO LET'S GO GET 'EM.
WE AWAIT YOUR MURDEROUS ORDER.
KER-CHUNK

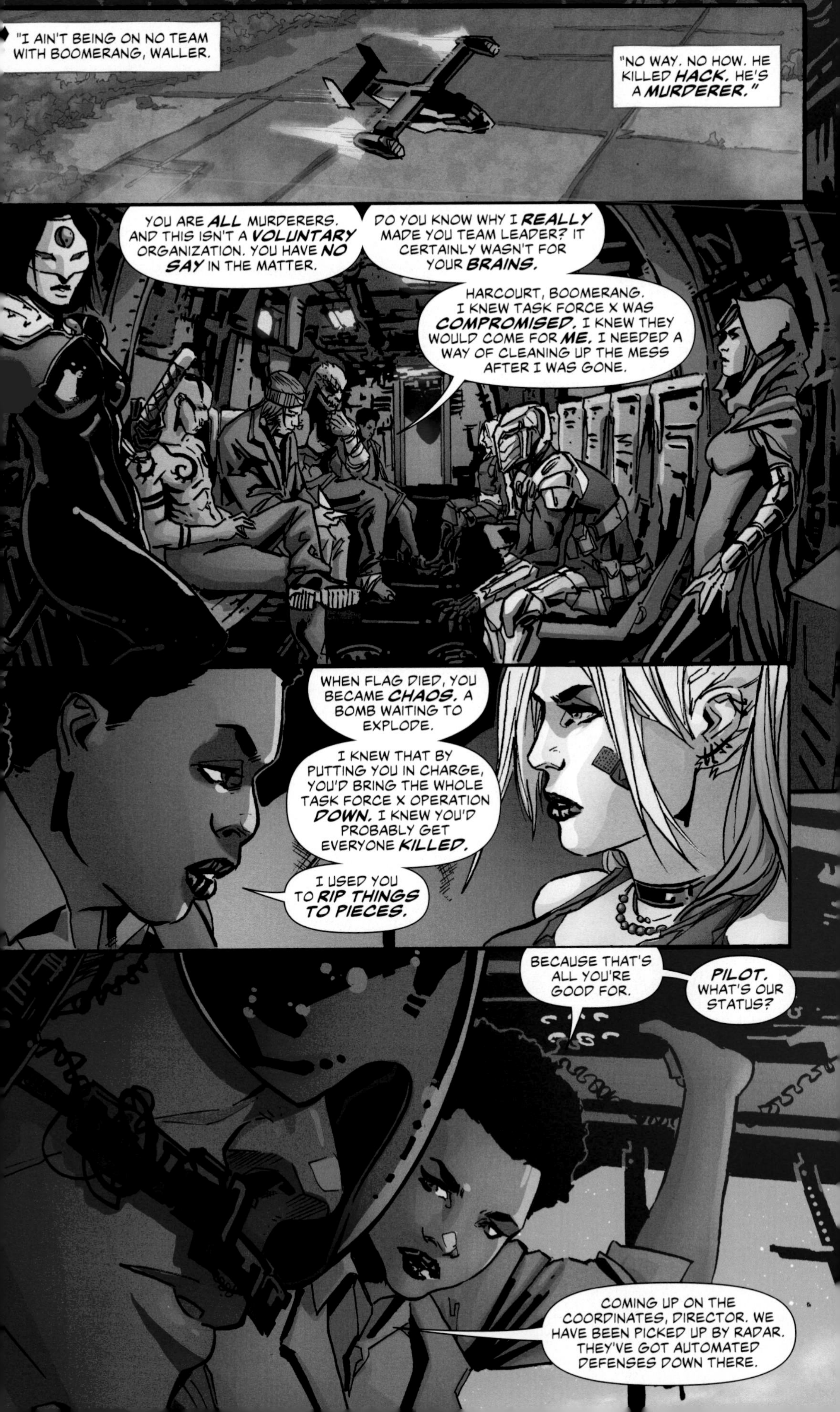
"I AIN'T BEING ON NO TEAM WITH BOOMERANG, WALLER.
"NO WAY. NO HOW. HE KILLED HACK. HE'S A MURDERER."
YOU ARE ALL MURDERERS. AND THIS ISN'T A VOLUNTARY ORGANIZATION. YOU HAVE NO SAY IN THE MATTER.
DO YOU KNOW WHY I REALLY MADE YOU TEAM LEADER? IT CERTAINLY WASN'T FOR YOUR BRAINS.
HARCOURT, BOOMERANG. I KNEW TASK FORCE X WAS COMPROMISED. I KNEW THEY WOULD COME FOR ME. I NEEDED A WAY OF CLEANING UP THE MESS AFTER I WAS GONE.
WHEN FLAG DIED, YOU BECAME CHAOS. A BOMB WAITING TO EXPLODE.
I KNEW THAT BY PUTTING YOU IN CHARGE, YOU'D BRING THE WHOLE TASK FORCE X OPERATION DOWN. I KNEW YOU'D PROBABLY GET EVERYONE KILLED.
I USED YOU TO RIP THINGS TO PIECES.
BECAUSE THAT'S ALL YOU'RE GOOD FOR.
PILOT. WHAT'S OUR STATUS?
COMING UP ON THE COORDINATES, DIRECTOR. WE HAVE BEEN PICKED UP BY RADAR. THEY'VE GOT AUTOMATED DEFENSES DOWN THERE.

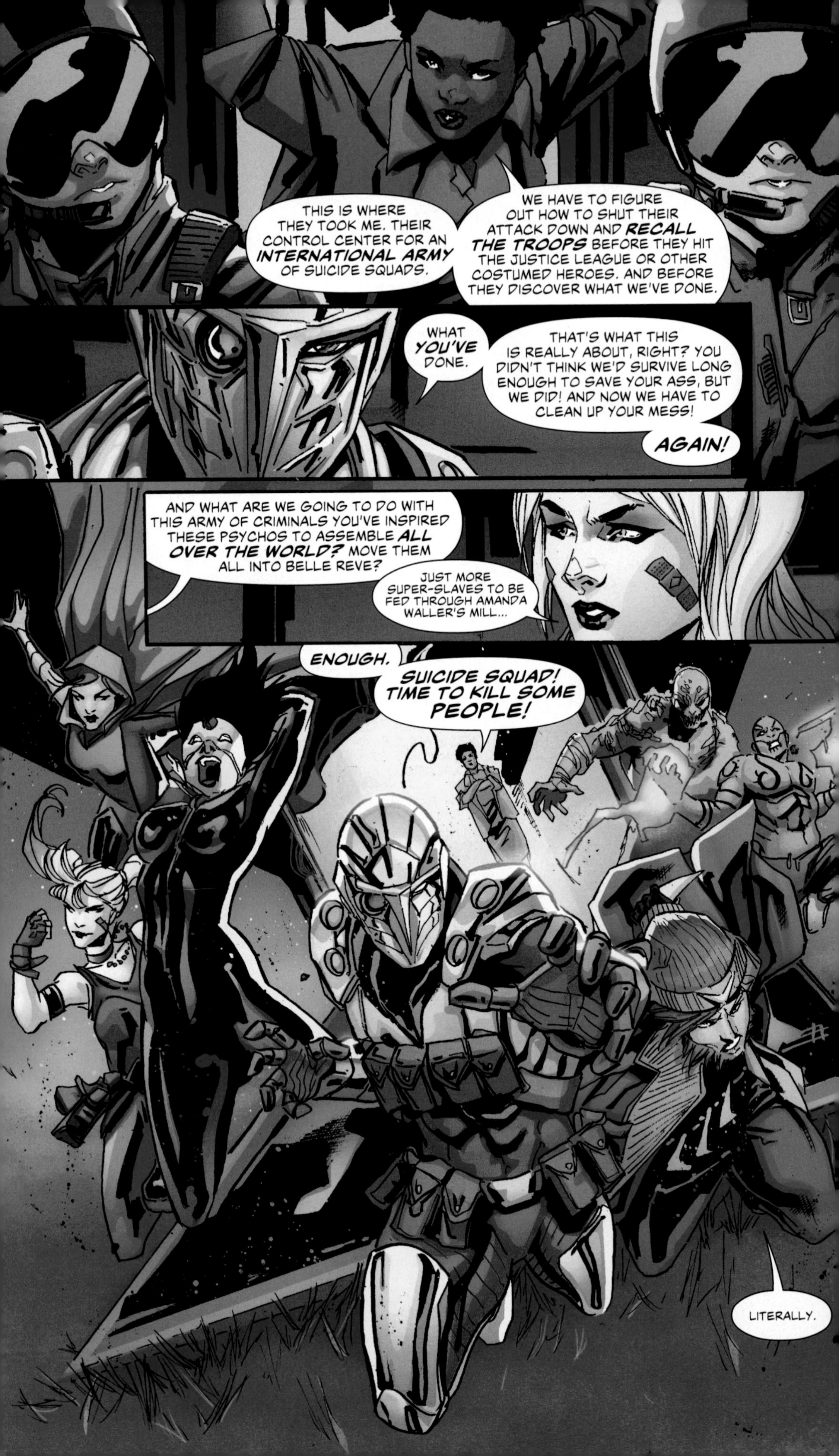
THIS IS WHERE THEY TOOK ME. THEIR CONTROL CENTER FOR AN INTERNATIONAL ARMY OF SUICIDE SQUADS.
WE HAVE TO FIGURE OUT HOW TO SHUT THEIR ATTACK DOWN AND RECALL THE TROOPS BEFORE THEY HIT THE JUSTICE LEAGUE OR OTHER COSTUMED HEROES. AND BEFORE THEY DISCOVER WHAT WE'VE DONE.
WHAT YOU'VE DONE.
THAT'S WHAT THIS IS REALLY ABOUT, RIGHT? YOU DIDN'T THINK WE'D SURVIVE LONG ENOUGH TO SAVE YOUR ASS, BUT WE DID! AND NOW WE HAVE TO CLEAN UP YOUR MESS!
AGAIN!
AND WHAT ARE WE GOING TO DO WITH THIS ARMY OF CRIMINALS YOU'VE INSPIRED THESE PSYCHOS TO ASSEMBLE ALL OVER THE WORLD? MOVE THEM ALL INTO BELLE REVE?
JUST MORE SUPER-SLAVES TO BE FED THROUGH AMANDA WALLER'S MILL...
ENOUGH.
SUICIDE SQUAD! TIME TO KILL SOME PEOPLE!
LITERALLY.

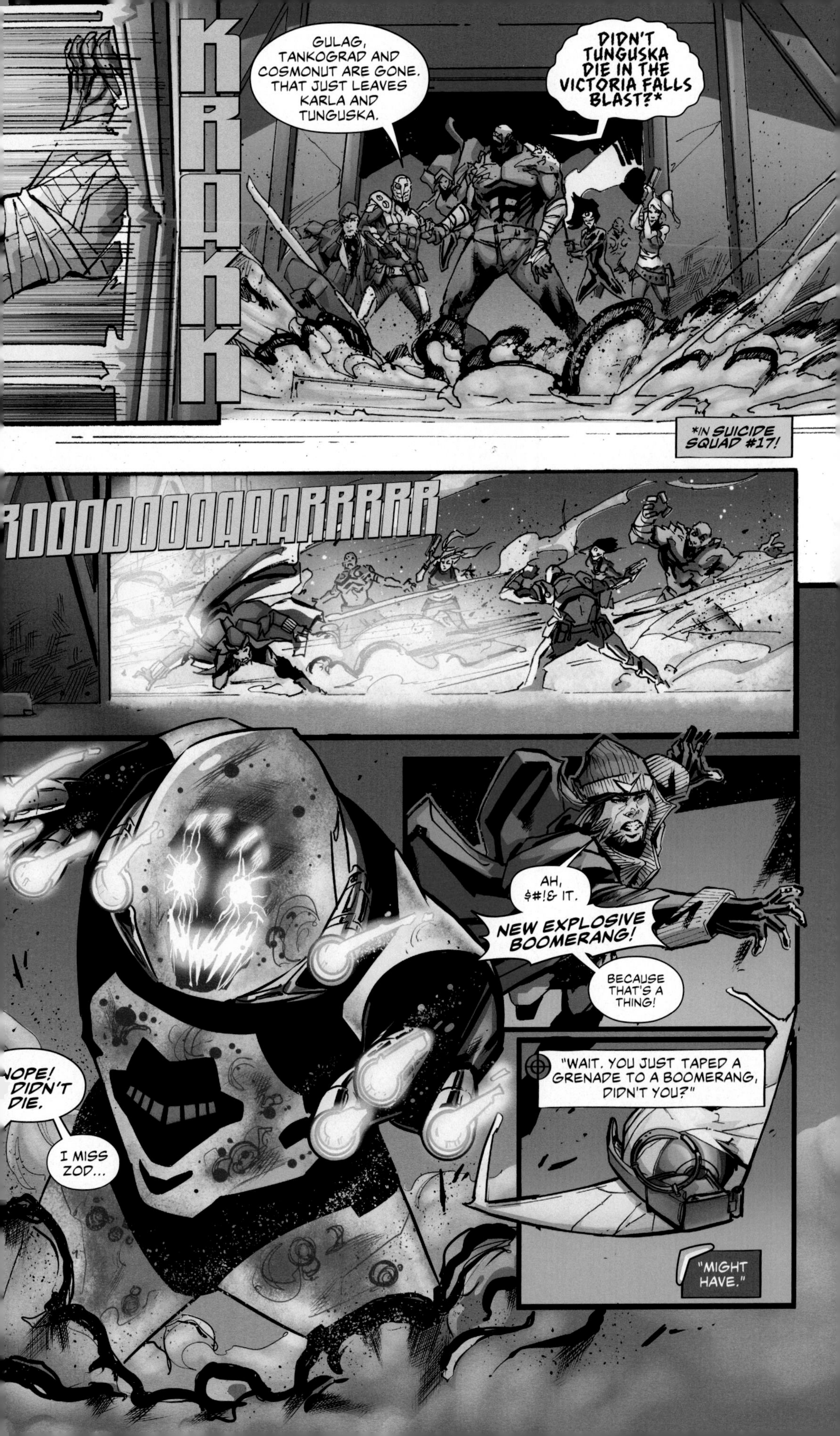
KRAKK
GULAG, TANKOGRAD AND COSMONUT ARE GONE. THAT JUST LEAVES KARLA AND TUNGUSKA.
DIDN'T TUNGUSKA DIE IN THE VICTORIA FALLS BLAST?*
*IN SUICIDE SQUAD #17!
ROOOOOOOAAARRRRR
AH, $#!& IT.
NEW EXPLOSIVE BOOMERANG!
BECAUSE THAT'S A THING!
NOPE! DIDN'T DIE.
I MISS ZOD...
"WAIT. YOU JUST TAPED A GRENADE TO A BOOMERANG, DIDN'T YOU?"
"MIGHT HAVE."

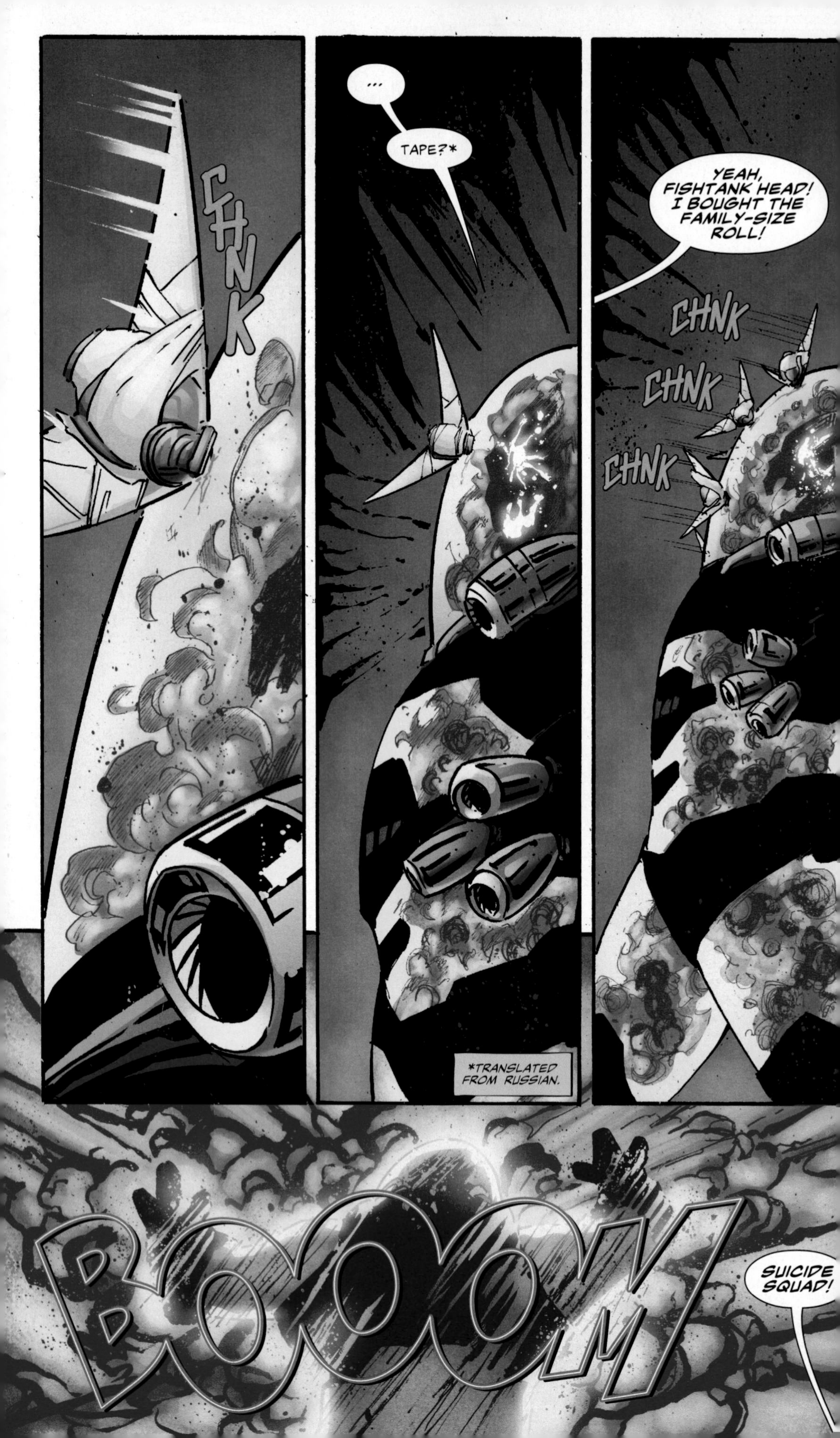

CHNK
...
TAPE?*
*TRANSLATED FROM RUSSIAN.
YEAH, FISHTANK HEAD! I BOUGHT THE FAMILY-SIZE ROLL!
CHNK
CHNK
CHNK
BOOOM
SUICIDE SQUAD!

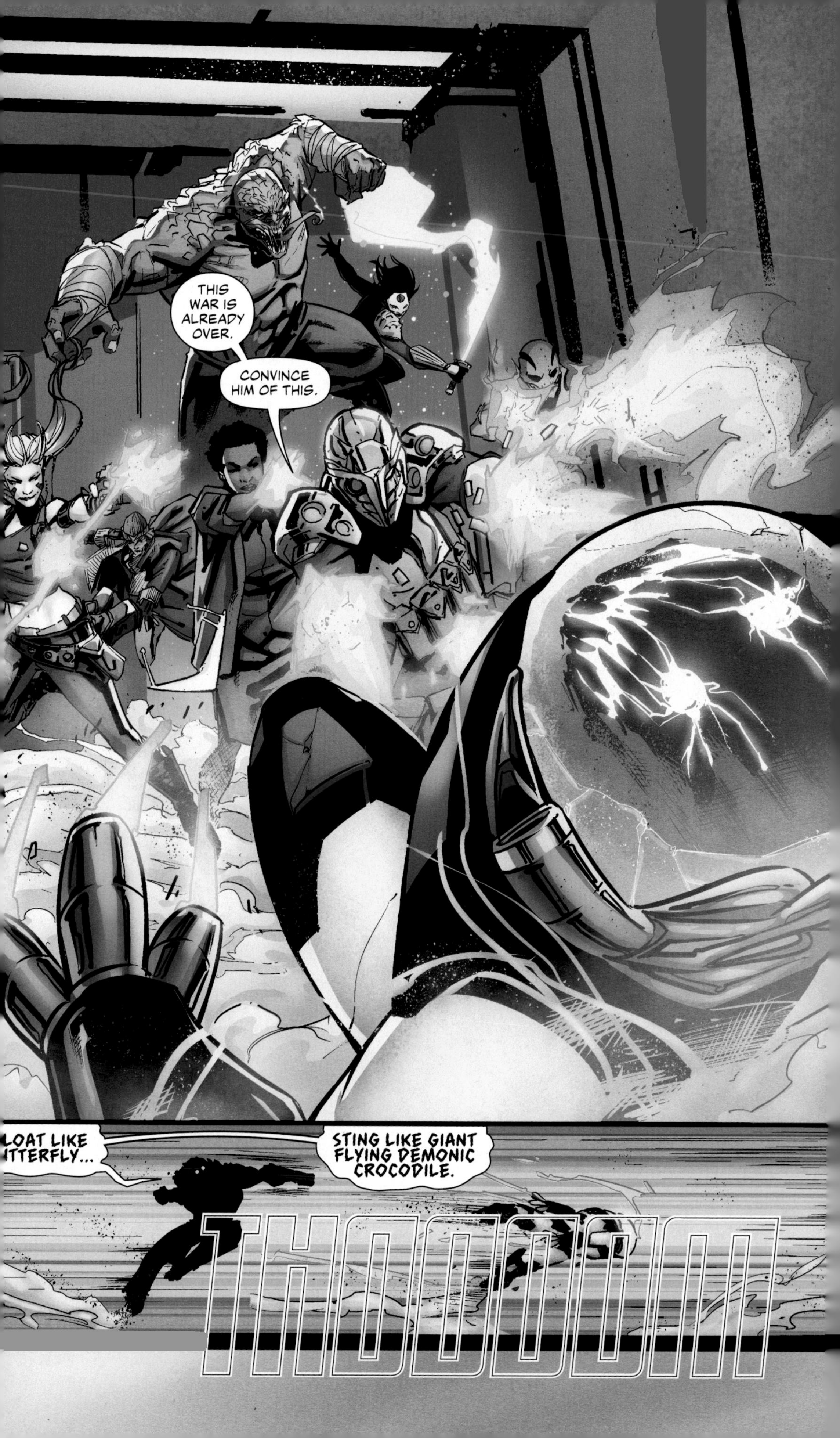
THIS WAR IS ALREADY OVER.
CONVINCE HIM OF THIS.
LOAT LIKE
ITTERFLY...
STING LIKE GIANT FLYING DEMONIC CROCODILE.
THOOOOM

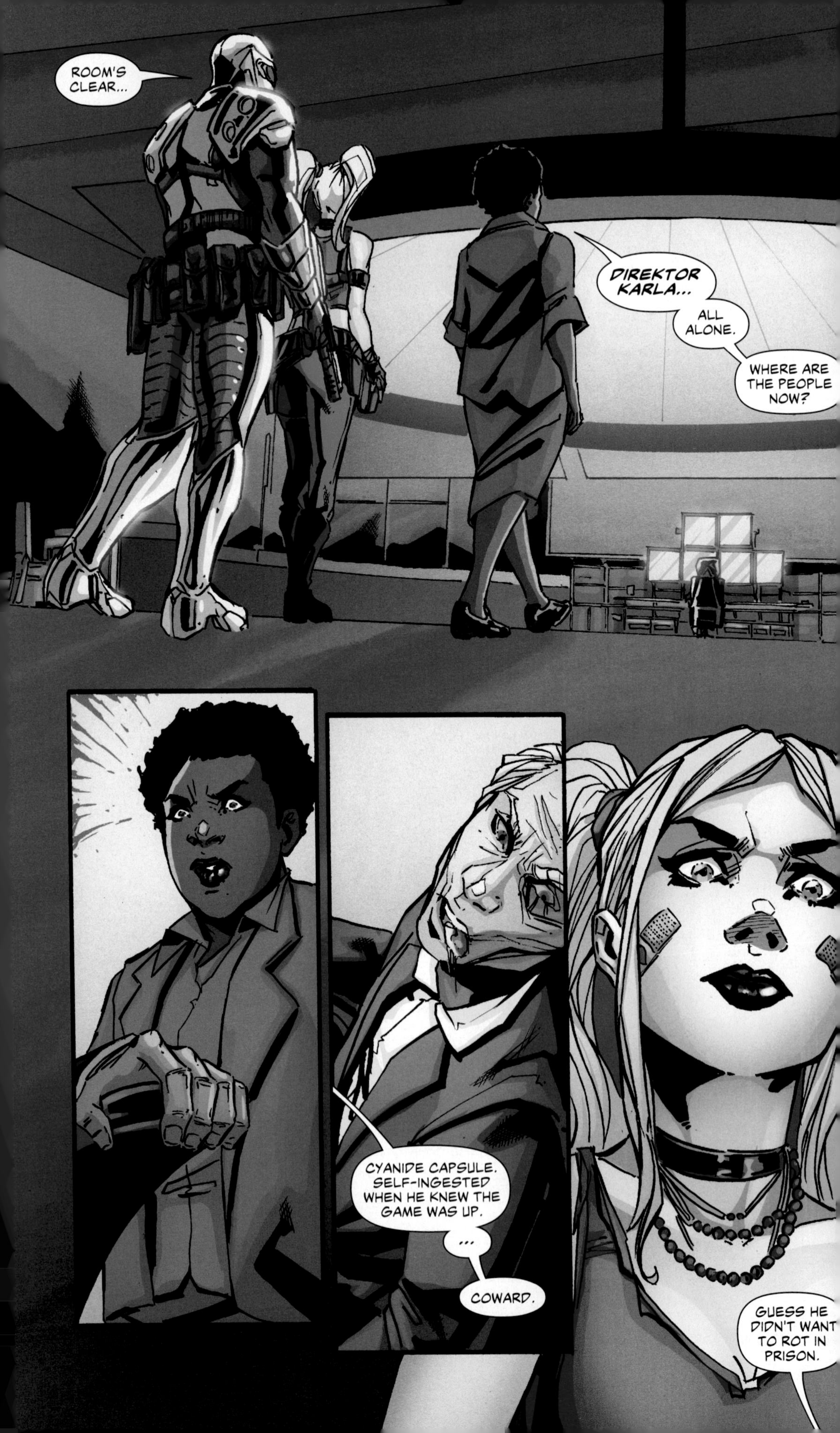
ROOM'S CLEAR...
DIREKTOR KARLA...
ALL ALONE.
WHERE ARE THE PEOPLE NOW?
CYANIDE CAPSULE. SELF-INGESTED WHEN HE KNEW THE GAME WAS UP.
...
COWARD.
GUESS HE DIDN'T WANT TO ROT IN PRISON.

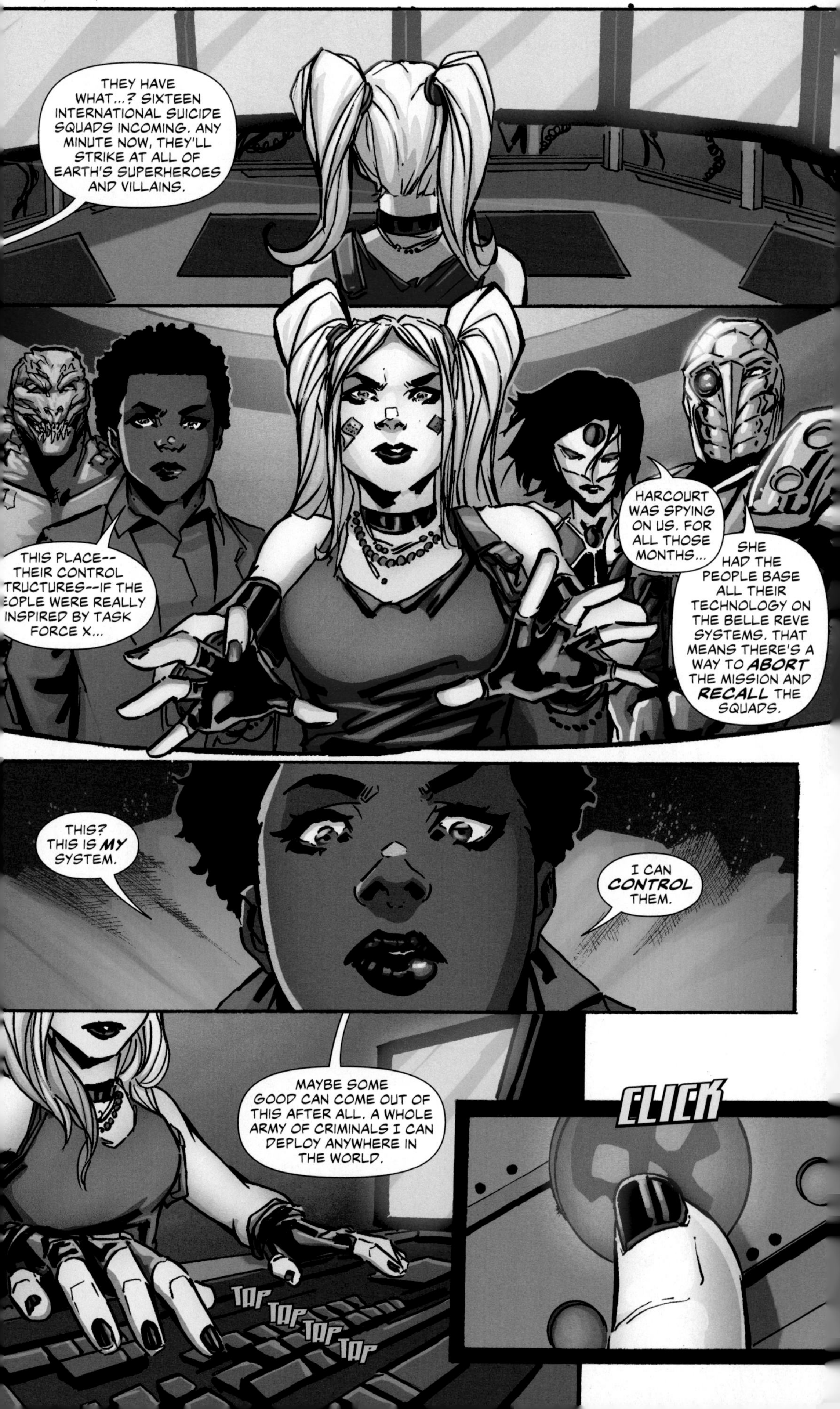

THEY HAVE WHAT...? SIXTEEN INTERNATIONAL SUICIDE SQUADS INCOMING. ANY MINUTE NOW, THEY'LL STRIKE AT ALL OF EARTH'S SUPERHEROES AND VILLAINS.
THIS PLACE-- THEIR CONTROL TRUCTURES--IF THE EOPLE WERE REALLY INSPIRED BY TASK FORCE X...
HARCOURT WAS SPYING ON US. FOR ALL THOSE MONTHS...
SHE HAD THE PEOPLE BASE ALL THEIR TECHNOLOGY ON THE BELLE REVE SYSTEMS. THAT MEANS THERE'S A WAY TO ABORT THE MISSION AND RECALL THE SQUADS.
THIS? THIS IS MY SYSTEM.
I CAN CONTROL THEM.
MAYBE SOME GOOD CAN COME OUT OF THIS AFTER ALL. A WHOLE ARMY OF CRIMINALS I CAN DEPLOY ANYWHERE IN THE WORLD.
TAP TAP TAP TAP
CLICK

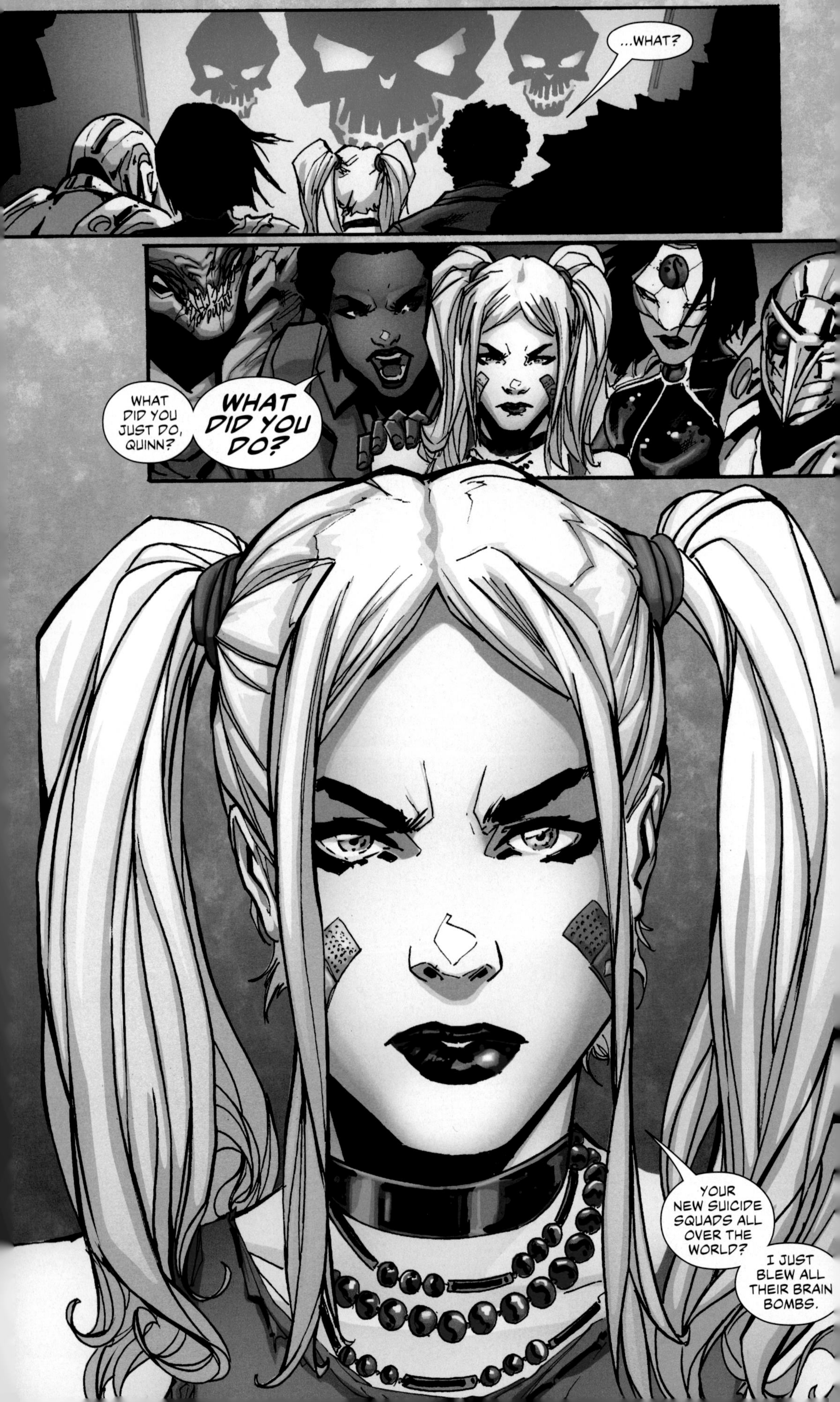
...WHAT?
WHAT DID YOU JUST DO, QUINN?
WHAT DID YOU DO?
YOUR NEW SUICIDE SQUADS ALL OVER THE WORLD?
I JUST BLEW ALL THEIR BRAIN BOMBS.

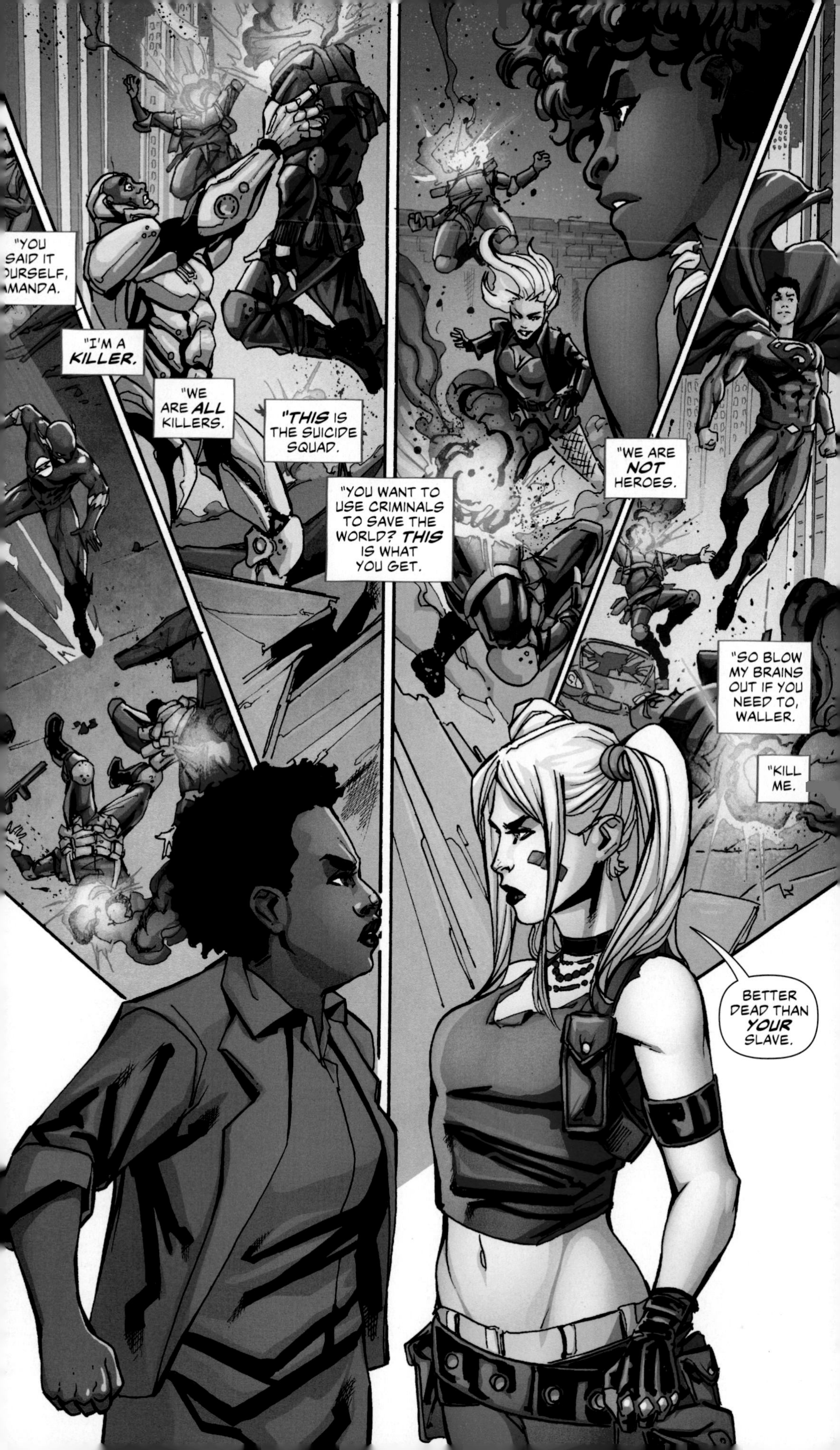
"YOU SAID IT OURSELF, AMANDA.
"I'M A KILLER.
"WE ARE ALL KILLERS.
"THIS IS THE SUICIDE SQUAD.
"YOU WANT TO USE CRIMINALS TO SAVE THE WORLD? THIS IS WHAT YOU GET.
"WE ARE NOT HEROES.
"SO BLOW MY BRAINS OUT IF YOU NEED TO, WALLER.
"KILL ME.
BETTER DEAD THAN YOUR SLAVE.

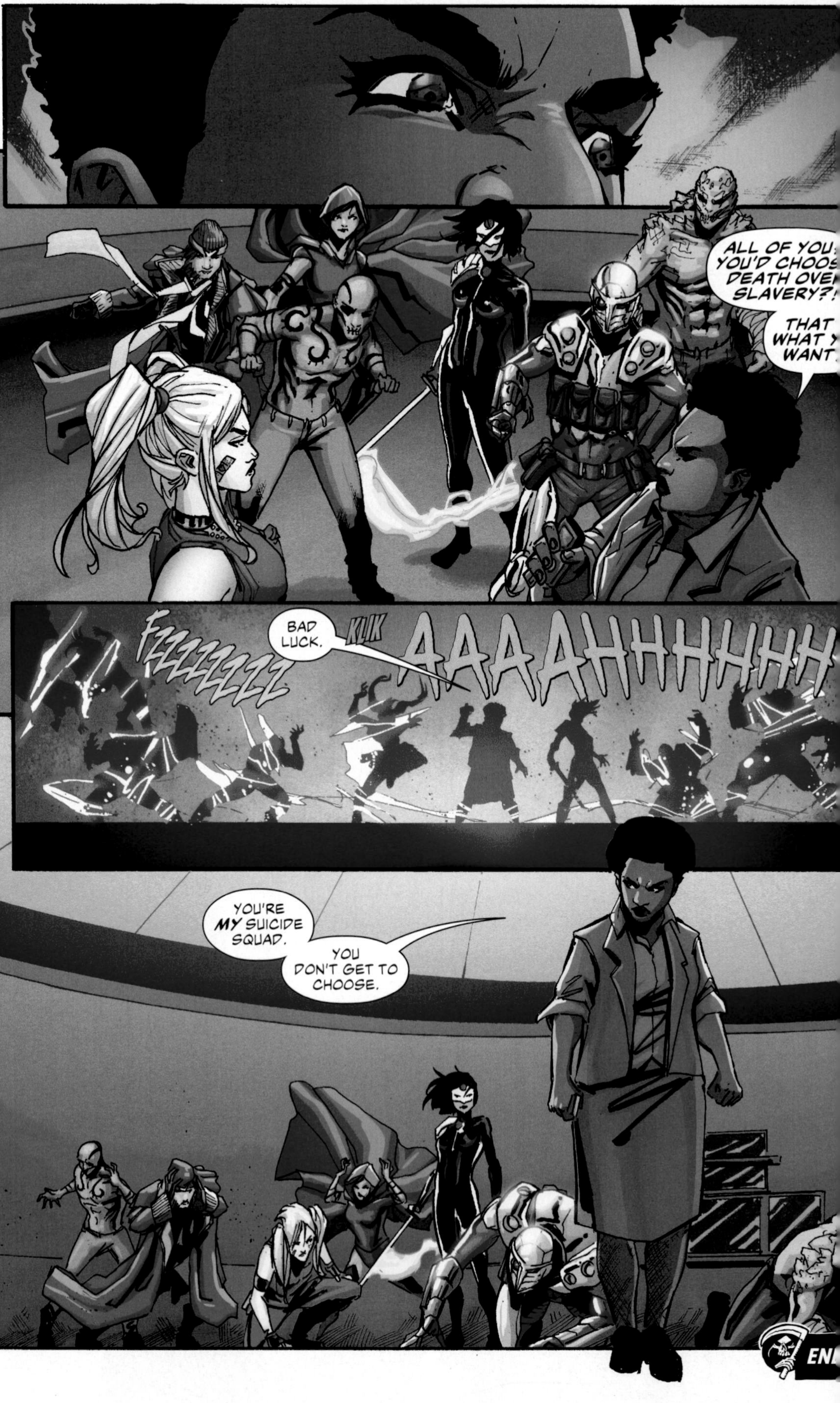

ALL OF YOU: YOU'D CHOOS DEATH OVER SLAVERY?!
THAT WHAT Y WANT
FZZZZZZZZ
BAD LUCK.
KLIK
AAAAHHHHHH
YOU'RE MY SUICIDE SQUAD.
YOU DON'T GET TO CHOOSE.
EN

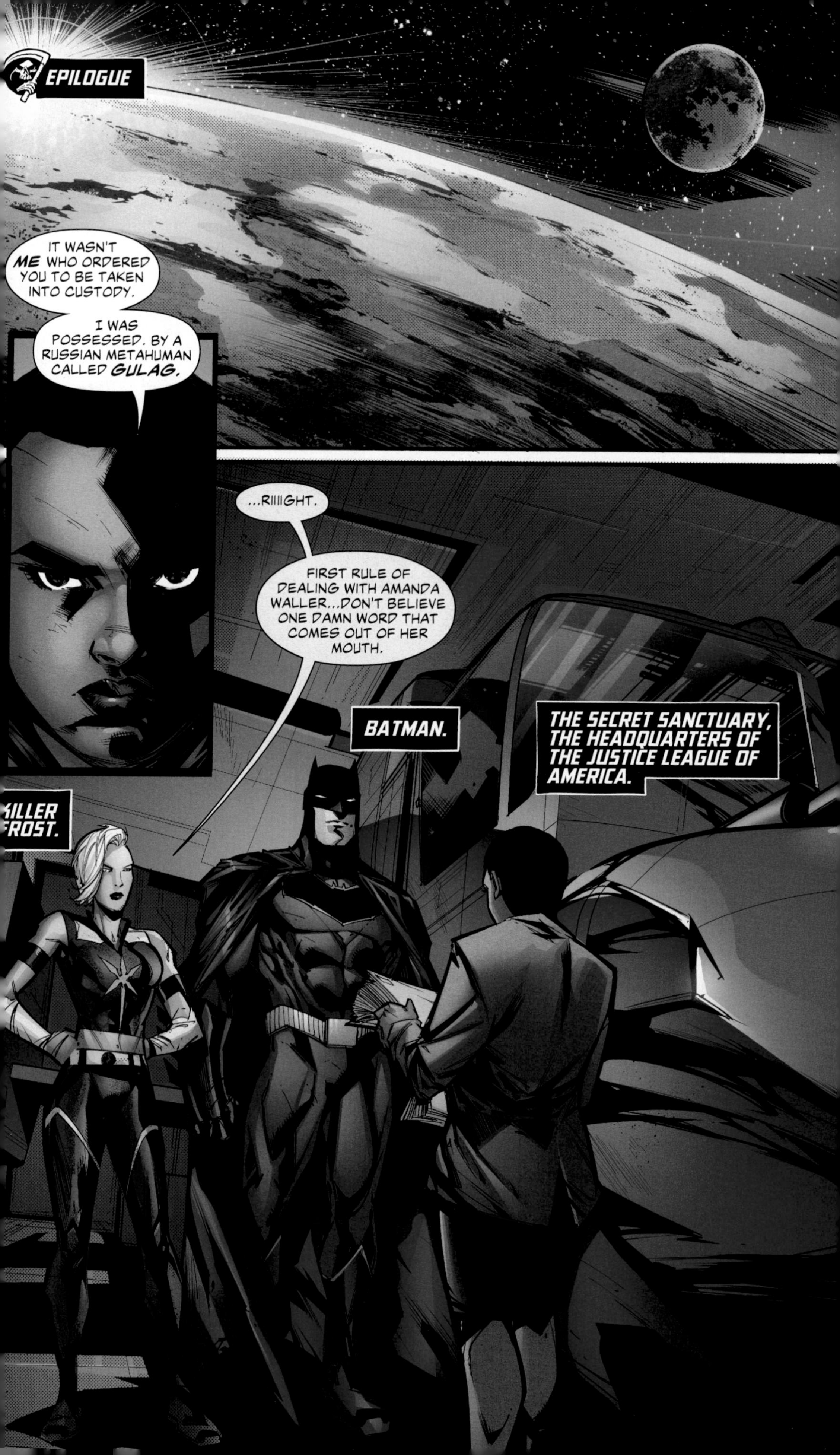
EPILOGUE
IT WASN'T ME WHO ORDERED YOU TO BE TAKEN INTO CUSTODY.
I WAS POSSESSED. BY A RUSSIAN METAHUMAN CALLED GULAG.
...RIIIIGHT.
FIRST RULE OF DEALING WITH AMANDA WALLER...DON'T BELIEVE ONE DAMN WORD THAT COMES OUT OF HER MOUTH.
BATMAN.
THE SECRET SANCTUARY, THE HEADQUARTERS OF THE JUSTICE LEAGUE OF AMERICA.

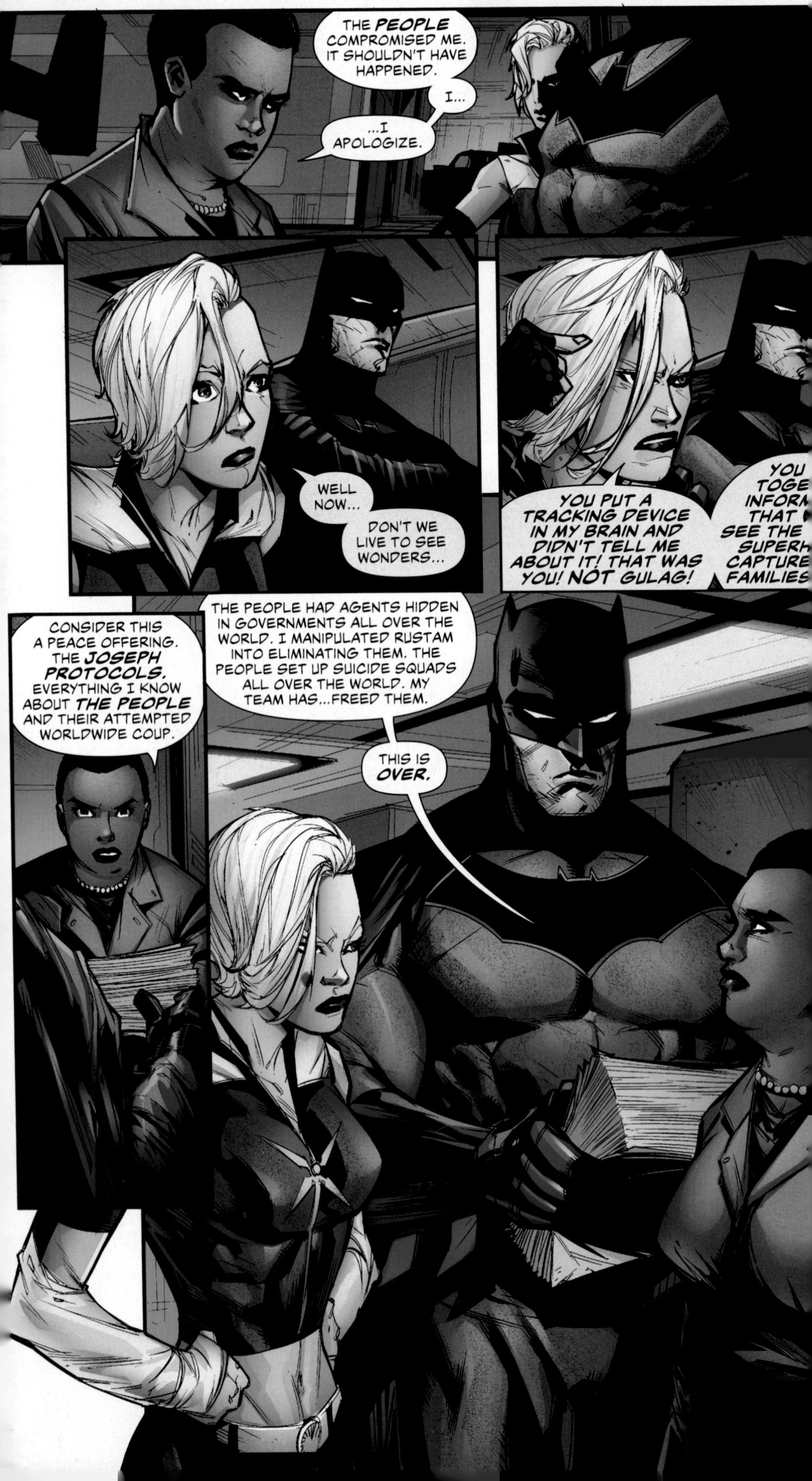

THE PEOPLE COMPROMISED ME. IT SHOULDN'T HAVE HAPPENED.
I...
...I APOLOGIZE.
WELL NOW...
DON'T WE LIVE TO SEE WONDERS...
YOU PUT A TRACKING DEVICE IN MY BRAIN AND DIDN'T TELL ME ABOUT IT! THAT WAS YOU! NOT GULAG!
CONSIDER THIS A PEACE OFFERING. THE JOSEPH PROTOCOLS. EVERYTHING I KNOW ABOUT THE PEOPLE AND THEIR ATTEMPTED WORLDWIDE COUP.
THE PEOPLE HAD AGENTS HIDDEN IN GOVERNMENTS ALL OVER THE WORLD. I MANIPULATED RUSTAM INTO ELIMINATING THEM. THE PEOPLE SET UP SUICIDE SQUADS ALL OVER THE WORLD. MY TEAM HAS...FREED THEM.
THIS IS OVER.

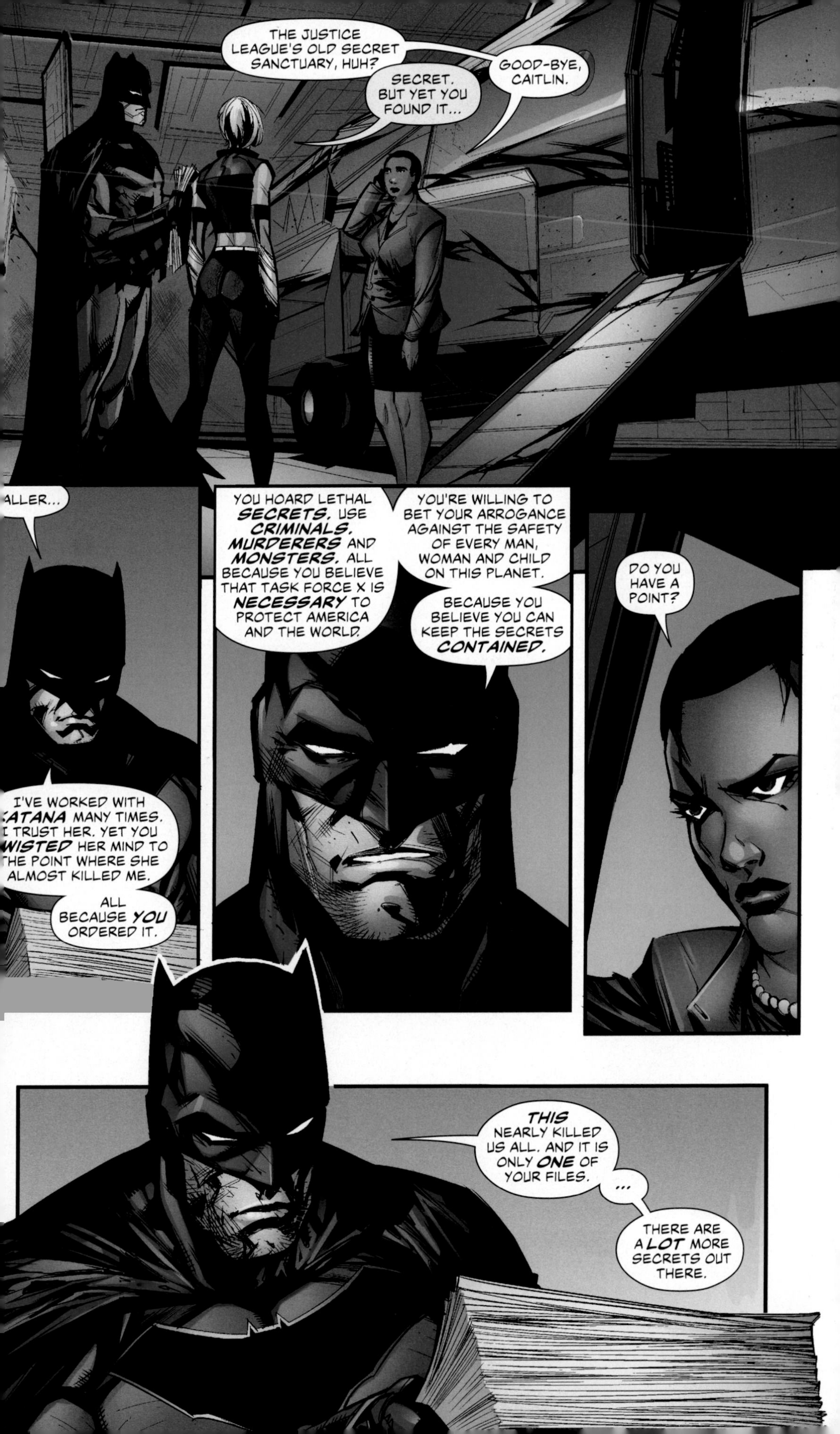
THE JUSTICE LEAGUE'S OLD SECRET SANCTUARY, HUH?
SECRET. BUT YET YOU FOUND IT...
GOOD-BYE, CAITLIN.
ALLER...
I'VE WORKED WITH KATANA MANY TIMES. I TRUST HER. YET YOU TWISTED HER MIND TO THE POINT WHERE SHE ALMOST KILLED ME.
ALL BECAUSE YOU ORDERED IT.
YOU HOARD LETHAL SECRETS. USE CRIMINALS, MURDERERS AND MONSTERS. ALL BECAUSE YOU BELIEVE THAT TASK FORCE X IS NECESSARY TO PROTECT AMERICA AND THE WORLD.
YOU'RE WILLING TO BET YOUR ARROGANCE AGAINST THE SAFETY OF EVERY MAN, WOMAN AND CHILD ON THIS PLANET.
BECAUSE YOU BELIEVE YOU CAN KEEP THE SECRETS CONTAINED.
DO YOU HAVE A POINT?
THIS NEARLY KILLED US ALL. AND IT IS ONLY ONE OF YOUR FILES.
...
THERE ARE A LOT MORE SECRETS OUT THERE.

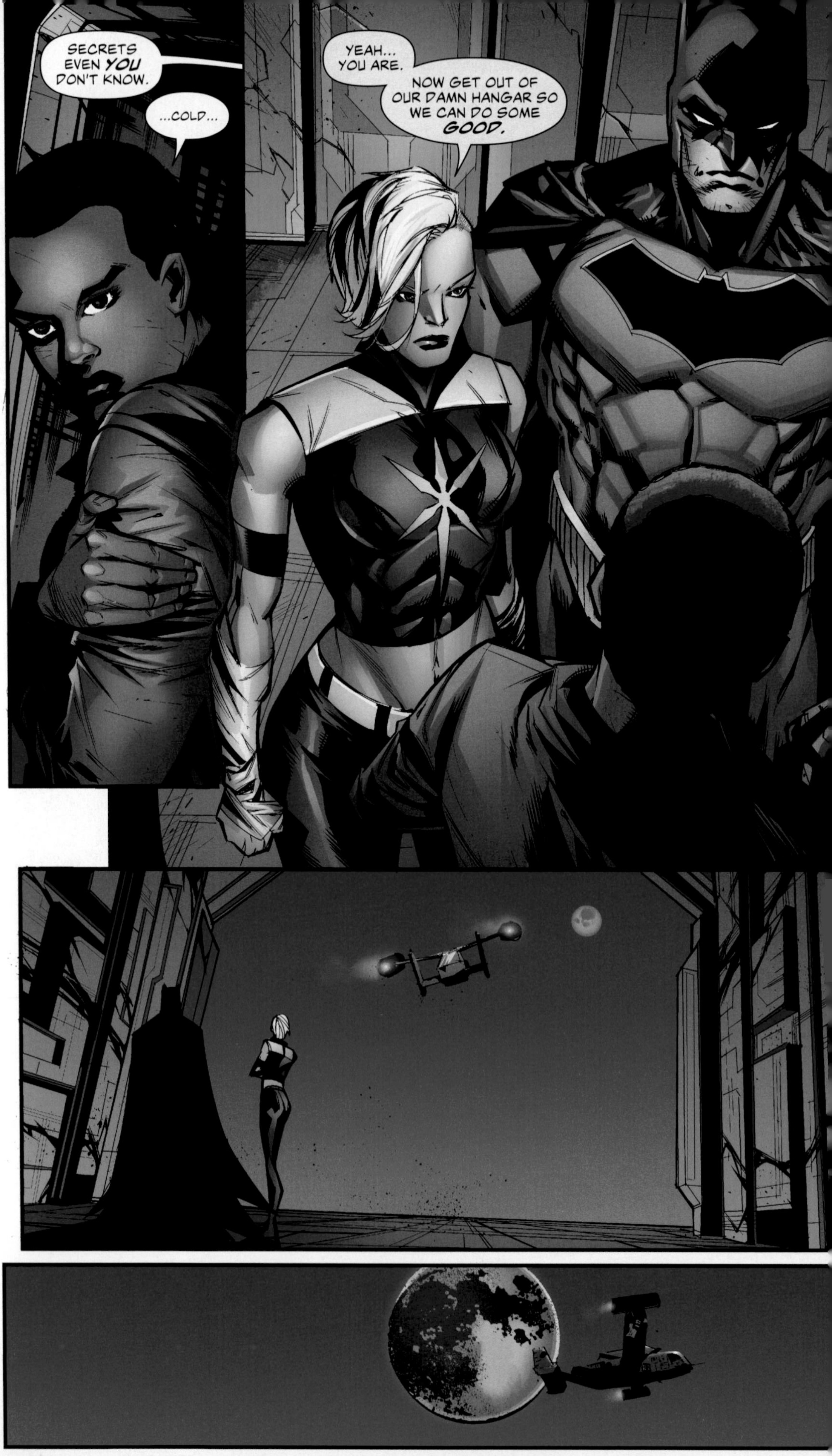
SECRETS EVEN YOU DON'T KNOW.
...COLD...
YEAH... YOU ARE.
NOW GET OUT OF OUR DAMN HANGAR SO WE CAN DO SOME GOOD.

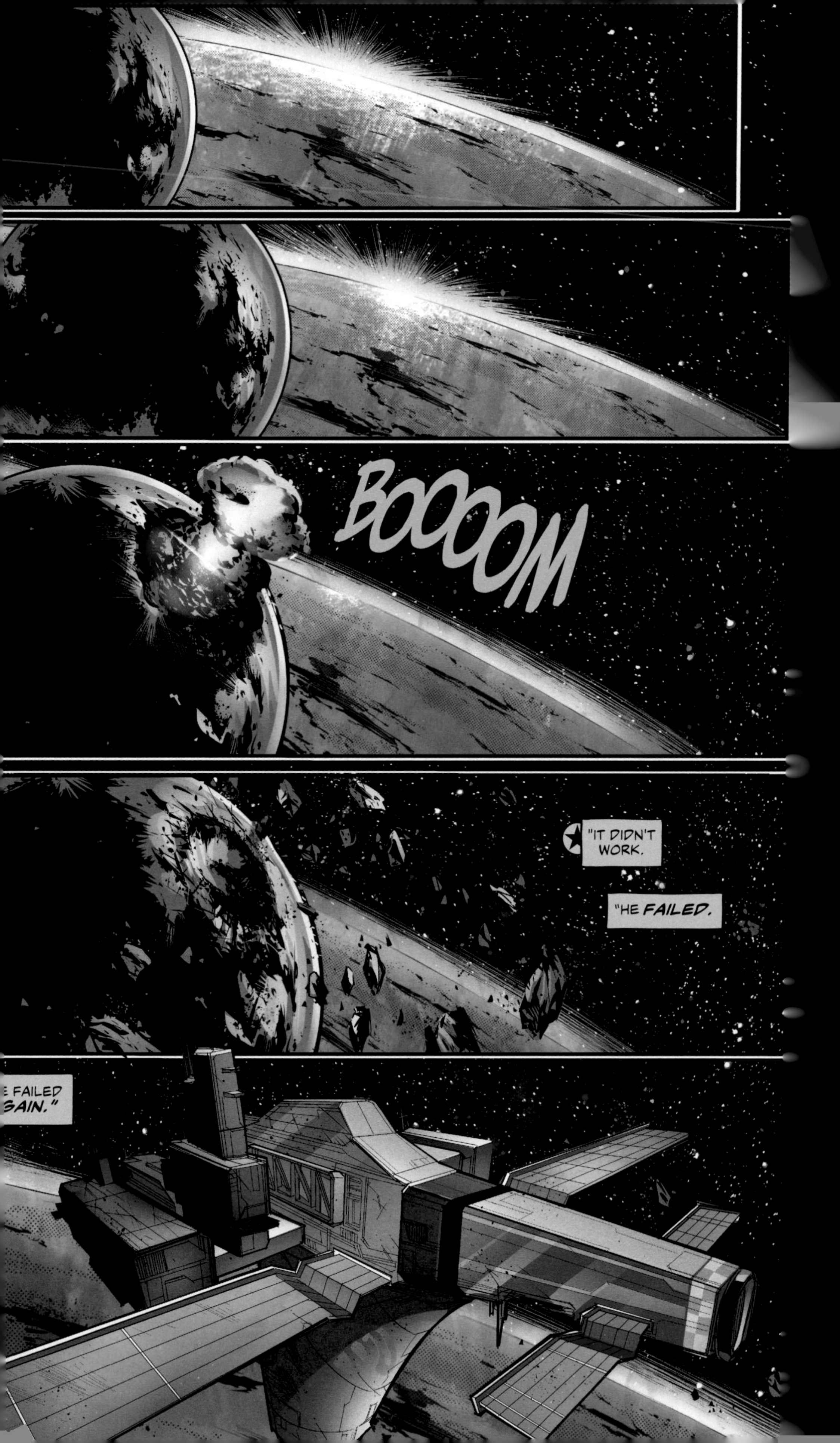
BOOOOM
"IT DIDN'T WORK.
"HE FAILED.
E FAILED
GAIN."

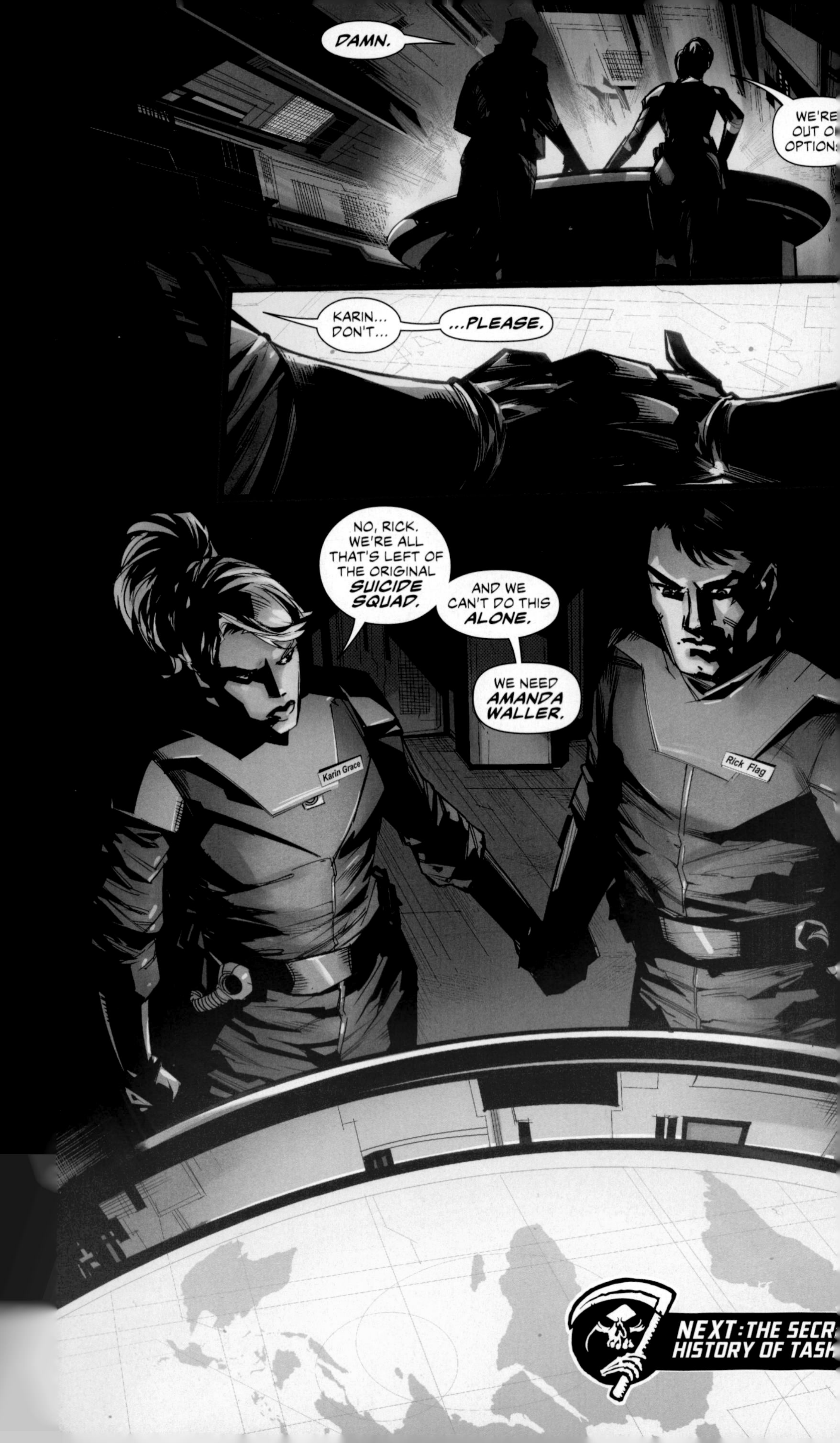
DAMN.
WE'RE OUT O OPTION
KARIN... DON'T...
...PLEASE.
NO, RICK. WE'RE ALL THAT'S LEFT OF THE ORIGINAL SUICIDE SQUAD.
AND WE CAN'T DO THIS ALONE.
WE NEED AMANDA WALLER.
Karin Grace
Rick Flag
NEXT: THE SECR HISTORY OF TASK

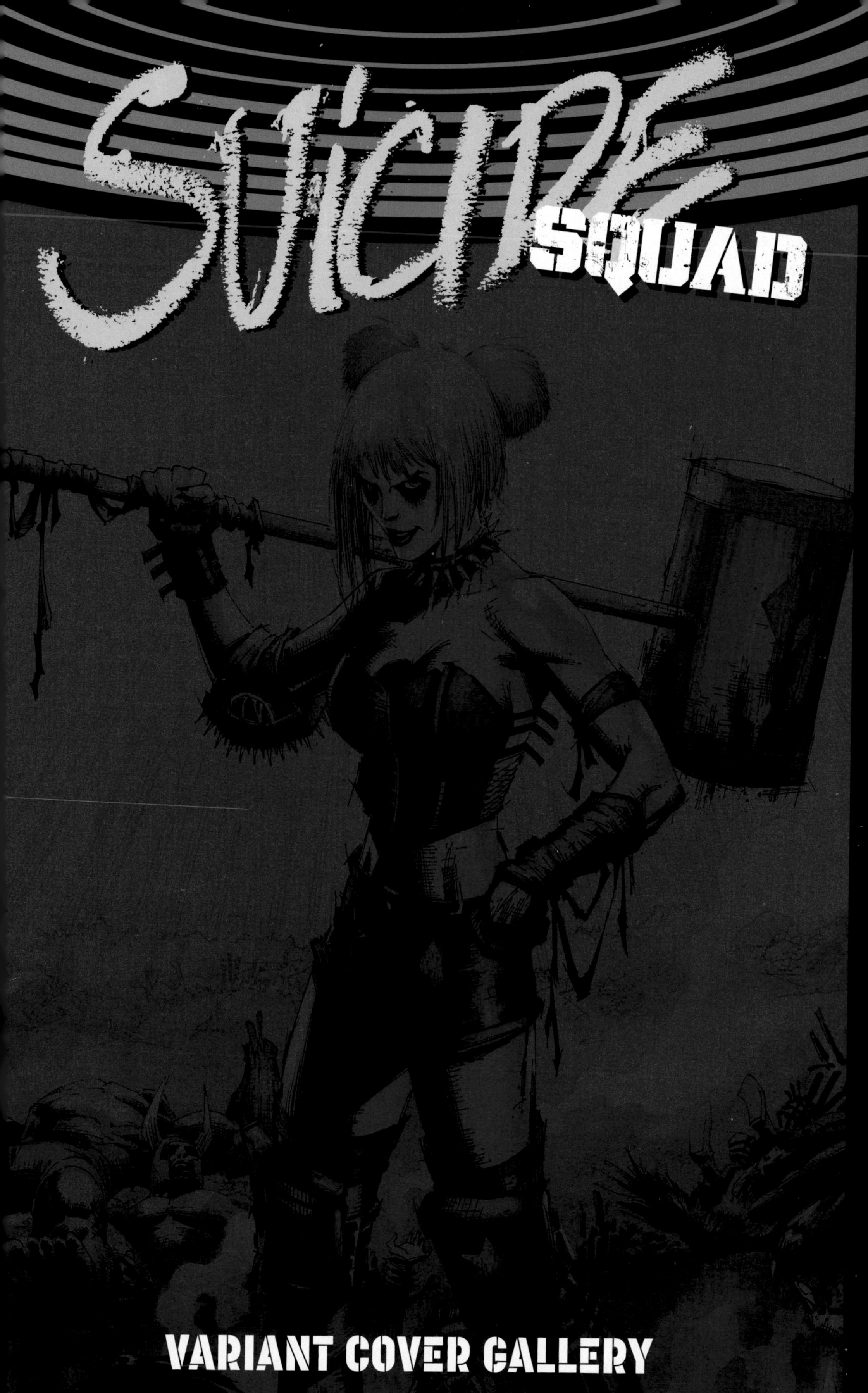
SUICIDE SQUAD
VARIANT COVER GALLERY

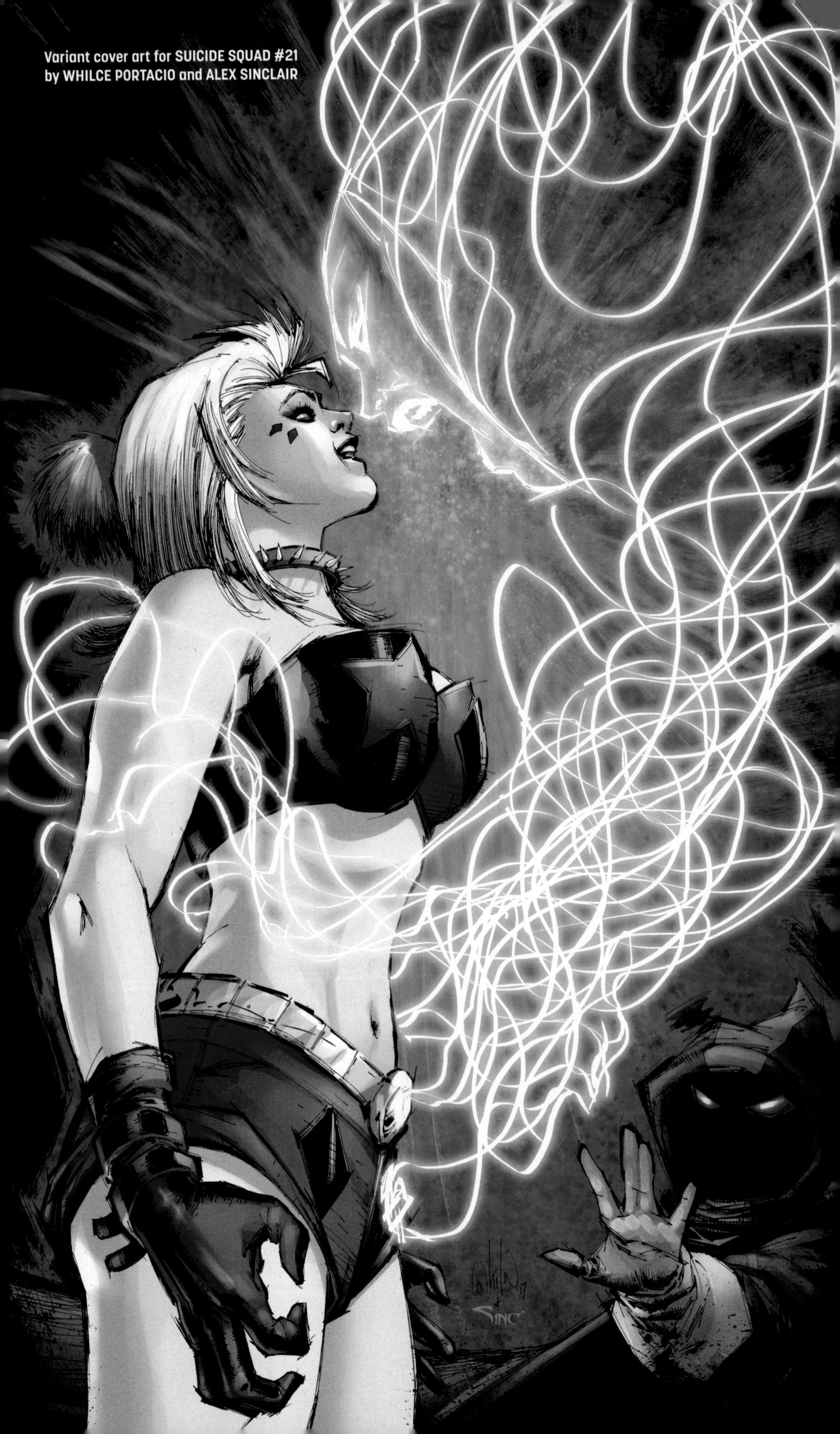

Variant cover art for SUICIDE SQUAD #21
by WHILCE PORTACIO and ALEX SINCLAIR

ariant cover art for SUICIDE SQUAD #22
y WHILCE PORTACIO and ALEX SINCLAIR

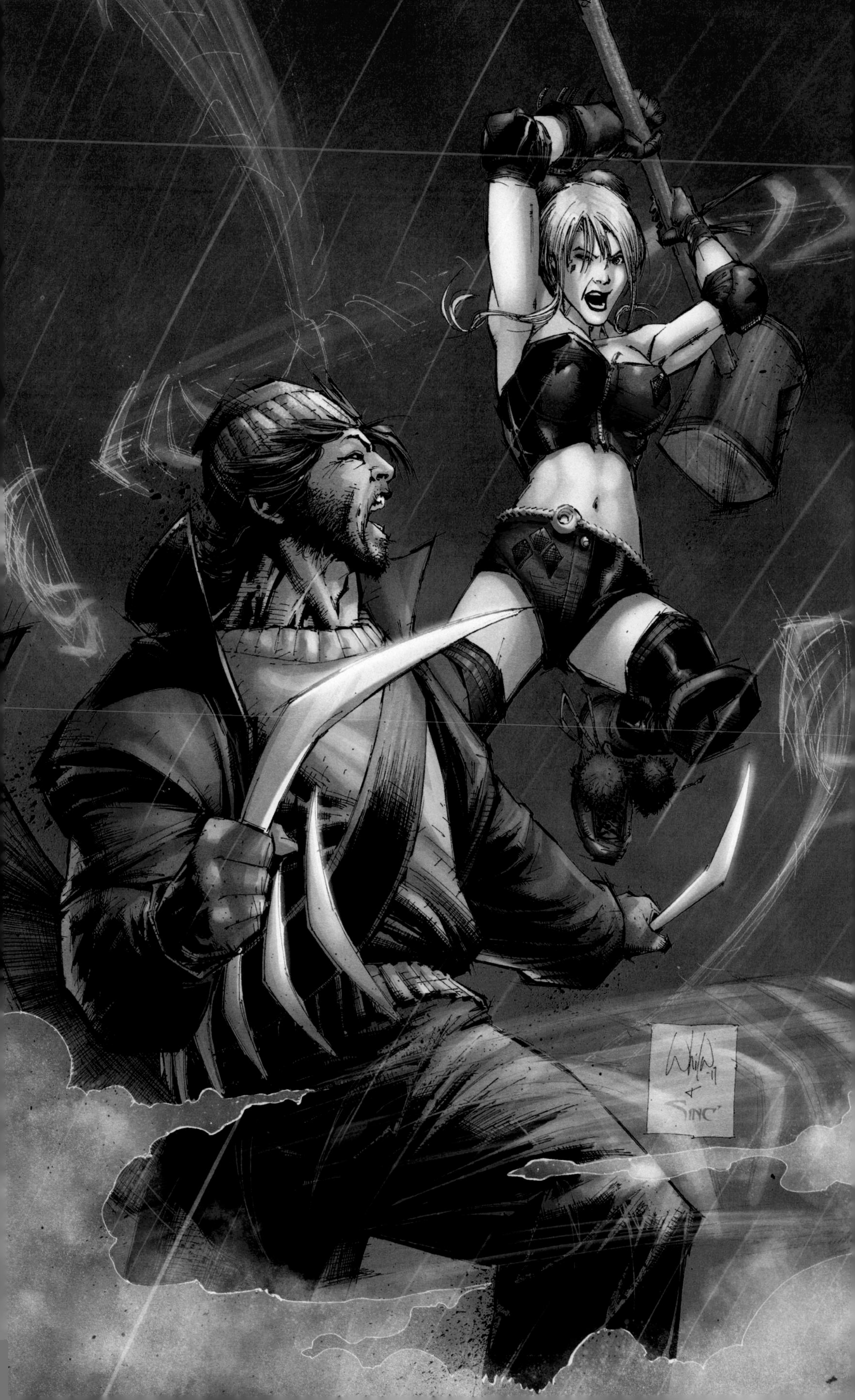

Variant cover art for SUICIDE SQUAD #23
by WHILCE PORTACIO and ALEX SINCLAIR

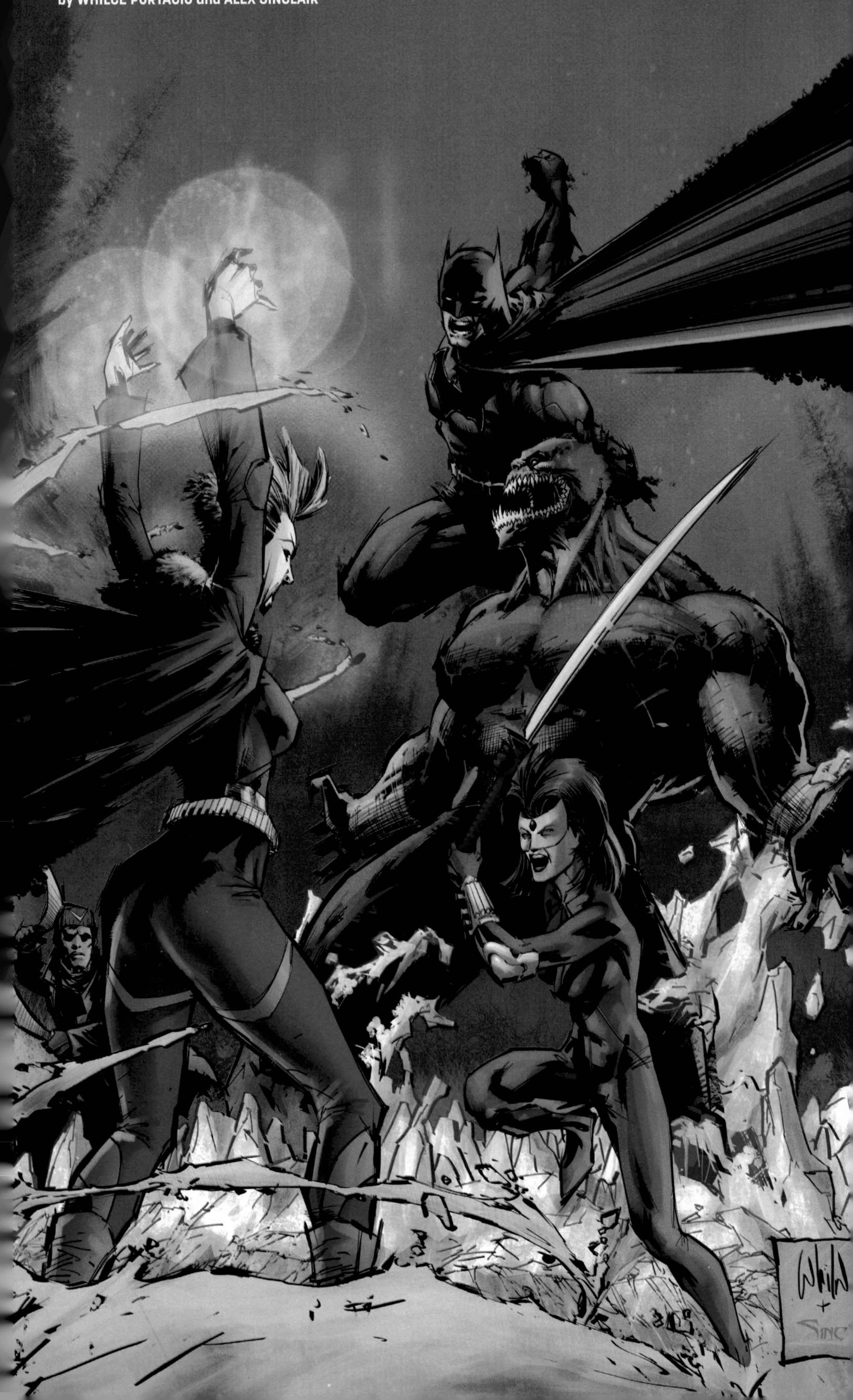

ariant cover art for SUICIDE SQUAD #24
WHILCE PORTACIO and ALEX SINCLAIR

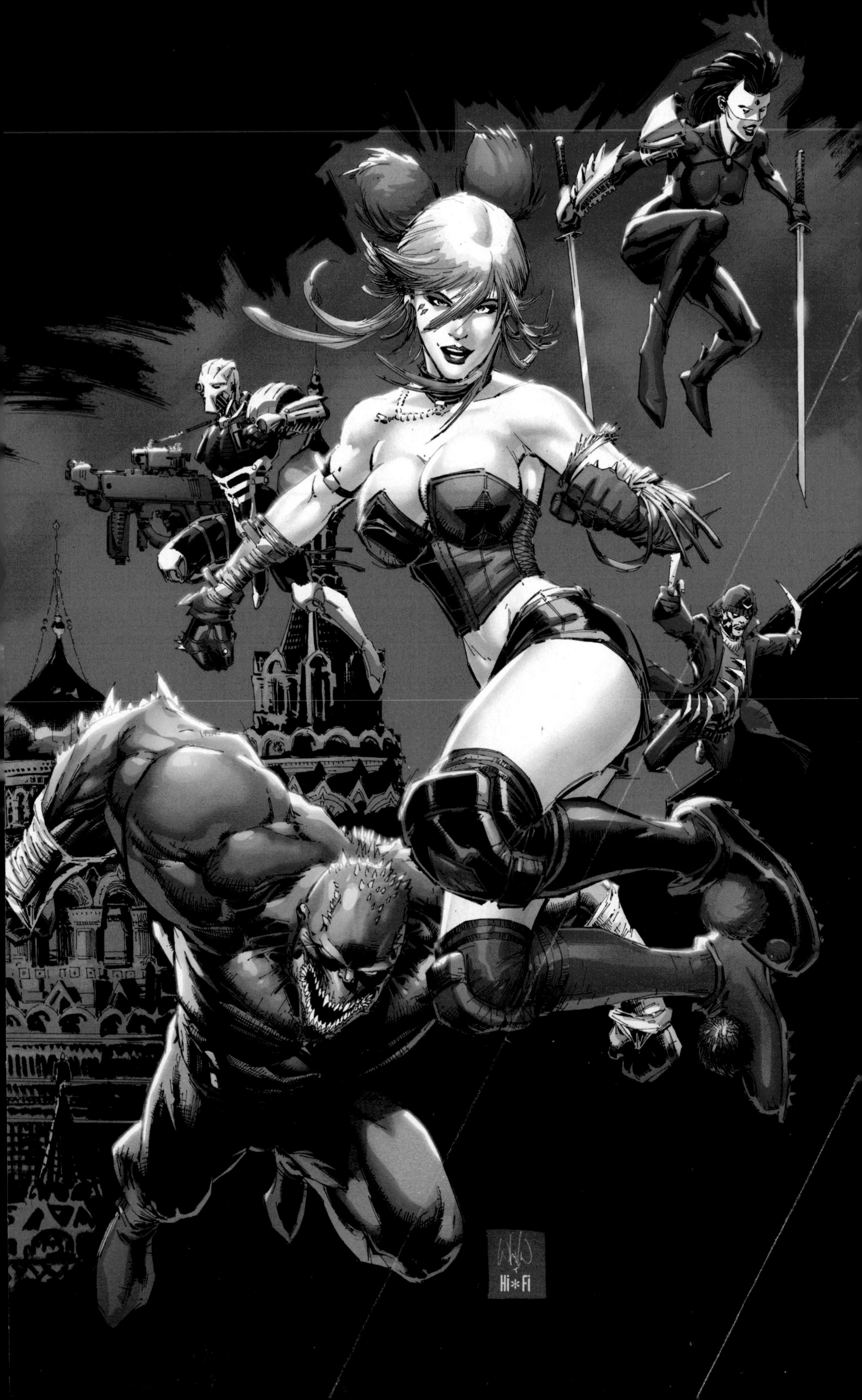
Hi*Fi

Variant cover art for SUICIDE SQUAD #25
by WHILCE PORTACIO and ALEX SINCLAIR

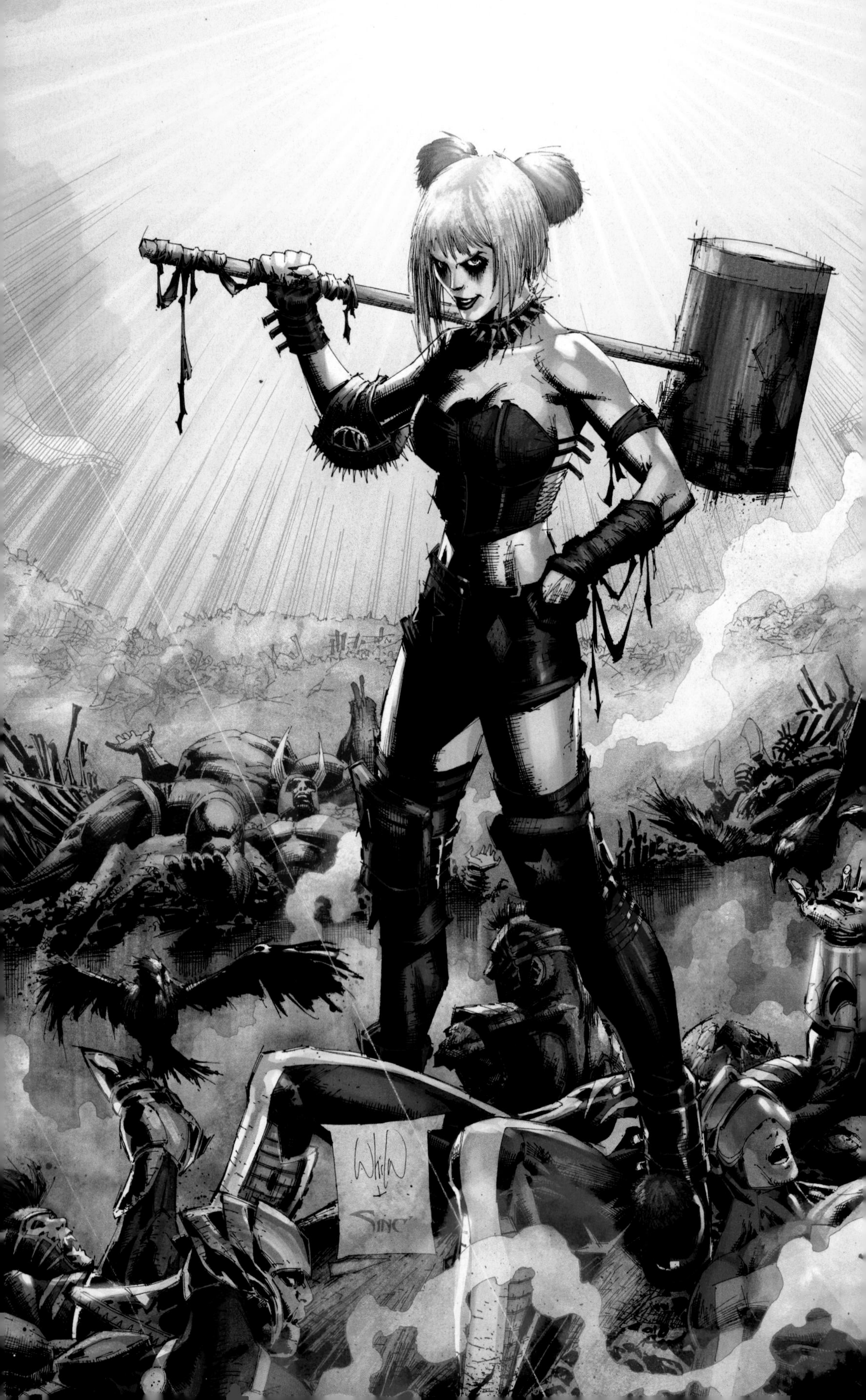